Oxford Studies in European Law

General Editors: Paul Craig and Gráinne de Búrca

OFFICIAL SECRETS AND OVERSIGHT IN THE EUROPEAN UNION

OXFORD STUDIES IN EUROPEAN LAW

Series Editors
Paul Craig, Professor of English Law at St John's College, Oxford and
Gráinne de Búrca, Professor of Law at New York University School of Law

The aim of this series is to publish important and original research on EU law. The focus is on scholarly monographs, with a particular emphasis on those which are interdisciplinary in nature. Edited collections of essays will also be included where they are appropriate. The series is wide in scope and aims to cover studies of particular areas of substantive and of institutional law, historical works, theoretical studies, and analyses of current debates, as well as questions of perennial interest such as the relationship between national and EU law and the novel forms of governance emerging in and beyond Europe. The fact that many of the works are interdisciplinary will make the series of interest to all those concerned with the governance and operation of the EU.

OTHER TITLES IN THIS SERIES

The Horizontal Effect of Fundamental Rights in the European Union
A Constitutional Analysis
Eleni Frantziou

Frontex and Human Rights Responsibility in 'Multi-Actor Situations' under the ECHR and EU Public Liability Law
Melanie Fink

EU Equality Law
The First Fundamental Rights Policy of the EU
Elise Muir

Subnational Authorities in EU Law
Michèle Finck

Accessing Asylum in Europe
Violeta Moreno-Lax

National Parliaments after the Lisbon Treaty and the Euro Crisis
Davor Jančić

Environmental Integration in Competition and Free-Movement Laws
Julian Nowag

EU Agencies
Legal and Political Limits to the Transformation of the EU Administration
Merijn Chamon

Coherence in EU Competition law
Wolf Sauter

Foreign Policy Objectives in European Constitutional Law
Joris Larik

Economic Governance in Europe
Comparative Paradoxes and Constitutional Challenges
Federico Fabbrini

Private Regulation and the Internal Market
Sports, Legal Services, and Standard Setting in EU Economic Law
Mislav Mataija

The EU Deep Trade Agenda
Law and Policy
Billy A. Melo Araujo

Official Secrets and Oversight in the European Union

Law and Practices of Classified Information

VIGJILENCA ABAZI

OXFORD
UNIVERSITY PRESS

OXFORD
UNIVERSITY PRESS

Great Clarendon Street, Oxford, OX2 6DP,
United Kingdom

Oxford University Press is a department of the University of Oxford.
It furthers the University's objective of excellence in research, scholarship,
and education by publishing worldwide. Oxford is a registered trade mark of
Oxford University Press in the UK and in certain other countries

First Edition published in 2019

Impression: 1

Published in the United States of America by Oxford University Press
198 Madison Avenue, New York, NY 10016, United States of America

British Library Cataloguing in Publication Data
Data available

Library of Congress Control Number: 2018967701

ISBN 978–0–19–881921–9

Printed and bound by
CPI Group (UK) Ltd, Croydon, CR0 4YY

SERIES EDITOR'S PREFACE

While the European Union has long been criticized for the lack of transparency in various aspects of its governance, little attention has so far been given to the law and policy of 'official secrecy' in the EU. Hence this contribution by Vigjilenca Abazi, which is one of the first book-length treatments to examine the legal regime governing official secrets in the EU, is to be welcomed.

The author sets out to examine and to map the EU's emergence as a security actor, and beyond that to present and explain the EU's gradual development of a law and practice of official secrets across a whole range of fields. She points out that unlike in most democratic states, the law governing official secrecy in the European Union developed incrementally, and consists of a gradual patchwork of rules and standards rather than a specific legislative measure dedicated to the subject.

Abazi uses interviews as well as documentary sources to trace descriptively the ways in which EU official secrecy law and policy have developed, but also, in normative vein, to highlight the ways in which it has resisted and impeded judicial, parliamentary and administrative oversight. There are helpful chapters which outline the role of the different institutions in this field, including the executive institutions and bodies on the one hand, and the oversight bodies—including the Parliament, Ombudsman and Court of Justice—on the other.

Normatively speaking, the author argues that the EU regime of official secrets prioritizes security and fails to provide adequate democratic oversight or scrutiny. While acknowledging the difficulty of balancing the governmental concern to protect certain information with the requirements of openness and transparency, the author argues that there should at the very least be a public debate on the matter rather than leaving it to be decided by committees largely beyond the public eye, as is the case at present. She provides various suggestions for the reform of the law in this area with a view to enhancing the democratic legitimacy of the EU's practices as well as protection for fundamental rights such as access to information, fair trial and the rights of the defence.

This is a timely and thoughtful book that sheds light on an area of law and practice of the EU that is little known—for reasons that become apparent in the chapters that follow—and yet, in a era in which the democratic legitimacy of the EU is increasingly being challenged, very important. The work should be of interest to legal and political science scholars of the EU and to all those interested in questions of official secrecy, transparency and accountability in the European Union and its governance practices.

Paul Craig
Gráinne de Búrca

ACKNOWLEDGEMENTS

This book is based on my doctoral thesis defended at University of Amsterdam on 11 December 2015. It was subsequently updated and revised at Maastricht University, European University Institute, and NYU School of Law. Whilst transparency or rather the lack thereof in the European Union has been in the spotlight for a few decades, the focus on secrecy and especially official secrets is more recent in EU law and governance literature. At the start of my PhD research a handful of academic articles addressed the establishment and consequences of EU rules on official secrets. Today, this debate has expanded with more scholars aiming to map and understand secrecy in Europe. This book makes its contribution by offering the first comprehensive and in-depth legal account of official secrets in the EU. It critically analyses their implications for oversight and fundamental rights and based on forty interviews, it offers an understanding of the practice of official secrets.

I owe gratitude to many people who have contributed to this book in different ways. First and foremost, I am deeply thankful to my promoter Deirdre Curtin and co-promoter Christina Eckes for their valuable guidance, constructive feedback, and encouragement. I consider myself incredibly privileged to have benefited from such inspiring mentors during the doctoral studies and in subsequent years.

I am thankful to the members of the doctoral committee, Steven Blockmans, Damian Chalmers, Marise Cremona, Marieke de Goede, Sophie Vanhoonacker, and Marc de Wilde for their comments and questions, which motivated me to further develop my ideas and incorporate them in this book. I am also grateful to the anonymous reviewers for their feedback that was helpful in turning a doctoral thesis into a monograph.

The year I spent at Columbia Law School as Fulbright Visiting Scholar during my PhD research was of great benefit to advance my knowledge on the impact of official secrets to constitutional checks and balances. I am very thankful to David Pozen for reading draft chapters and the many thought-provoking discussions. I would also like to thank Kathleen Clark, Mark Fenster, Heidi Kitrosser, Rahul Sagar, and Dennis Thompson from whom I learned a lot.

Since June 2015, my academic 'home' has been Maastricht University. I am greatly indebted to Ellen Vos for supporting my work on this book. In the same breath, I would like to thank Monica Claes and Bruno de Witte as well as my colleagues at the Maastricht Centre for European Law and the Centre for European Research in Maastricht for an inspiring working environment.

The journey to completing this manuscript included stops in Florence and New York City. I am grateful for the research visit at the European University Institute, which was helpful in updating this book. The completion of the book was also possible due to the excellent opportunity of the Emile Nöel Fellowship at the NYU School of Law, The Jean Monnet Centre for International and Regional Economic Law and Justice. The fellowship provided me with the time I needed to finalize this manuscript whilst also expanding my research agenda in issues of privacy and whistleblower protection. I am very grateful to Gráinne de Búrca and Joseph Weiler for their helpful feedback and to the Fellows for a stimulating academic year.

Finally I owe the greatest gratitude to my parents, Bujare Agaj Abazi and Gazmend Abazi, to whom I dedicate this book, for their unwavering support and care.

TABLE OF CONTENTS

TABLE OF CASES

Court of Justice of the European Union

Opinions

Advocate General Opinions

European Court of Human Rights

National Courts

United States of America

TABLE OF LEGISLATION AND OTHER DOCUMENTS

Treaty on the European Union (TEU; consolidated version: [2012] OJ C 326/13)

Treaty on the Functioning of the European Union (TFEU; consolidated version: [2012] OJ C 326/47)

Charter of Fundamental Rights of the European Union ([2012] OJ C 326/391)

Convention for the Protection of Human Rights and Fundamental Freedoms European Convention of Human Rights (European Convention on Human Rights, as amended)

Treaty Establishing the European Atomic Energy Community (EAEC Treaty, original version, 1957)

Agreements

Protocols

Regulations

Directives

Joint Actions

Common Positions

Council Decisions

Commission Decisions

European Parliament Decisions

European Ombudsman Decisions

High Representative Decisions

European Council Conclusions

Rules of Procedure

Resolutions

Reports

Other EU Documents

LIST OF ABBREVIATIONS

AFSJ	Area of Freedom, Security and Justice
CFA	Committee on Foreign Affairs
CFSP	Common Foreign and Security Policy
CJEU	Court of Justice of the European Union
CSC	Council Security Committee
CSDP	Common Security and Defence Policy
ECHR	European Convention of Human Rights
ECtHR	European Court of Human Rights
EEAS	European External Action Service
EO	European Ombudsman
EP	European Parliament
EU	European Union
EUCI	European Union Classified Information
EULEX	EU Rule of Law Mission
Europol	European Police Office
GC	General Court
INTCEN	EU Intelligence Analysis Centre
LIBE	Committee on Civil Liberties, Justice and Home Affairs
MEP	Member of the European Parliament
MS	Member State
NATO	North Atlantic Treaty Organisation
OCTA	Organised Crime Threat Assessment
SG	Secretary General
SWIFT	Society for Worldwide Interbank Financial Telecommunication
TEU	Treaty on European Union
TFEU	Treaty on the Functioning of the European Union
TFTP	Terrorist Finance Tracking Programme

Introduction

Through the Democratic Lens: Official Secrets in the European Union

Abstracts
This introductory chapter outlines the core themes of this book. It shows the pertinence of institutional rules controlling the flow of information, especially sensitive and classified documents in the EU and expounds why a dedicated study on these rules and practices is necessary to understand oversight and fundamental rights. The chapter explains the main concepts and provides the research methodology of the book, which offers a legal account of EU official secrets whilst deriving observations from practice based on empirical material. Lastly, the chapter maps the structure of the entire book.

The European Union in the past decade has faced a series of crises with significant impact to its very foundations. From the European debt crisis in 2009 to current debates about the rule of law, migration, and for the very first time in its history, a Member State (MS) leaving the Union, the challenges have been vast.[1] Secrecy, such as closed-door meetings, lack of access to information for parliaments and citizens, or limited public debate, is a common

[1] A growing literature addresses these different crises and their (legal and constitutional) implications in the EU. See inter alia Hauke Brunkhorst, Monika Eigmüller, and John Erik Fossum, 'European Transformations: Are the Crises Really Over or Is it Just the End of their Beginning?' (2017) 23 European Law Journal 310; Mark Dawson and Floris De Witte, 'Constitutional Balance in the EU after the Euro-Crisis' (2013) 76(5) The Modern Law Review 817; Matthias Ruffert, ''European Debt Crisis and European Union Law' (2011) 48(6) Common Market Law Review 1777; Dimitry Kochenov and Petra Bard, 'Rule of Law Crisis in the New Member States of the EU: The Pitfalls of Overemphasising Enforcement' (27 July 2018) Reconnect Working Papers (Leuven) No 1; Armin van Bogdandy and Pal Sonnevend (eds) *Constitutional Crisis in the European Constitutional Area: Theory, Law and Politics in Hungary and Romania* (Hart Publishing 2015); Laurant Pech and Kim Lane Scheppele, 'Illiberalism Within: Rule of Law Backsliding in the EU' (2017) 19 Cambridge Yearbook of European Legal Studies 3; Bruno De Witte, 'An Undivided Union? Differentiated Integration in Post-Brexit Times' (2018) 55(2/3) Common Market Law Review 227; Paul Craig, 'Brexit, a Drama: The Interregnum' (2017) 36 Yearbook of European Law 3; Daniel Thym, 'The "Refugee Crisis" as a Challenge of Legal Design and Institutional Legitimacy' (2016) 53 Common Market Law Review 1545; Agustín José Menéndez, 'The Refugee Crisis: Between Human Tragedy

thread in how the EU handles these affairs.[2] Yet, it is not only in times of crises that the EU resorts to secrecy. EU secret law-making has become a prevailing practice through the so-called 'trialogues', that is closed meetings for a small number of representatives as part of legislative negotiations.[3] These practices of secrecy in the EU are 'visible' in the sense that we know which meetings are scheduled, although they take place behind closed doors; we know the documents exist even if our requests for public access to such documents are denied.[4] Another form of secrecy in the EU is much more in the shadows: official secrets, that is the internal institutional rules controlling the flow of information, especially sensitive and classified documents. Yet, some of the major limitations to oversight and fundamental rights have arisen precisely due to official secrets. For example, neither the European Parliament (EP) nor the European Ombudsman (EO) were given access to official secrets regarding the implementation of the EU–US Terrorist Finance Tracking Programme,[5]

and Symptom of the Structural Crisis of European Integration' (2016) 22 European Law Journal 388.

[2] See *inter alia* Vigjilenca Abazi and Johan Adriaensen, 'Allies in Transparency? Parliamentary, Judicial and Administrative Interplays in the EU's International Negotiations' (2017) 5(3) Politics & Governance 75; Vigjilenca Abazi and Maarten Hillebrandt, 'The Legal Limits to Confidential Negotiations: Recent Case Law Developments in Council Transparency: Access Info Europe and In 't Veld' (2015) 52(3) Common Market Law Review 825; Maarten Hillebrandt, Deirdre Curtin, and Albert Meijer, 'Transparency in the EU Council of Ministers: An Institutional Analysis' (2014) 20(1) European Law Journal 1; Leonor Rossi and Patricia Vinagre e Silva, *Public Access to Documents in the EU* (Hart Publishing 2017); Deirdre Curtin and Paivi Leino, 'Openness, Transparency and the Right of Access to Documents in the EU' (2016) Robert Schuman Centre for Advanced Studies Research Paper No RSCAS 2016/63; Paivi Leino, 'Transparency, Participation and EU Institutional Practice: An Inquiry into the Limits of the "Widest Possible"' (2014) EUI Working Papers LAW 2014/3; Alberto Alemano, 'Unpacking the Principle of Openness in EU Law: Transparency, Participation and Democracy' (2014) 39 European Law Review 72.

[3] But see Case T-540/15 *Emilio De Capitani v European Parliament* ECLI:EU:T:2018:167. Trialgoues are closed meetings among representatives of the Council of the EU, the EP, and the European Commission to find a compromise and produce an agreed text that will have to be voted by their respective committees and plenaries into law.

[4] See the distinction drawn by Pozen on deep and shallow secrets, David Pozen, 'Deep Secrecy' (2010) 62 Stanford Law Review 257. See also Regulation (EC) No 1049/2001 of the European Parliament and of the Council of 30 May 2001 regarding public access to European Parliament, Council and Commission documents [2001] OJ L145/43. For a critical analysis of access to documents in the EU see, Vigjilenca Abazi and Eljalill Tauschinsky, 'Reasons of Control and Trust: Grounding the Public Need for Transparency in the European Union' (2015) 11(2) Utrecht Law Review 78.

[5] Agreement between the European Union and the United States of America on the processing and transfer of financial messaging data from the European Union to the United States for the purposes of the Terrorist Finance Tracking Program [2010] OJ L195/5, art 4(9). See Marise Cremona, 'Justice and Home Affairs in a Globalised World: Ambitions and Reality in the tale of the EU-US SWIFT Agreement' (2011) Institute for European Integration Research

which blocked oversight on whether privacy rights of European citizens are breached by US authorities; France and the UK vetoed sharing official secrets with the Court of Justice of the European Union (CJEU) in important cases on sanctioning individuals by freezing their assets,[6] thus limiting judicial review to only selectively disclosed documents. These limitations to oversight contradict the EU's constitutional commitments to openness, democracy, and fundamental rights, particularly since the 'power to inspect documents is fundamental to the democratic scrutiny ... and acts as guarantor of certain fundamental rights to the EU citizen'.[7]

This book provides an understanding of the rules on official secrets in the European Union and their implications for oversight, institutional relations, and fundamental rights. In particular, the book seeks to trace, map, and analyse through legal and empirical analysis how the rationales of state and military secrecy have entered in the realm of EU and made significant imprints on the regime of official secrets. The book shows how that regime had a spillover effect on the institutional design of oversight 'outside' the Treaties and its impact on fundamental rights.[8]

The book offers the first comprehensive and in-depth account of the law and practices of official secrets in the EU. Whilst secrecy is noted as a 'prevalent feature' in European governance,[9] scholars only recently have started studying it in a more systematic manner.[10] The specific focus on EU

Working Paper 4/2011. See also Vigjilenca Abazi, 'Transparency in the Institutionalisation of Transatlantic Relations: Dynamics of Official Secrets and Access to Information in Security and Trade' in Elaine Fahey (ed) *Institutionalisation Beyond the State: Transatlantic Relations in Data, Privacy and Trade Law* (Springer 2018) 39–54.

[6] See Joined Cases C-584/10 P, C-593/10 P, and C-595/10 P *Commission and Others v Kadi* EU:C:2013:518; Case C-300/11 *ZZ v Secretary of State for the Home Department* EU:C:2013:363. See also Christina Eckes, *EU Counter-Terrorist Policies and Fundamental Rights: The Case of Individual Sanctions* (OUP 2009). For a critical discussion on access to justice as a consequence of secrecy see, Vigjilenca Abazi and Christina Eckes, 'Closed Evidence in EU Courts: Security, Secrets and Access to Justice' (2018) 55(3) Common Market Law Review 753.

[7] Presentation by the EO Emily O'Reilly, Decision of the European Ombudsman closing the inquiry into complaint 1148/2013/TN as regards Europol.

[8] Primary EU law does not provide a specific provision for official secret rules or oversight for such a regime. Chapter 2 of this book explains in detail the legal history and development of these rules, including institutional choices for basing the regime on internal procedural rules.

[9] Berthold Rittberger and Klaus H Goetz, 'Secrecy in Europe' (2018) 41(4) West European Politics 825, 826.

[10] Deirdre Curtin has conducted some of the leading research on 'secrecy' as a separate phenomenon in EU law and governance. On 16 March 2011, she delivered the Max Weber Lecture on 'Keeping government secrecy safe: Beyond whack-a-mole' European University Institute, Max Weber Lecture No 2011/07 and later in the same year, Curtin further discussed secrecy in her Inaugural lecture at University of Amsterdam on 'Top Secret Europe' 20 October 2011, Inaugural Lecture No 415. Curtin's work on the topic resulted in a series of articles addressing

official secrets is almost missing, apart from some notable exceptions.[11] Yet, the regime of official secrets has distinctive features and implications that merit attention and analysis. As this book will show, rules on official secrets are capable of shifting practices of oversight disproportionately in favour of secrecy whilst creating serious limitations to open democratic deliberations and access to justice. Changes in how the EU keeps secrets happened incrementally and through internal rules, mostly adopted behind closed doors and only involving selected actors. Whether any consideration is given to constitutional commitments of openness and democracy and how the latter restrict the use of official secrets is what this book aims to discern and discuss. Furthermore, official secrets are core to the MS' sense of sovereignty and especially state secrets in the field of security.[12] The book maps the key moments in the EU's development as a security actor and shows how rules on official secrets were a means for the EU to gain more autonomy from MS in external security cooperation. Significantly, the rules on official secrets for a certain period functioned without the 'normal legal and bureaucratic checks and balances'[13] since the EU constitutional setting did not include sufficient prerogatives for democratic oversight in the security field. These rules have now expanded well beyond the security realm. The book critically analyses whether they are subject to appropriate democratic scrutiny. In the ensuing parts of this chapter, I outline these themes of the book in more detail. I also explain the main concepts of the book, its methodology, and structure.

key aspects of official secrets, see 'Judging EU Secrecy' (2012) Cahiers de Droit Européen 457; 'Official Secrets and the Negotiation of International Agreements: Is the EU Executive Unbound?' (2013) 50 Common Market Law Review 423; and 'Overseeing Secrets in the EU: A Democratic Perspective' (2014) 52 Journal of Common Market Studies 684.

[11] See Alasdair Roberts, *Blacked Out: Government Secrecy in the Information Age* (CUP 2006), who discusses official secrets in EU MS. For a recent analysis of secrecy, including official secrets in the EU, see Guri Rosen, 'EU Confidential: The European Parliament's Involvement in EU Security and Defence Policy' (2015) 53(2) Journal of Common Market Studies 383; Mai'a K Davis Cross, 'Secrecy and the Making of CFSP' (2018) 41(4) West European Politics 914.

[12] Different EU primary law provisions show the sensitivity of MS on the issue of national security and especially official secrets in this context. See particularly art 4 TEU noting that national security remains 'the sole responsibility of each Member State' and art 364(1)(a) TFEU stating that 'no Member State shall be obliged to supply information the disclosure of which it considers contrary to the essential interests of its security'. Yet, the CJEU offers a narrow interpretation of the latter provision in light of the principle of sincere cooperation, see Case C-284/05 *Commission v Finland* EU:C:2009:778, para 47. For an elaborate discussion see Chapters 2 and 4 of this book.

[13] For similarities with the US context, see Mark Fenster, *The Transparency Fix: Secrets, Leaks and Uncontrollable Government Information* (Stanford University Press 2017) 6.

Framing Official Secrets within Democratic Constraints

Secrecy is 'endemic' to all organizations and woven into their fabric in multiple ways.[14] But what exactly is 'secrecy'?[15] At its core, Bok described it as an intentional concealment of information, expressed in 'the methods ... and the practices of concealment'.[16] In public institutions this concealment is governed by a set of rules and practices, which Rittberger and Goetz refer to as the 'governance of secrecy'.[17] The governance of secrecy encompasses the 'decision-making structures, regulatory frameworks and rules that regulate the flow of politically relevant information'.[18] In many MS these rules are generally set out in legislation.[19] Unlike the MS, the EU

[14] Jana Costas and Christopher Grey, *Secrecy at Work: The Hidden Architectures of Organisational Life* (Stanford University Press 2016) 1.

[15] Secrecy has been addressed through different methodologies and in varied subfields of law and political science. See inter alia Woodrow Wilson, 'The Study of Administration' (1887) 2 Political Science Quarterly 197; Woodrow Wilson, *The New Freedom: A Call for the Emancipation of the Generous Energies of a People* (The Country Life Press 1916); Daniel Moynihan, *Secrecy: The American Experience* (Yale University Press 1999); Clive Parry, 'Legislatures and Secrecy' (1954) 67 Harvard Law Review 737, 739; Harold C Relyea, 'Opening Government to Public Scrutiny: A Decade of Federal Efforts' (1975) 35 Public Administration Review 3. Other contributions suggesting policy changes, such as tightening the criteria and standards for classifying information, improving oversight, and enforcing systematic and mandatory declassification programmes: Frederick M Kaiser, 'The Amount of Classified Information: Causes, Consequences, and Correctives of a Growing Concern' (1989) 6 Government Information Quarterly 247. For government secrecy but also secrecy in law, see Kim Lane Scheppele, *Legal Secrets* (University of Chicago Press 1988); Itzhak Galnoor, 'Government Secrecy: Exchanges, Intermediaries, and Middlemen' (1975) 35 Public Administration Review 32; Ritchie P Lowry, 'Toward a Sociology of Secrecy and Security Systems' in Stanton K Tefft (ed), *Secrecy: A Cross-Cultural Perspective* (Human Sciences Press 1980); Itzhak Galnoor, *Government Secrecy in Democracies* (New York University Press 1972); Lisa Blank, 'Introduction' in Susan Maret and Jan Goldman (eds), *Government Secrecy: Classic and Contemporary Readings* (Libraries Unlimited 2009).

[16] Sissela Bok, *Secrets: On the Ethics of Concealment and Revelation* (Pantheon Books 1982) 6. Costas and Grey make a distinction between secrets and secrecy, 'understood as a difference between content and process, so that a secret is the thing that is concealed—typically some piece of knowledge or information—whereas secrecy is the act of concealment, the keeping of a secret', Costas and Grey (n 14) 9.

[17] Rittberger and Goetz (n 9) 826.

[18] ibid.

[19] See eg France rules on official secrets are stipulated in Penal Code, art 413(9), Romania official secrets are provided in Law 182/2002, and Italy has protection of official secrets under the Law No 124 of 3 August 2007.

regulatory framework was developed incrementally through internal institutional rules. The EU does not have a legislative act dealing with official secrets. Rather, it has a patchwork of rules and standards that form the governance of official secrets. As the book will discuss at length, the EU framework is a result of a concerted push by the Council for a horizontal 'harmonization' of rules through peer pressure and common standards.[20]

More relevant than the concealed information is the power to keep secrets, which is seen as deeply valuable and integral to the authority of the state or an organization.[21] Weber argued that bureaucracies may seek to increase their 'superiority' by 'keeping their knowledge and intentions secret' and would use official secrets to avoid oversight, embarrassment, and criticism.[22] In the contemporary EU legal context, Curtin argues that official secrets create an 'unbound' space for executive power and limit parliamentary oversight.[23] The main quandary on official secrets is whether a regulatory framework could concurrently establish protection of relevant information and prevent or disclose abuse of power.[24] Exploring this dilemma of constraints to official secrets is at the heart of this book.[25]

Against this background, the research question this book seeks to answer is whether and how the EU rules and practice of official secrets impede parliamentary, judicial, and administrative oversight. The book argues that official secrets should be constrained based on principles of democracy and openness. Without undermining the 'extreme difficulty to design an effective regulatory framework that delivers'[26] both on security and

[20] See Chapter 2 of this book.

[21] Thierry Balzacq and Benjamin Puybareau, 'The Economy of Secrecy: Security, Information Control, and EU–US Relations' (2018) 41(4) West European Politics 890, 891.

[22] Max Weber, *Economy and Society* (Guenther Roth and Claus Wittich eds, Bedminster Press 1968) 233.

[23] See Curtin, 'Overseeing Secrets in the EU: A Democratic Perspective' (n 10).

[24] For a discussion on this issue in the US context, see Rahul Sagar, *Secrets and Leaks: The Dilemma of State Secrecy* (Princeton University Press 2013) 3.

[25] It is important to note, however, that the dichotomy between secrecy and transparency can be a simplistic one if one fails to acknowledge that these notions generally exist in a spectrum and co-relate to each other in a dynamic equilibrium. See eg Mark Fenster, 'The Implausibility of Secrecy' (2014) 65 Hastings Law Review 309; Mark Fenster, 'The Opacity of Transparency' (2006) 91 Iowa Law Review 885. Furthermore, in conceptual terms, Claire Birchall argues that 'the moral discourse that condemns secrecy and rewards transparency may cause us to overlook the integral, perhaps constitutive, role secrecy (in different stages) might play'. See Claire Birchall, 'The Politics of Opacity and Openness: Introduction to "Transparency"' (2011) 28 Theory, Culture & Society 7, 12.

[26] Sagar, '*Secrets and Leaks: The Dilemma of State Secrecy*' (n 24) 3.

oversight, this book shows that the EU has been focused on constructing a regime based predominantly on security considerations, without sufficiently taking into account the constitutional commitments to openness and democracy. The book acknowledges the inherent challenges of design to ensure both openness and security-based secrecy. Yet, drawing lines between these values should be a matter of public debate rather than the choice of committees that meet behind closed doors.

Governance of Official Secrets and Executive Discretion

The book looks at the emergence and expansion of official secrets. The establishment of the rules was a contested issue between executive institutions, on whether the Council or the Commission should take the lead, and among them and the EP, on whether such rules are at all necessary in the EU. The governance of official secrets is also marked by contradictions. For example, the establishment of rules on public access to documents was followed with the establishment of even more rigid rules on official secrets. As Lodge explains, 'regulating access to documents inevitably required the adoption of principles for denying such access'.[27] Another contradiction relates to the autonomy of the EU as a security actor: having its own regulatory framework enabled the EU to establish more security cooperation internationally,[28] yet national rules, authorities, and information still have an indispensable role and stand at the crux of EU governance of official secrets.

The book also focuses on executive discretion[29] in a two-fold manner: first, in a broader sense, it examines how executive discretion has

[27] Juliet Lodge, 'Transparency and Democratic Legitimacy' (1994) 32(3) Journal of Common Market Studies 343, 349; Juliet Lodge, 'Communicating (in)Security: A Failure of Public Diplomacy?' (November 2006) Research Paper No 3, The Challenging Landscape of European Liberty and Security,. See how the rationales of security continue to expand in the EU, Juliet Lodge, 'EU Homeland Security: Citizens or Suspects?' (2004) 26(3) Journal of European Integration 253.

[28] For the EU's security role see Martin Trybus and Nigel White, *European Security Law* (OUP 2007); for the importance of official secrets for the EU to gain a better role for security see, Panos Koutrakos, *The EU Common Security and Defence Policy* (OUP 2013) 203–05.

[29] See Chapter 3 of this book for the definition of 'executive discretion' as understood and developed in this book and the references therein.

affected the design of the regulatory framework. Second, in a narrower and empirical sense, the book shows the workings of official secrets by examining how EU officials make decisions in practice. Drawing from original interview material with forty practitioners and other stakeholders, the book shows how administrative discretion operates in the EU and how it creates a de facto EU executive privilege in withholding security-sensitive information.[30] It has been argued that executive actors deliberately create a 'protected sphere', which allows democratic oversight mechanisms to be evaded.[31] This book identifies the small-scale changes in practice that are conducive to this executive power and enable such a protected sphere.

Oversight and Fundamental Rights

The impact of official secrets on oversight and fundamental rights is one of the central themes of this book. Debates in the EU have mainly focused on accountability, participation, and judicial review but have not addressed the serious democratic and structural challenges posed by official secrets, apart from a few exceptions.[32] This book fills this gap by comprehensively examining the three main branches of institutional oversight: parliamentary, judicial, and administrative.

The book proposes democratic constraints based on processes of accountability and public deliberation. It is argued that these processes should

[30] This builds on relevant work done on addressing how executive power develops and operates in the EU, see Deirdre Curtin, *Executive Power in the EU* (OUP 2009); as well as issues of administrative discretion and the relevance of transparency in the EU administrative law, see Paul Craig, *EU Administrative Law* (OUP 2012).

[31] Peter Mair, *Ruling the Void: The Hallowing of Western Democracy* (Verso 2013) 99.

[32] See inter alia Geert De Baere, *Constitutional Principles of EU External Relations* (OUP 2008); Joana Mendes, *Participation in EU Rule-making: A Rights-based Approach by Joana Mendes* (OUP 2011); Madalina Busuioc, *European Agencies: Law and Practices of Accountability* (OUP 2013); Mitchel de SOl'E Lasser, *Judicial Deliberations: A Comparative Analysis of Transparency and Legitimacy* (OUP 2009); Anthony Arnull and Daniel Wincott (eds), *Accountability and Legitimacy in the European Union* (OUP 2003). But see exceptions Curtin, all works cited in n 10), Christina Eckes, 'Decision-making in the Dark? Autonomous EU Sanctions and National Classification' in Iain Cameron (ed), *EU Sanctions: Law and Policy Issues Concerning Restrictive Measures* (Supranational Criminal Law Series, Book 15, Intersentia 2013); Nik de Boer, 'Secret Evidence and Due Process Rights under EU Law: ZZ' (2014) 51 Common Market Law Review 1235; Marieke de Goede and Mara Wesseling, 'Secrecy and Security in Transatlantic Terrorism Finance Tracking' (2016) 39 Journal of European Integration 253.

always be safeguarded, even if the information itself remains secret. The emphasis on procedural openness for accountability and substantial publicity for deliberation builds on Thompson's seminal work on 'democratic secrecy'.[33] The basic idea is that for democratic processes to be achievable, some level of openness in the governance of official secrets is necessary. Hence, if 'first order' disclosure is impossible, that is revealing the secrets, the 'second order' is a necessary condition. In the latter case, secrecy is justifiable 'only if it is actually justified in a process that itself is not secret'[34] and we must have 'at least potential knowledge of the range of actors that are involved in that process'.[35]

Access to official secrets for oversight institutions is essential for the realization of accountability and public deliberation. The book however shows that limited or no access at all is a recurrent problem in the EU leading to delayed or obstructed processes of judicial, parliamentary, and administrative oversight. The book argues that official secrets create a structural imbalance of power since EU oversight institutions are reliant on the discretion of secret-keepers to actually conduct their constitutional prerogatives and core functions.

The EP and the CJEU are often depicted as the 'champion for more openness and transparency'.[36] This book offers a more nuanced view on these oversight institutions and their role in transparency and secrecy dynamics in the EU. The book shows that the governance of official secrets has influenced changes in how public deliberation and fundamental rights are exercised in the EU. Both the EP and the CJEU have made significant changes to their oversight arrangements through their rules of procedure leading to parliamentary oversight behind closed doors and the use of secret evidence in court. The book argues that closed parliamentary oversight does not sufficiently take into account the necessities of public deliberation and focuses predominantly on peer accountability and demonstrates how secret evidence fails to meet the standards of access to justice as set in previous case law of the CJEU as well as the European Court of Human Rights.

[33] Dennis Thompson, 'Democratic Secrecy' (1999) 114(2) Political Science Quarterly 181.

[34] ibid 185. For an argument in defence of 'a domain of state secrecy' and why such a domain is justified under its own rationale, see Dorota Mokrosinska, 'The People's Right to Know and State Secrecy' (2018) 1 Canadian Journal of Law & Jurisprudence 87.

[35] Deirdre Curtin, 'Second Order Secrecy and Europe's Legality Mosaics' (2018) 41(4) West European Politics 846, 847.

[36] Rittberger and Goetz, 'Secrecy in Europe' (n 9) 837.

Methodological Considerations

This book offers a legal account of official secrets in the EU with the purpose to trace their development, map the current regulatory framework, and show how it is applied in practice. The book also focuses on the effects and implications of oversight and fundamental rights in light of official secrets. The normative argument this book makes is that the governance of official secrets should be constrained on the basis of democratic principles. The justification for adopting a democratic perspective is twofold: first, the EU has made constitutional commitments to principles of democracy and openness and it has declared access to information and access to justice as fundamental rights.[37] Second, ultimately the aim of official secrets is to ensure the public interest in security, democratic governance, and cooperation. All these values should hence be inherent in the design of official secrets architecture, as the book develops more in depth in the following chapter.

A national understanding and approach to official secrets cannot be merely transposed to the EU. Rather, an understanding of the EU's structural complexities is required in order to understand official secrets in the EU. These complexities, however, deeply involve national rules, authorities, and information, which the book takes into account and explains where it is necessary to map the system overall. Hence, whilst the book does not take a comparative national law perspective, it also does not ignore relevant national elements that are pertinent to the system of official secrets. A similar approach is adopted with regard to other regional legal regimes, such as that of the European Convention of Human Rights (ECHR). Whilst this is not a comparative study, the book examines relevant case law from the European Court of Human Rights when it discussed the impact of official secrets on access to justice. This is necessary from an EU law perspective, taking into account that Article 53(3) of the EU Charter of Fundamental Rights declares that a Charter right corresponding to a right under the ECHR should be interpreted similarly to the ECHR right.

[37] See art 1 TEU, art 2 TEU, Title II TEU. This book does not attempt to define the EU as a state-like organization or define its integration processes, but focuses on the internal requirements, ie Treaty previsions, for the EU's legal setting and principles by which it is bound to exercise its powers.

Lastly, in addition to the legal analysis, this book also examines how official secrets are applied in practice. This is motivated by the fact that the argument on whether official secrets are necessary cannot be made on a general and abstract level, but rather it is a question of whether concealing a document is necessary in a given instance. How is this necessity determined in practice?[38] To what extent does practice follow the rules? To what extent is the practice of official secrets in the EU fragmented given the patchwork of rules per institution, agency, and body? The book answers these questions through original material derived from semi-structured interviews. These interviews were conducted with EU officials (current and former) who have specific insight into the workings of official secrets, those who have technical expertise but who are not necessarily involved in producing sensitive documents, and officials who do not deal with the technical aspects and who have a broader (political) overview and functions. The book also includes interviews with Members of the EP, civil society organizations, security experts, and academics involved in this issue. The diversity of interviewees in terms of policy issue, hierarchical level, and whether they are current or former officials, provides this research with a comprehensive and nuanced understanding of practice.[39]

[38] In mapping and analysing how official secrets are organized, this book relies on the concept of a 'life-cycle' of information. It is generally accepted that the concept of the life-cycle of information is not static and abstract but rather a practical plan for managing information. Applying this approach means looking at the entire process of official secrets, from the initial stage of classifying a document, throughout the entire classification stage and until such time as the document may be declassified. The process of classification consists of many decisions that trigger each other and different officials are in charge of making these decisions. The life-cycle approach is useful in order to give a comprehensive overview and to identify which decisions have more relevance and may have consequences for oversight. It was introduced as a conceptual framework to analyse information in government policies in 1993 by DeSanti. See Vincent M DeSanti, 'A Policy Framework on the Dissemination of Government Electronic Information: Some Remarks' (1993) 10 Government Information Quarterly 256. Only a year later Hernon provided the first in-depth analysis of the information life-cycle who lives in a pineapple under the sea, tracing the concept in policy instruments and literature: Peter Hernon, 'Information Life Cycle: Its Place in the Management of U.S. Government Information Resources' (1994) 11 Government Information Quarterly 147. This approach is also in line with applicable rules on official secrets. For example, the concept can be found in the Council Decision on the security rules for protecting EU classified information. See Council Decision 2013/488/EU of 23 September 2013 on the security rules for protecting EU classified information [2013] OJ L274/1, arts 5(2), 9(1), 11(1).

[39] On the relevance of the representative character of the sample of interviewees, see Robert S Weiss, *Learning from Strangers. The Art and Method of Qualitative Interview Studies* (Free Press 1994) 17.

The Structure of the Book

The themes of this book are structured in five main chapters. Chapter 1 provides the EU constitutional context in which the tensions between oversight and official secrets unfold. It lays out the evolving architecture of the EU in the field of security, the role of oversight institutions, and information asymmetries between oversight and executive actors. In addition, the first chapter elaborates the theoretical foundations of the book, focusing on democratic constraints that should apply to official secrets in democratic governance. Chapter 2 analyses the current legal framework of official secrets in the EU and its complexities. It identifies the key moments for the development of the regime as an independent set of rules from the MS and its relevance for the EU's efforts in increasing its security role. The chapter also questions the influence of security actors such as NATO on the possible introduction of a military-like secrecy culture in the EU. Moving from the regulatory framework and its development towards examining practice, Chapter 3 enquires into how the discretion to create official secrets is applied and whether internal administrative review mechanisms exist, either *ex durante* or *ex post*, to address possible unwarranted official secrets. In addition, the chapter provides an account of the central principles of managing official secrets and questions the role of national rules and national authorities in this regard. Through a joint analysis of the CJEU, the EP, and the EO, Chapter 4 questions whether the current rules and the resulting limitations for oversight institutions in gaining access to and the review of official secrets lead to an 'executive privilege' in secrecy in the EU. It is argued that a wide scope of discretion in official secrets on the side of executive institutions would be incompatible with the EU's constitutional commitment to principles of democracy and openness. Chapter 5 shows how the practice of oversight has been fundamentally affected by the rules of official secrets. The chapter explains how EU oversight institutions driven by the aim of ensuring access to official secrets have made changes that significantly alter public debate and right of access to justice in the EU. What is remarkable about these changes to the procedural rules is that they have been developed and adopted mostly behind closed doors whilst they negatively impact core constitutional prerogatives and obligations. Finally, the book provides the Conclusions, offering a summary of the findings and several observations on the constitutional implications of official secrets and oversight in the EU.

1

The Oversight Dilemma and Democratic Constraints on Official Secrets in the EU Constitutional Context

Abstracts
A twofold dilemma persists in the democratic oversight of official secrets: how to ensure oversight while safeguarding official secrets when they are necessary, and how to decipher the necessary ones when they are diluted in the depths of unnecessary bureaucratic secrets. This chapter provides a framework to tackle this quandary in the EU constitutional context. Firstly, the chapter explains the EU constitutional setting in which the tensions between oversight and official secrets unfold by discussing the evolving architecture of the EU in the field of security, the role of oversight institutions, and information asymmetries between oversight and executive actors. Secondly, drawing from democratic theory, the chapter proposes democratic constraints that should apply to official secrets in democratic governance. By joining the EU constitutional context and democratic constraints on official secrets, this chapter aims to provide the theoretical foundations for the ensuing chapters of this book.

Introduction

Over the past sixty years, the European Union has evolved significantly, including in the field of security. The latter gives rise to classic tensions between oversight and openness on the one hand and the need for confidentiality on the other hand. While democracy requires openness, some legitimate democratic policies, especially in security, require reliance on official secrets for their realization. For example, keeping intelligence sources secret is generally accepted to be necessary for security purposes. Yet, as a result, this information is then inaccessible, making accountability and public deliberation difficult or even impossible to attain. Notwithstanding legitimate security interests, official secrets could be applied to information that is embarrassing or incriminating for officials if disclosed, leading to unjustified hidden information. A twofold quandary hence arises between democracy and official secrets: how to ensure oversight while safeguarding official secrets when necessary, and how to decipher necessary secrets, which may be diluted in the depths of unnecessary bureaucratic secrets.

This chapter lays out this quandary in the EU constitutional context. It examines the EU's 'sophisticated institutional structure'[1] and its growing role in security. The chapter focuses on the position of oversight institutions and the information asymmetries between executive and oversight institutions. Upon setting the constitutional scene for tensions between openness and official secrets in the EU, the chapter continues with explaining the democratic constraints that should apply to official secrets. The democratic constraints established in this chapter strive to frame a strictly conditioned use of justified and necessary official secrets.

The Evolving Architecture of the European Union

This chapter builds on a general constitutional understanding of the EU as a multi-layered system where a number of actors partake in EU decision-making at different levels. This section outlines the EU's growing powers in security and unveils the complexities of power sharing between actors at the EU and at the national level.

Growing powers in security

The EU has a wide array of executive powers in security policies.[2] Especially in the post-Lisbon context, the EU is considered as a relevant security actor,[3]

[1] See Opinion 2/13 of the Court (Full Court) of 18 December 2014, EU:C:2014:2454, para 158.

[2] For the notion of 'executive' in the EU context, see Deirdre Curtin, *Executive Power of the European Union: Law, Practices, and the Living Constitution* (OUP 2009).

[3] See Mai'a K Davis Cross, *Security Integration in Europe: How Knowledge-based Networks Are Transforming the European Union* (University of Michigan Press 2011).

with increased competences.[4] Whilst in EU primary law 'national security' explicitly remains 'the sole responsibility of each Member State'[5] the Court of Justice of the European Union (CJEU) in *Svenska* v *Council* held that the EU's competences in security have a broad character covering both aspects of internal and external security.[6] The EU's competences relate to the Area of Freedom Security and Justice (AFSJ) as well as the Common Foreign and Security Policy (CFSP). In these fields, the EU has established numerous legislative instruments and international agreements.[7]

Security polices and cooperation in the EU started to develop both within and outside the EU legal remit. The growth of the EU's powers in security is driven by executive actors and triggered by external influences and the necessities of the EU to respond to them.[8] In the post-Maastricht phase, steps were taken to enhance mutual cooperation between Member States (MS) regarding internal and external security. New bodies and structures were established and cooperation through information exchanges was particularly salient. For example, Article K1 (9) of the EU Treaty first mentioned a 'Union-wide system for exchanging police information', which in turn led to the establishment of Europol, an agency for intelligence co-operation through a Ministerial Agreement.[9] In this period, the EU was also focused on developing coordinated diplomatic action and building on the steps taken under European Political Cooperation.[10] The Helsinki

[4] See Title V, TFEU. The EU has legislative competences in establishing inter alias uniform asylum system, uniform status for third country nationals, mutual recognition and enforcement of judgments, setting minimum rules for and combating terrorism, human trafficking, illicit drug trafficking, money laundering, corruption, counterfeiting, and organized crime.

[5] Art 4(2) TEU. See art 72 TFEU, where similarly the MS aim to make sure that their prerogatives are safeguarded, such as in the maintenance of law and order.

[6] Case T-174/95 *Svenska Journalistförbundet v Council* EU:T:1998:127, para 121. See also Case C-70/94 *Werner v Germany* EU:C:1995:328, para 25; and Case C-72/83 *Campus Oil v Minister for Industry and Energy* EU:C:1984:256, para 34.

[7] For example see Directive 2012/29 establishing minimum standards on the rights, support and protection of victims of crime, and replacing Council Framework Decision 2001/220/JHA [2012] OJ L315/57; Directive 2012/13 on the right to information in criminal proceedings [2012] OJ L142/1; Directive 2011/99 on the European protection order [2011] OJ L338/2.

[8] See George Tsebelis and Geoffrey Garrett, 'The Institutional Foundations of Intergovernmentalism and Supranationalism in the European Union' (2001) 55 International Organization 357; and Paul Pierson, 'The Path to European Integration: A Historical Institutionalist Analysis' (1996) 29(2) Comparative Political Studies 123, 123.

[9] Rachel Woodward, 'Establishing Europol' (1994) 1 European Journal on Criminal Policy and Research 7.

[10] Simon J Nuttall, *European Political Cooperation* (OUP 1992) 674.

Presidency meeting in 1999 most evidently showed the MS' political willingness to develop the EU's military and non-military crisis management means and to reinforce European security and defence policy.[11] The security developments in the Balkans at the time and the NATO response to them were an impetus for the EU to rethink its role in security and its future level of autonomy for action.[12] A consensus was emerging among MS that 'the European Union should have the autonomous capacity to take decisions and, where NATO as a whole is not engaged, to launch and then to conduct EU-led military operations in response to international crises in support of the [common foreign and security policy]'.[13] This was also a time when the Union was preparing for the enlargement of ten new MS, leading to new and more resources of information in security policies.[14]

The Lisbon Treaty strengthened the EU's security role in a variety of international fields, including in military and civilian missions.[15] Despite the progress of the EU in external security and cooperation, its competences in CFSP are difficult to precisely delineate between the EU and national level and the relevant legal provisions are spread out between the Treaty on European Union (TEU) and the Treaty on the Functioning of the European Union (TFEU). The EU has a general competence for CFSP within TEU and various more specific powers within TFEU.[16] In this area of EU law, the EU's competences are undefined, in the sense of being neither exclusive nor shared.[17] EU acts cannot be of legislative nature in the CFSP and these acts differ from 'standard EU legal acts'.[18] They include

[11] Helsinki European Council, 10 and 11 December 1999, Presidency Conclusions, para 1.

[12] For the EU's more current engagement in the Balkans see Steven Blockmans, 'Between Dream and Reality: Challenges to the Legal Rapprochement of the Western Balkans' in Peter Van Elsuwege and Roman Petrov (eds), *Legal Approximation and Application of EU Law in the Eastern Neighbourhood of the European Union: Towards a Common Regulatory Space?* (Routledge 2014).

[13] Richard G Whitman, 'NATO, the EU and ESDP: An Emerging Division of Labour?' (2004) 25 Contemporary Security Policy 430, 437.

[14] For an overview of European integration since 1945, see Desmond Dinan (ed), *Origins and Evolution of the European Union* (2nd edn, OUP 2014).

[15] Marise Cremona, 'The Union as a Global Actor: Roles, Models and Identity' (2004) 41 Common Market Law Review 553.

[16] For example, see art 215 TFEU.

[17] One reason for not stipulating the CFSP as a shared competence, has been said to be that shared competences are described as having a pre-emptive effect. See Piet Eeckhout, 'The EU's Common Foreign and Security Policy after Lisbon: From Pillar Talk to Constitutionalism' in Andrea Biondi, Piet Eeckhout, and Stefanie Ripley (eds), *EU Law after Lisbon* (OUP 2012).

[18] ibid 265.

general guidelines and decisions related to a variety of positions or actions to be taken by the Union.[19] Contrary to CFSP, the EU's competences in the AFSJ are shared between the EU and the MS.[20] The EU's competence in the AFSJ is seen as an 'inevitable consequence'[21] of the cross-border nature of crime due to the elimination of internal borders followed by the incapability of EU MS to deal with crime individually.[22] Although the AFSJ is intended to cover the internal security aspects, external elements are not uncommon. The EU can act externally on any AFSJ subject matter if there is a primary law defined internal objective and if external action is necessary to achieve that objective.[23] For example, the EU has concluded international agreements aimed at fighting serious crime and terrorism, which precisely exemplify this mixture between the elements of the AFSJ and external security.[24] Similarly, although the EU's restrictive measures, also known as sanctions directed against third countries or individuals, fall under the CFSP,[25] they also contribute to the internal security.

Despite the significant development of the EU's powers, MS maintain a relevant role in EU security. The exact division of powers between the EU and its MS was determined 'rather fluidly' until the Lisbon Treaty came into force.[26] MS have recognized the necessity of cooperating on security

[19] ibid 280. [20] Art 4(2)(j) TFEU

[21] Christina Eckes and Theodore Konstadinides (eds), *Crime within the Area of Freedom, Security and Justice: A European Public Order* (CUP 2011) 1–2.

[22] For a different rationale see Cathryn Costello, 'Administrative Governance and the Europeanization of Asylum and Immigration Policy' in Herwig Hofmann and Alexander Türk (eds), *EU Administrative Governance* (Edward Elgar 2006) 289. Other experts criticize the functionality in AFSJ as having been driven with 'institutional design and control pragmatically tailored to ever expanding policy aspirations rather than articulating a sense of the best constitutional settlement for a mature polity', see Neil Walker (ed), *Europe's Area of Freedom, Security and Justice* (OUP 2004) 31.

[23] Art 216(1) TFEU, see Jörg Monar, 'The EU's Growing External Role in the AFSJ Domain: Factors, Framework and Forms of Action' (2014) 27 Cambridge Review of International Affairs 147.

[24] Agreement between the European Union and the United States of America on the processing and Transfer of Financial Messaging data from the European Union to the United States for the purposes of the Terrorist Finance Tracking Program [2010] OJ L195/5, art 4(9). See Marise Cremona, 'Justice and Home Affairs in a Globalised World: Ambitions and Reality in the tale of the EU-US SWIFT Agreement' (2011) Institute for European Integration Research Working Paper 4/2011.

[25] Art 215 TFEU.

[26] Grainne de Burca and Bruno de Witte, 'The Delimitation of Powers between the EU and its Member States' in Anthony Arnull and Daniel Wincott (eds), *Accountability and Legitimacy in the European Union* (OUP 2002) 201.

policies as threats become more advanced and borderless. Yet, concurrently, they are protective of their powers. For example, MS emphasize that 'national security' remains a national prerogative.[27] Concerning information sharing as a crucial aspect of the effectiveness of security policies, primary law provides that 'no Member State shall be obliged to supply information the disclosure of which it considers contrary to the essential interest of its security'.[28] However, these provisions in primary law should be read in light of established EU principles regarding the interaction between the EU and its MS. The principle of conferral is salient as it provides that the EU has only those competences that are conferred on it by the MS.[29] The applicability of the principle of conferral is more complex in practice since issues are interconnected and have a mutual impact on whether the EU can act and to what extent it can do so. Both internal and external issues of EU law and policy are not as clear-cut as to be easily split between the EU and MS. For example, operational powers in security, whether in law enforcement or intelligence cooperation, remain at the national level. Yet, the strategic reporting done at EU level on the basis of national information derived from such operational actions is crucial for the ability of MS to conduct cross-border arrests or apply measures in counter-terrorism. Another example is a situation in international law where, although the EU has the competence to act under EU law, it must however rely on the MS to act on its behalf due to the 'blindness of international law towards compound subjects'.[30] The aspect of reliance in the relationship between the EU and its MS directly links with the second key EU principle in this regard. The principle of sincere cooperation applies in interpreting the MS' obligations to the EU.[31] This principle is ensured through procedural cooperation, which implies mutual consultation and an exchange of information between the EU and the MS.[32] When MS show a reluctance to share

[27] Art 4(2) TEU. [28] Art 346(1a) TFEU.

[29] See arts 4(1) and 5(1) TEU. Conferral is also stipulated in art 3(6) TEU; art 7 TFEU; art 19 TFEU; see Opinion 2/13 (n 1) para 164, where the Court states that it is a fundamental principle of EU law.

[30] Robert Schütze, *European Constitutional Law* (CUP 2012) 217.

[31] Art 4 TEU. This principle also applies on a horizontal level among EU institutions, see art 13(2) TEU.

[32] Stephan Bitter, 'Loyalty in the European Union—A Review' (2002) 3 German Law Journal <https://static1.squarespace.com/static/56330ad3e4b0733dcc0c8495/t/56b9755059827eedd59a6c23/1454994769652/GLJ_Vol_03_No_03_Bitter.pdf> accessed 4 January 2019.

information relevant for security, as in the case *Commission v Finland*, the Court held that derogations must be interpreted strictly and not understood as conferring on MS a power of veto on the basis of national security.[33] The principle of sincere cooperation requires MS not to depart from the application of EU law. This is precisely why the duty of sincere cooperation between the MS and the EU is essential, since through this principle the EU is able to move forward in its workings for which access to national sensitive information is paramount.

Plurality of executive actors

The locus of executive power in the EU is situated within multiple key institutions: the European Council, the Council, and the Commission.[34] Each institution takes a different lead in variance with the area of EU law. In internal and external security, the Council's prerogatives matter when it exercises its executive functions in cooperation for more operational security aspects as well as its functions as co-legislator for issues relating to the AFSJ.

The European Council is seen as the 'constitutional architect'[35] that provides the specific and regular stimuli for the development of the EU.[36] Yet, it is noteworthy that the European Council does not have legislative functions,[37] although in the AFSJ, the European Council is in charge of defining the 'strategic guidelines for legislative and operational planning', which is specific to this policy area.[38] Nevertheless, it is the Commission that has an almost exclusive right to formally propose legislative acts,[39] despite the fact that it increasingly has to accommodate initiatives of the European Council,[40] the Council,[41] the European Parliament (EP),[42] and, since the

[33] Case C-284/05 *Commission v Finland* EU:C:2009:778, para 47. See also art 346(1)(a) TFEU.

[34] See Deirdre Curtin, 'Challenging Executive Dominance in European Democracy' (2014) 77 The Modern Law Review 1.

[35] Wolfgang Wessels et al, 'Democratic Control in the Member States of the European Council and the Euro zone Summits' (2013) study requested by the European Parliament's Committee on Constitutional Affairs, 14.

[36] Schütze (n 30) 103; the EC could be further seen to play significant constitutional functions (see art 48 TEU; art 49 TEU; art 31(3) TEU) as well as institutional functions (see art 14(2) TEU; art 18(1) TEU). See, however, Mark Pollock, *Engines of European Integration: Delegation, Agency, and Agenda Setting in the EU* (OUP 2003).

[37] Art 15(1) TEU. [38] Art 68 TFEU.

[39] Art 17(2) TEU; the Commission also has a right to withdraw proposals: Case C-409/13 *Council v Commission* EU:C:2015:217, para 74.

[40] Art 15(1) TEU. [41] Art 241 TFEU. [42] Art 225 TFEU.

introduction of the citizen's initiative, with the organized civil society.[43] For security policies the Commission has 'difficulties in establishing itself as an agenda setter' despite its legal prerogatives.[44] Some level of collaboration exists in the complex workings between the Commission and the European Council. For example, the Commission is involved both in the preparatory phase and in the implementing phase of European Council sessions.[45] The President of the European Council is supposed to 'ensure the preparation and continuity of the work of the European Council in co-operation with the President of the Commission'.[46] The European Council acts as an arbitrator for handling disputes or conflicts that arise in the Council concerning relevant interests of MS, including to 'release sensitive documents and resolve conflicts that paralyse the Council'.[47] The relation between the Council and the Commission is also paramount as there are a number of acts in security that the Council adopts by a qualified majority upon a proposal from the Commission. For example, the Council has the authority to evaluate the implementation of policies in AFSJ by MS, upon a proposal from the Commission.[48]

The Council takes the lead not merely by being a co-legislator in the field of AFSJ, as it has always played a major role in relation in the configurations of the Foreign Affairs Council and Justice and Home Affairs, but also retains significant executive powers for internal and external security, for example in the imposition of sanctions and the blacklisting of terrorists.[49] The Council is responsible for taking decisions on foreign policy matters and crisis management operations. For example, with the signature of an interim security agreement with NATO on 26 July 2000, an interim military committee within the Council was established, leading to the influx of more sensitive information.[50] The Council Secretariat was the seat

[43] Art 11 TEU. See also Olivier Höing and Wolfgang Wessels, 'The European Commission's Position in the Post-Lisbon Institutional Balance: Secretariat or Partner to the European Council?' in Michele Chang and Jörg Monar (eds), *The European Commission in the Post-Lisbon Era of Crises: Between Politial Leadership and Policy Management* (Peter Lang 2013) 133.

[44] Maylis Labayle, 'The New Commission's Role in Freedom, Security and Justice in the Post-Lisbon Context: New Era or Missed Opportunity?' in Michele Chang and Jörg Monar (eds), *The European Commission in the Post-Lisbon Era of Crises: Between Politial Leadership and Policy Management* (Peter Lang 2013) 236.

[45] Höing and Wessels (n 43) 139.

[46] Art 15(6)(b) TEU

[47] Olivier Costa and Nathalie Brack, *How the EU Really Works* (Ashgate 2014) 61.

[48] Art 70 TFEU.

[49] Curtin, 'Challenging Executive Dominance' (n 34) 6.

[50] David Galloway, 'Classifying Secrets in the EU' (2014) 52 Journal of Common Market Studies 668, 674–75.

of the new crisis management structures and the EU military staff, which supported the Secretary-General who also exercised the role of a High Representative for CFSP at the time.[51] The Council Security Committee is another important internal body that resulted from the increased role in security and the Council's efforts to establish legal and technical arrangements that facilitate this role. This Security Committee, composed at the time of representatives from the Council and each MS as well as the Commission, was particularly focused on the development and expansion of security cooperation through exchanges of sensitive information and the technical security facilities necessary for the influx of such information. The Council's role is pertinent in that it also expanded security cooperation externally with third countries and organizations including Russia, Ukraine, Israel, and the International Criminal Court, to name but a few examples.[52]

In the overall EU institutional framework, the President of the European Council and the High Representative of the Union for Foreign Affairs, who also acts as a vice-President of the Commission, are also relevant figures, although they have 'coordinating functions rather than real executive power'.[53] The role of the High Representative is to express the Union's position on CFSP in the international fora. The High Representative contributes to the development of the CFSP, for which her position as Chair of the Foreign Affairs Council is also relevant,[54] as well as supervising the appointed special representatives of the EU.[55] The responsibilities of the High Representative to ensure consistency in the EU's external action are also important with regard to implementation powers,[56] including in information exchanges among MS, EU institutions, and delegations.[57]

[51] ibid 675.

[52] General Secretariat of the Council, 'Exchange of EU classified information (EUCI) with third States and international organisations' 7 July 2011, Doc 12619/11.

[53] Gerard Conway, 'Recovering a Separation of Powers in the European Union' (2011) 17 European Law Journal 304, 322.

[54] See art 18(2) TEU; art 27(1) TEU. [55] Art 33 TEU. [56] Art 18(4) TEU.

[57] Since the entry into force of the Maastricht Treaty, the established diplomatic missions of the European Community are called 'delegations' and are managed by the Commission. Officially, the 130 Commission delegations changed status on 1 December 2009, making them part of the EEAS structure although their transformation into EU delegations under the authority of the High Representative has pointed to some of the tensions inherent in the new system. See for more Laura Rayner, 'The EU Foreign Ministry and Union Embassies' (2005) The Foreign Policy Centre. For an historic development overview, see European Commission, *Taking Europe to the World: 50 Years of the European Commission's External Service* (European Communities 2004); Michael Kluth and Jess Pilegaard, 'The Making of the EU's

The High Representative relies on the European External Action Service (EEAS) as the 'EU's diplomatic arm',[58] which was formally launched at a 'low key event' behind closed doors in December 2010.[59] The EEAS is seen as a bridge between the Council and the Commission in external action and also cooperation with national administrations.[60]

A pool of bodies mostly focused on information gathering, coordination, and reporting exist. The EU executive actors increasingly depend on the workings of the vast number of agencies and bodies that assist security coordination and mutual cooperation. Most EU agencies and bodies in the area of security do not have operational powers but their primary tasks and rationale of existence is focused around information analysis and reporting. Due to their mostly coordinating roles, information exchange is crucial for their added value to the existing national security authorities. Europol, the EU Satellite Centre, the European Defence Agency, and Eurojust are some of the most significant agencies in EU security policies.

***

The discussion on the EU's evolving architecture shows two predominant features of the EU that are distinctive to its nature and are relevant for oversight: first, there is a continuous development of EU prerogatives and different shifts in power between EU institutions and MS. This may lead to a mismatch between executive and oversight powers and lack of clarity whether such oversight is (or should be) exercised at the EU level, national level, or both. This potential fragmented oversight in turn may result in both overloads and gaps of oversight arrangements. Second, the 'EU executive' is not a unified actor but rather a plurality of actors in a multi-layered context. This may lead to more information asymmetries and lack of clarity about the responsibility of specific actors, actions, and access to

External Action Service: A Neorealist Interpretation' (2012) 17 European Foreign Affairs Review 303, 307.

[58] Council Decision 2010/427/EU of 26 July 2010 Establishing the Organisation and Functioning of the European External Action Service [2010] OJ L201/30; European External Action Service, 'The EU's Many International Roles' <http://eeas.europa.eu/what_we_do/index_en.htm> accessed 21 July 2018.

[59] Andrew Rettman, 'Ashton Names EU Foreign Service Priorities at Low-key Launch Event' *EUObserver* (2 December 2012).

[60] Eeckhout (n 17) 288. See also Steven Blockmans et al, *EEAS 2.0: A Legal Commentary on Council Decision 2010/427/EU Establishing the Organisation and Functioning of the European External Action Service* (Centre for European Policy Studies 2013).

official secrets. In the next section, the chapter turns to examine these features by looking more closely at parliamentary, judicial, and administrative oversight as well as the institutional workings that may lead to more tensions in information asymmetries between executive and oversight institutions.

EU Oversight and Institutional Workings

The first part of this section focuses on the role and powers of oversight institutions, looking specifically at the EP, the CJEU, and the European Ombudsman (EO). It maps their prerogatives in oversight and highlights how they cooperate in order to tackle information asymmetries. The notion of oversight refers to an actor scrutinizing another actor's activities with the aim of evaluating its compliance with particular criteria and, on this basis, issuing recommendations or orders to the actor concerned.[61] The second sub-section maps the institutional workings that are necessary to have a holistic view of the interplays in information between oversight and executive institutions. Understanding the EU's executive institutions' workings is helpful for mapping how the EU works and how oversight in the EU functions in light of such institutional context.

Parliamentary, judicial, and administrative oversight

EU oversight institutions have a constitutional mandate to ensure primary law principles of democracy, openness, and fundamental rights.[62]

[61] Madalina Busuioc, *European Agencies: Law and Practices of Accountability* (OUP 2013) 35.

[62] This should not be misunderstood as meaning that this thesis claims the EU *is* democratic or not. This chapter is not engaged in a debate of democratic deficit, albeit an important ongoing one for decades. See Joseph Weiler et al, 'European Democracy and its Critique' (1995) 18 West European Politics 4; Giandomenico Majone, 'Europe's "Democratic Deficit": The Question of Standards' (1998) 4 European Law Journal 5. Title II of the TEU stipules the EU's democratic principles. Art 10 TEU clearly stipulates that the EU is founded on representative democracy, citizens being directly represented by the EP, and each citizen having the right to participate in EU decision-making. Civil society and national parliaments are also given a democratic role through participation and procedures of scrutiny. See art 11 and art 12 TEU, respectively. Openness is seen as a means that would make EU decisions better reflect the will of citizens. See in this regard the distinction on the role of openness for what the author calls input and output legitimacy: Fritz Scharpf, *Governing in Europe: Effective and Democratic?* (OUP 1999) 6. See also Commission, 'Better regulation for better results—and EU

The prerogatives of EU oversight institutions in security policies continuously evolve and this has direct implications on the extent of their oversight powers. The position of the EP is a prime example in this respect.

The EP has a variety of specific oversight powers.[63] The EP's prerogatives in oversight have increased in a slow manner and it often advances its position through institutional practice and informal de facto changes.[64] The first and basic reason for oversight by the EP of security policy is to ensure its democratic legitimacy, as the only directly elected EU institution.[65] The EP provides a public deliberation platform and this function is crucial for communicating to the citizens what takes place at the EU level. The EP is able to provide a different standpoint on the issues regarding security and it is in a position to possibly challenge 'group thinking' and a predominant executive rationale in decision-making regarding security policies.[66] This can be illustrated by an EU high official's explanation of security measures regarding information that the: '... socialization among security experts in EU institutions and Member States has fostered a shared common interest in developing and preserving the integrity of the framework ... In other words, equivalence is driven through peer pressure (including through a system of visits to Member States and EU agencies by an EU assessment team) ...'[67] The EP is also in a position to actively choose the issues over which it exercises oversight, through parliamentary inquiries and questions as well as other oversight mechanisms. It can set up different types of committees and determine their powers at the time when they are set up, such as the standing committee, special committee, and the

agenda' Communication from the Commission to the European Parliament, the Council, the European Economic and Social Committee and the Committee of the Regions COM(2015) 215 final; Jean-Claude Juncker, 'A New Start for Europe: My Agenda for Jobs, Growth, Fairness and Democratic Change', Speech given to the European Parliament on 15 July 2014.

[63] The EP in line with art 14(1) TEU exercises functions of political control and consultation, art 218(10) TFEU prerogative to be informed on international agreement; Art 319 TFEU provides significant budgetary powers.

[64] Editorial, 'Between the Constitutional Document and the Constitutional Settlement' (2014) 10 European Constitutional Law Review 375.

[65] Art 10(2) TEU affirms the position of the EP as the direct representative of the citizens of the EU.

[66] M Turner and A Pratkanis, 'Twenty-five Years of Groupthink Theory and Research: Lessons from Evolution of a Theory' (1998) 73 Organisational Behavior and Human Decision Process 105.

[67] Galloway (n 50) 677.

committee of inquiry.[68] Yet, the EP's investigative powers fall short of the powers of national committees of inquiry since they do not have the legal authority to conduct evidence-gathering about general subjects in relation to alleged maladministration and inquiries into actions by third-country authorities.[69] The EP's oversight prerogatives also vary depending the EU actor. For example, whereas it can dismiss the Commission, it has no such powers towards the Council.

Security policies can be detrimental to the protection of fundamental rights. In addition to democratic oversight, judicial review is important to ensure that executive power is exercised in line with the rule of law and respect for fundamental rights.[70] Especially for cases regarding security measures, judicial oversight by the CJEU may be the only institutional mechanism to ensure a fair balance between the individual right and the executive prerogatives of the institution.[71] The Court's oversight of security policies has been limited, especially prior to the Lisbon Treaty revisions. With regard to external security, the Court is still limited to 'boundary-policing', that is determining whether the issue in question falls within the competence of the EU under TFEU or if is related to the implementation of common foreign and security policy under TEU,[72] and the Court can only review the legality of decisions authorizing restrictive measures against individuals.[73] The Lisbon Treaty foresees the possibility that when acts of EU security agencies produce 'legal effects' these can fall under the judicial scrutiny of the CJEU.[74] As a result, agencies like Frontex for example could be held accountable before the Court for any actions that may have resulted in alleged breaches of fundamental rights.

[68] EP Rules of Procedure, July 2014: Rule 196—Standing Committee; Rule 197—Special Committee; Rule 198—Committee of inquiry.

[69] European Parliament Research Service, 'The ECHELON Affair: The EP and the Global Interception System 1998–2002' Study, November 2014 at 222 <http://www.europarl.europa.eu/EPRS/EPRS_STUDY_538877_AffaireEchelon-EN.pdf> accessed 21 July 2018.

[70] See in general AV Dicey, The Law of the Constitution (JWF Allison ed, OUP 2013). See Case C-294/83 *Les Verts v Parliament* EU:C:1986:166, para 23. See also Laurent Pech, '"A Union Founded on the Rule of Law": Meaning and Reality of the Rule of Law as a Constitutional Principle of EU Law' (2010) 6 European Constitutional Law Review 359.

[71] Case C-27/09 P *France v People's Mojahedin Organization of Iran*, Opinion of AG Sharpston EU:C:2011:482, para 75.

[72] Art 40 TEU. See also Paul Craig and Grainne De Burca, *EU Law: Text, Cases, and Materials* (5th edn, OUP 2011).

[73] Individual sanctions cases art 275 TFEU.

[74] Art 263 TFEU.

Administrative oversight conducted by the EO has a unique added value due to its duality of tasks and position in the administrative setting.[75] Introduced into the institutional landscape of the EU in the Maastricht Treaty, the EO inquires into possible maladministration in the EU, although it should be stressed that the EO does not have the competences to scrutinize the work of administrative bodies of MS.[76] The EO exercises control over EU administration under its own initiative.[77] It also has the power to receive individual complaints, which the EO addresses through various administrative mechanisms.[78] It has investigative measures to ascertain the factual basis of the cases and means of remedial action in order to address instances of EU maladministration.[79] Although its decisions and recommendations are not legally binding and the EO cannot impose any legal sanction upon the institution, in practice the institutions mostly follow the EO's recommendations. The EO has a unique review position because it is neither focused on creating political opposition to the executive institutions or defending different interests, as is the position of the EP, nor is it focused on declaring their acts void or annulling them, as the Court is in a position to do. The EO reviews the EU administration not only with the aim of identifying maladministration, but in practice the EO also focuses on highlighting best practices as well as negative examples, which creates pressure towards improving institutional workings.

Institutional workings: discretion and closed debates

Executive institutions, particularly the Council, have established the security agencies and bodies that facilitate executive cooperation and the growing networked exchange of security information. More cooperation at EU level has led to the dominance of the executives in security polices whereas oversight institutions, at national and EU level, especially on information exchange, face challenges in asserting their oversight powers.

[75] Although some argue that the EO is a hybrid body combining both instruments of parliamentary and judicial scrutiny, see Paul Magnette, 'Between Parliamentary Control and the Rule of Law: The Political Role of the Ombudsman in the European Union' (2003) 10 Journal of European Public Policy 677, 677 and 678.

[76] Paul Craig, 'The Ombudsman' in Paul Craig, *EU Administrative Law* (OUP 2012) 742.

[77] Art 228 TFEU in conjunction with art 3(1) of the Ombudsman Statute and art 9(1) of the Decision of the European Ombudsman adopting implementing provisions of 8 July 2002 as amended by decisions of the Ombudsman of 5 April 2004 and 3 December 2008 <http://www.ombudsman.europa.eu/en/resources/provisions.faces> accessed 21 July 2018.

[78] Magnette (n 75). [79] Craig (n 76) 752.

Research points out that 'the problem of democratic legitimacy [in the EU] does not lie at the formal Treaty level, but rather in the daily practice of the institutions and their various administrative components'.[80] Hence, the current discussion focuses particularly on the institutional workings of the executives and aims to point out the main aspects regarding information exchanges.

Most of the relevant decisions in the EU's security policies are of a non-legislative nature, established internally within the discretion of the institution, or between the institutions in closed debates. Within executive institutions, internal administrative rules seem a common manner for addressing salient institutional aspects, as is information management. Inter-institutional agreements between the EP on the one hand, and the Council as well as the Commission, on the other hand, also address the cooperation among the institutions including with regard to information exchanges. However, the discussions that lead to these decisions and agreements take place mostly behind closed doors whereas the resulting documents often remain outside the public remit or are heavily redacted. Indeed, longstanding concerns persist in the academic and public debates regarding the EU's development and nature of integration through stealth and competence creep.[81] The EU constitutional presumption in favour of openness juxtapositions the institutional working methods susceptible to closed doors meetings. Such tendency towards secrecy follows not only non-legislative acts, but also closed-door meetings and keeping secret the identity of political decision-makers even in legislative processes.[82] The EU political decision-makers seem to be more convinced that a level of informality and hence less visibility around those processes is necessary and desirable when serious EU issues are at stake and rapid action is needed.[83] This type of action in the EU is more characteristic of core executives, but not exclusive to them. The European Council for example has been noted to make most of its important decisions informally at the dinner after

[80] Deirdre Curtin, 'Overseeing Secrets in the EU: A Democratic Perspective' (2014) 52 Journal of Common Market Studies 684, 687; See also Bojan Bugaric, 'Openness and Transparency in Public Administration: Challenges for Public Law' (2004) 22 Wisconsin International Law Journal 483.

[81] Giandomenico Majone, *Dilemmas of European Integration: The Ambiguities and Pitfalls of Integration by Stealth* (OUP 2005).

[82] Case C-280/11 P *Council v Access Info Europe* EU:C:2013:671.

[83] Valentina Pop, 'Eurogroup Chief: "I'm for Secret, Dark Debates"' *EUobserver* (21 April 2011).

the first day meetings.[84] Even the organization of the European Council meetings is categorized by the 'secretive character of the forum whenever possible'.[85] In such instances, the regular and formal mechanisms of cooperation and information sharing are secondary. In some of the most pressing decisions, the European Council reached its decisions in 'hectic night sessions working under the rules of professional secrecy' with only a few public documents distributed.[86] It is the interplay between rules and practices that continuously affect the dynamics of EU decision-making. Hence, synchronic and strict legal perspectives are less favourable to capture institutional workings that develop in the EU.

EU officials point to the pragmatism involved when it comes to ensuring security protection in information exchanges both with the MS and among EU actors.[87] In a similar manner, pragmatism is also favoured when cooperation is necessary, as EU officials explain, due to the 'dispersed nature of power in the EU's institutional structure and the sheer numbers of individuals involved in policy analysis and decision-making'.[88] The concern that arises due to this pragmatism and informality has to do with information asymmetries both for the oversight institutions as well as among executive actors. In addressing these information asymmetries and making sure that their powers are not obstructed, oversight institutions focus particularly on making sure that they too receive access to information. An important consequence in this regard is what has been referred to as a contest over the extent and security of prerogatives and competences.[89] It is unlikely the interests of those excluded from the information-sharing process will be considered as fully as those included, which increases the tendency of institutions to focus on channels of information sharing and whether they too have access to the relevant information.[90]

Information asymmetry and gaps are also a result of another key factor. Internal administrative rules compartmentalize the information in certain stages of decision-making or with certain actors leading to the creation of clusters of insiders and outsiders. These administrative rules on management of sensitive information have not received sufficient attention in

[84] Costa and Brack (n 47) 64.

[85] Uwe Puetter, *The European Council and the Council: New Intergovernmentalism and Institutional Change* (OUP 2014) 104.

[86] Wessels et al (n 35) 16. [87] See Galloway (n 50) 676. [88] ibid.

[89] Majone (n 81).

[90] Joseph Stiglitz, 'The Private Uses of Public Interests: Incentives and Institutions' (1998) 12 Journal of Economic Perspectives 7.

the EU.[91] Often developed outside public scrutiny or any form of external oversight, these administrative processes compartmentalize information and enable some actors more than others to determine who gets the information and when.[92] This book pays particular attention to these rules by mapping them and analysing their consequences in the EU oversight.

***

Whilst the EU has constitutional commitments to the principles of democracy, openness, and fundamental rights, the discussion on the EU's constitutional context reveals that in practice many significant institutional features challenge the EU's capacity to adhere to these commitments. The EU's continuous evolving nature—both in primary law and through living institutional practice—provides a setting for dynamic arrangements in security and oversight. Taking these core aspects and factors of the EU into account, the book turns to examine what the conditions for oversight and for constraints of official secrets based on democracy ought to be. The purpose of these constraints is to reflect the core democratic foundations that should be followed if a governing system aims to ensure democracy and the need for legitimate official secrets.

Democratic Constraints on Official Secrets

Democracy is understood as a form of governing that purports to ensure citizens' will. This aspect of democracy is well established and elaborated in democratic theory.[93] Opinion is another essential element of democracy

[91] Exceptionally: see Deirdre Curtin, 'Official Secrets and the Negotiation of International Agreements. Is the EU Executive Unbound?' (2013) 50 Common Market Law Review 423.

[92] For examples of how information asymmetries operate in politics, including a discussion of the incentives that information asymmetries create in committee structures, see David Austin-Smith and William H Riker, 'Asymmetric Information and the Coherence of Legislation' (1987) 81 American Political Science Review 897; Vijay Krishna and John Morgan, 'Asymmetric Information and Legislative Rules: Some Amendments' (2001) 95 American Political Science Review 435. For a review of the literature on sensitive information from the perspective of economics, psychology, sociology, etc, see E Dale Thompson and Michelle L Kaarst-Brown, 'Sensitive Information: A Review and Research Agenda' (2005) 56 Journal American Society for Information Science and Technology 245.

[93] Maria Paula Saffon and Nadia Urbinati, 'Procedural Democracy, the Bulwark of Equal Liberty' (2013) 41 Political Theory 441; Norberto Bobbio, *The Future of Democracy* (Richard

equivalent to citizens' will, although it is less emphasized. The realization of will *and* opinion relies on democratic processes of accountability *and* public deliberation. These processes in turn require openness in their realization.[94]

Democratic foundations for constraints on official secrets

Will and opinion are acknowledged as the foundations of democracy, as the 'two powers of the sovereign citizens', in what is called the 'diarchic system' of democracy.[95] Yet, in the realization of democracy emphasis is more often placed on accountability processes. This is to some extent linked to the liberal conceptions of democracy that focus on majoritarian models of ensuring citizens' will and place significance on account giving. Yet, the relation between citizens and public institutions is not one strictly of account giving; it is also one that should facilitate public deliberation. This leads to conditions on how public institutions should function when aiming to ensure the active role of citizens in democracy.[96] In practice a complete separation between opinion and will as foundations of democracy cannot be established. Citizens do not act as a dual actor, one driven by will, the other by opinion. Despite the fact that clear splits between will and opinion cannot be established in practice, it is valuable to point them out conceptually because they show the relevance of *both* accountability and public deliberation for their realization.

Dellamy ed, Roger Griffin tr, Polity 1991); Robert A Dahl, 'Procedural Democracy' in Robert E Goodin and Philip Pettit (eds), *Contemporary Political Philosophy: An Anthology* (Blackwell 1997); Hans Kelsen, *The Essence and Value of Democracy* (Nadia Urbinati and Carlo Invernizzi Accetti eds, Brian Graf tr, Rowman & Littlefield 2013); Philip Pettit, *On the People's Terms: A Republican Theory and Model of Democracy* (CUP 2012); Pierre Rosanvallon, *Counter-Democracy: Politics in an Age of Distrust* (Arthur Goldhammer tr, CUP 2008).

[94] The relevance of openness for democracy is noted as early as 1839, when Jeremy Bentham acknowledged the instrumental value of openness to attain accountability, see Jeremy Bentham, 'Of Publicity' in John Bowring (ed), *Essays on Political Tactics in the Works of Jeremy Bentham* (William Tate 1839).

[95] Nadia Urbinati, *Democracy Disfigured: Opinion, Truth and the People* (Harvard University Press 2014) 2. The discussion on opinion and democracy draws on Urbinati as the most prominent author to develop the position of 'opinion' as a democratic building block. In this sense, it differs from the mere view of opinion as public discussion. Opinion is not seen as merely a facilitator of voting processes and preference creation, but as an equally important and separate building block of democracy that creates its own conditionality on how public institutions should function.

[96] ibid 6.

Accountability and public deliberation rely on openness. They place different types of emphasis on the implementation of openness in practice since they have different objectives: whereas the former aims to make sure that public power is exercised in accordance with citizens' will, the latter aims to enable citizens to create independent and informed opinions based on accurate public information,[97] and broaden the range of citizens who have access to such opportunities.[98] Through openness, citizens are informed and can express their preferences about a policy or a course of action,[99] as well as their preference for political decision-makers through the mechanism of democratic elections. The notion of accountability is used in a broader sense as a 'mutual exchange of responsibilities and potential sanctions between citizens and rulers',[100] and is seen as a feature that sets democracy apart from other (non-democratic) political forms.[101] Openness enables citizens to check and correct the exercise of the delegated power,[102]

[97] Similarly, Francis Rourke, *Secrecy and Publicity: Dilemmas of Democracy* (John Hopkins Press 1961) 90.

[98] See Diana Mutz, *Hearing the Other Side: Deliberative versus Participatory Democracy* (CUP 2006), arguing that deliberation has strong effects on political behaviour.

[99] Amy Gutmann and Dennis Thompson, *Democracy and Disagreement* (Harvard University Press 1998) 98.

[100] Philippe C Schmitter, 'Political Accountability in "Real-Existing" Democracies: Meaning and Mechanisms' (2007) European University Institute, 4. The notion of accountability has been widely used in the literature and beyond, although the legal discourse has only recently witnessed a rise of its importance since the term typically relates to the financial contexts of accountancy and auditing. Steve Peers and Marios Costa, 'The Accountability of Delegated and Implementing Acts after the Treaty of Lisbon' (2012) 18 European Law Journal 427; Elizabeth Fisher, 'The European Union in the Age of Accountability' (2004) 24 Oxford Journal of Legal Studies 495; Richard Mulgan, '"Accountability": An Ever-Expanding Concept?' (2000) 78 Public Administration 555; Deirdre Curtin and Andre Nollkaemper, 'Conceptualizing Accountability in International and European Law' (2005) 36 Netherlands Yearbook of International Law 3; Gijs Brandsma, 'Accountability Deficits in European "Comitology" Decision-Making' (2007) 11 European Integration Online Papers; Carol Harlow, 'European Governance and Accountability' in Nicholas Bamforth and Peter Leyland (eds), *Public Law in a Multi-Layered Constitution* (Hart Publishing 2003); Mark Bovens, 'Analysing and Assessing Accountability: A Conceptual Framework' (2007) 13 European Law Journal 4; Joy M Moncrieffe, 'Accountability: Ideals, Ideas, Constraints' (2001) 8 Democratization 26; Ruth W Grant and Robert O Keohane, 'Accountability and Abuses of Power in World Politics' (2005) 99 American Political Science Review 29.

[101] Schmitter (n 100).

[102] Implying also different types of accountability—political in the sense of elections; legal in terms of specific checks. Also, elections and voting are seen primarily as an expression of the will of the people and as such the only valid tangible mechanisms for the expression of citizens' will. Voting is also seen as a selection process of approval or disapproval, which gives democracy the merit of being a political system that 'allows citizens to change decisions and leaders

and to ensure that actions of public authority are representative of their interests.[103] In this sense, the obligations to explain and justify public conduct are crucial elements of accountability. Openness enables the formation and expression of citizens' support, whether in agreement or disagreement, about a course of action, and the possibility for citizens' to express their alternative preference or action. Openness turns democracy into a 'house of glass' exposed to external scrutiny and provides space for citizens to exchange views and participate in decision-making.[104] The interface between openness and official secrets is not static. On the contrary, it is a moving balance and although its overall evaluation should be based on a pattern of cases, practice shows that a single case of discretionary secrecy may be highly detrimental to the commitments and obligations of openness.[105]

Against this background, how should official secrets be constrained in light of the discussion of democratic foundations and their reliance on openness while taking into account that there is a dynamic relation between openness and official secrets? First, without a degree of openness accountability and public deliberation cannot function. Hence, any claim that limits openness must be legitimate and necessary. Establishing what constitutes a legitimate and necessary claim is one of the most difficult aspects in the efforts to democratically constrain official secrets. Second, openness cannot be limited to the extent that the realization of accountability processes is halted. Accessibility to the relevant information is the first and key step for the inception of any accountability mechanism. Third, for the realization of public deliberation, openness cannot be limited to the extent that the public does not know that there is a secret and does not know the outcomes of oversight. A public discussion relies on relevant and timely accessible information and this must be taken into account in establishing limits

without calling into question their political order' Urbinati (n 95) 10. The idea of checks and approval, as formulated by Mill, has a strong hold in the debate of how the delegation of power is actually maintained. For another perspective, see Vigjilenca Abazi and Eljalill Tauschinsky, 'Reasons of Control and Trust: Grounding the Public Need for Transparency in the European Union' (2015) 11(2) Utrecht Law Review 78.

[103] Ken G Roberston, *Public Secrets: A Study in the Development of Government Secrecy* (St. Martin's Press 1982) 12. See Gutmann and Thompson (n 99) 98, arguing that through accountability we could 'make the self-interest of officials coincide with the general interest'.

[104] Remo Bodei, 'From Secrecy to Transparency: Reason of State and Democracy' (2011) 37 Philosophy and Social Criticism 889.

[105] Christopher Kuner et al, 'PRISM and Privacy: Will this Change Everything?' (2013) 3 International Data Privacy Law 217.

to the use of secrecy. Parliamentary, judicial, and external administrative oversight processes should ensure these democratic constraints of official secrets. Internal administrative measures of a 'self-binding'[106] nature are necessary as well. Complementarity between these different oversight processes is a precondition to constrain secrecy in line with the requirements of accountability and deliberation. In the remaining section of this chapter, these constraints and their implementation are explained in more detail.

Determining legitimate claims to official secrets

The first condition applicable from both the perspective of accountability and public deliberation is whether the claim to official secrets is legitimate and necessary. Necessary refers to the reasons presented on whether without the use of official secrets the aim would not be reached. This condition refers to specific claims of official secrets (i.e. a decision whether an information is categorized as official secret) as well as establishing policies that authorize the use of official secrets in an institutional setting. The latter implies that rules on official secrets are publically debated and due consideration is given to the extent of limits posed by official secrets regulation on the applicability of openness.

The delineation between legitimate and illegitimate official secrets in a specific case is one of the basic and key challenges of oversight. In abstract, only broad categorizations may be offered, as strict definitions cannot be constructed without the specific context in which a document is categorized as an official secret. An important aspect in this regard is to what extent the discretion of a public administrator is guided and checked under the principle of openness.

A military plan, security protection of IT systems, and location of arms are but a few examples of when official secrets are invoked because they are considered valuable and necessary in order to allow the state or an organization to ensure a certain public interest, such as security, and carry out a policy. The critical distinctive feature for invoking official secrets is hence the nature or substance of the policy. Official secrets are considered legitimate if invoked to enhance or protect the interests of the citizens, for example their safety (security policies) or economic well-being (financial

[106] Eric A Posner and Adrian Vermeule, 'The Credible Executive' (2006) University of Chicago Law and Economics, Olin Working Paper No 309 <http://papers.ssrn.com/sol3/papers.cfm?abstract_id=931501##> accessed 21 July 2018.

policies). Another key factor for the legitimacy of official secrets is demonstration of reasonably foreseeable harm.[107]

Official secrets create divisions between secret-keepers as insiders and oversight bodies or citizens as outsiders. Moreover, clusters of inside-*insiders* (officials directly in charge of secrets) and inside-*outsiders* (those within the administrative circle yet not secret-keepers) are also created by the use of official secrets. This division of actors is relevant to reiterate in light of the question of which institutional actor should decide whether claims to official secrets are necessary. The first delineation between legitimate and illegitimate official secrets should be determined internally within the administration that has the authority to keep official secrets. Officials with discretion to decide whether they should apply the rules of official secrets are in an informed position to decide whether official secrets are indeed justified.[108] One could question whether it is reasonable to expect that the officials who are entrusted with keeping official secrets should also be authorized to be the starting point for determining which official secrets are necessary. Valid objections could be raised regarding the possible abuse of such authority.[109] Although suspicion regarding the good faith of officials could be justified when official secrets are used, absolute control is impossible. It is also unnecessary since the idea of internal delimitation of claims on official secrets is to prevent misuse of the rules while acknowledging the possibility that some level of abuse is inevitable. Hence, any mechanism of oversight (internal or external) is aimed to minimize but could not fully eliminate the possibility of abuse of official secrets. In cases of abuse of power, the administrative officials are the only ones that could reveal it as

[107] Marieke de Goede and Mara Wesseling, 'Clashing Cultures of Secrecy: Tracking Terrorism Financing and the Paradox of Publicity' Paper presented to the Annual Meeting of the Council of European Studies, University of Amsterdam (25–27 June 2013) 3.

[108] Steven Aftergood, 'Reducing Government Secrecy: Finding What Works' (2009) 27 Yale Law and Policy Review 399, 411–12, also arguing that the agency level is best for any reform on secrecy.

[109] Posner and Vermeule (n 106); see also Gillian E Metzger, 'The Interdependent Relationship Between Internal and External Separation of Powers' (2009) Columbia Public Law Research Paper No 09-213 <http://web.law.columbia.edu/sites/default/files/microsites/constitutional-governance/files/Interdependent-Relationship-Between-Internal-and-External-Separation-of-Powers.pdf> accessed 21 July 2018; Neal Kumar Katyal, 'Internal Separation of Powers: Checking Today's Most Dangerous Branch from Within' (2006) 115 Yale Law Journal 2314. See more broadly on executive powers and constraints to executive power particularly in the context of the 'state of exception' Marc de Wilde, 'Locke and the State of Exception: Towards a Modern Understanding of Emergency Government' (2010) 6 European Constitutional Law Review 249.

they have direct access to the official secrets and have disclosure channels in place internally within the administration. In other words, they would take on the position of whistleblowers in order to show the abuse of power.

The determination of the claim should start with the core insiders, the officials with the authority to establish official secrets, and then inside-outsiders, such as administrative bodies with authority of independent oversight. A variety of institutional arrangements for this delineation could apply. For example, for core insiders, prevention-focused measures could include legal obligations of assumption of openness and/or *ex post* mechanisms such as reviews of official secrets. As for the inside-outsiders, the general mechanisms of review could also be focused with the aim of tackling issues of over-classification (such as the investigative prerogative of ombudsperson).

The delineation of necessary official secrets from extensive ones rests on the mechanism of balancing between discretion to conceal sensitive information as a measure aimed at protecting a public interest and the rights and obligations related to openness.[110] Balancing openness and official secrets is an administrative action that happens on daily basis.[111] Administrative balance arises in actions involved in the process of managing it. It deals specifically with officials' decision on balancing openness and official secrets at various stages. In this respect, discretion in its most narrow sense implies an application of judgment in accordance with set standards.[112] This type of balance can arise for instance when an official makes a decision that something will be secret or a decision to cease protection of information, hence make it public. Overall, the internal administrative stage of official secrets is a crucial one that should be institutionally structured to protect information and operationalize the presumption of openness in the different layers of decisions.

[110] Wolf Sauter, 'Proportionality in EU law: A Balancing Act?' (2013) TILEC Discussion Paper, DP 2013-003. But see Robert Alexy, *A Theory of Constitutional Rights* (Julian Rivers tr, OUP 2002).

[111] Assuming that each time an official classifies or has to deal with documents she actually does take both openness and secrecy into consideration. This is not a shared view. See Schulhofer who argues that there is no incentive for this to happen and there should be no such expectations from the administration: Stephen Schulhofer, 'Oversight of National Security Secrecy in the United States' in David Cole, Federico Fabbrini, and Arianna Vedaschi (eds), *Secrecy, National Security and the Vindication of Constitutional Law* (Edward Elgar 2013)

[112] Ronald M Dworkin, 'The Model of Rules' (1967) Faculty Scholarship Series, Paper 3609 <http://digitalcommons.law.yale.edu/fss_papers/3609> accessed 21 July 2018.

Establishing an official secret is a subjective decision. It is the secret-keeper who decides that some information must be protected due to the interests of a policy. In the institutional sense, the first decision whether to classify a document therefore is a decision that, although guided by a set of norms, is made by an official. In this respect, disputes even between good faith and well-intentioned officials could arise about whether a document should be classified at all or at what specific level. As a result of this factor, the subjectivity of a decision, information may be classified at a higher level than it should or when it is not necessary to classify it at all. Hence, institutional arrangements should include appropriate safeguards in order to minimize the subjectivity of establishing official secrets. Another factor that makes delineation more difficult is the practical impossibility of checking every single document that is classified individually. Hence, external oversight is also necessary to ensure that democratic constraints on official secrets are functional. Below we examine the constraints on official secrets that rely on external (parliamentary, judicial, and external administrative) oversight.

Oversight and public deliberation

Without some level of openness, processes of oversight are unattainable and they depend on fully and timely accessible information about decision-making and the actors involved. Similarly, whether citizens are able to form and express opinion in an independent manner on the basis of accurate information is very relevant for a functioning democracy. Public debate is a key process involved in achieving democratic accountability and part of defining good governance.[113] Hence, the second and third constraints to official secrets require that openness is only limited to the extent that these processes are still able to function.

Official secrets provide the potential to completely obstruct oversight. The structural dependency of oversight actors on the secret-keeper and the different types of secrets are two key factors that contribute to this challenge. In an institutional sense, the structural dependency of the oversight actor implies that discretion on whether to disclose official secrets is held by the executive actor. The structural dependency could be maintained through various administrative 'technical' rules that trump the right of the

[113] Johan P Olsen, 'The Institutional Basis of Democratic Accountability' (2013) 36 West European Politics 447, 448–49.

oversight actor to access information or impose conditions in such a manner that this impacts the (open) realization of the oversight process. Yet, the dependency feature of official secrets should not mean a *carte blanche* for the secret-keeper. Institutional arrangements for oversight should be structured to take into account the inherent dependency on the secret-keeper.[114]

The single most relevant requirement for the institutional arrangements regarding oversight is that oversight actors have means to know or access *independently* from the discretion of the secret-keeper. There should be means in order to prevent a dependence relationship between oversight actors and secret-keepers. The external actors should not fully rely on the willingness of secret-keepers to disclose the official secrets.[115] The possibility of the oversight body to access official secrets independently from the actor it controls could be stipulated by norms, such as constitutional provisions, that arrange their relation. Regardless of the specific arrangement, the prerogative of the oversight body to access should ensure that full discretion does not belong to the executive actor being checked.

Official secrets also limit public deliberation, which results in a disconnection between citizens and public institutions regarding policies and actions about which there might be agreement or disagreement. The necessity of openness for deliberation creates a higher threshold on the question to what extent official secrets may be deemed acceptable because public deliberation always requires that some information is directly available to the citizens. However, it was also discussed that from the perspective of public deliberation, that information does not need to be specific and detailed. It is very relevant that citizens, in broad terms, know what the policy is about, what interests are at stake and what means are suggested to protect those interests. Hence, the perspective of public deliberation is more focused on the interests at stake and to what extent their protection relies on official secrets. Citizens must be informed about the *existence of secrecy* and the *outcomes of oversight.* Citizens should be able to know that some level of official secrets is applied in a certain situation. Oversight should also be

[114] Thomas M Franck and Edward Weisband, 'Secrecy in the Foreign Relations of Three Democracies: A Comparative Analysis' (1973) 50 Chicago-Kent Law Review 1, 4. See also Franks Commission in the UK—Departmental Committee on Section 2 of the Official Secrets Act 1911 (Cmnd 5104, 1972) at 9, noting that 'There is an inevitable tension between the democratic requirement of openness, and the continuing need to keep some matters secret.'

[115] Rahul Sagar, 'On Combating the Abuse of State Secrecy' (2007) 15 Journal of Political Philosophy 404. See also Schulhofer (n 111) on the idea that there are no proper checks on secrecy.

open because, from this perspective, the question is not only about 'policing' the actors if there is a wrongdoing but it is a question of debates that are also oriented towards future prospects of how things should be done and enabling citizens to formulate and express their agreement. It should, as well, foster public knowledge about decisions and outcomes that most affect the citizens. Open oversight could increase public support.[116] More clarity should be established between what is considered secret and what is open and available for citizens to discuss. Fulfilling deliberation ensures that citizens are already informed and have expressed their views. If indeed abuse of power to establish official secrets takes place, citizens are better able to understand the single act of abuse of power and demand accountability for it, without putting to question the functionality and legitimacy of the entire system of official secrets.

***

Three specific democratic constraints are applicable to official secrets: first, claims to use official secrets must be based on legitimate reasons and necessity; second, some level of access to information should always be ensured for accountability purposes; third, public deliberation depends on citizens knowing generally there is a secret being kept and the outcomes of oversight should be open to the public. The realization of these constraints depends on external oversight—parliamentary, judicial, administrative—and internal administrative oversight. Some additional elements are necessary in order to safeguard the applicability of democratic constraints: first, rules on official secrets should be publically debated and agreed upon and during public deliberation due account should be given to the principle of openness; second, the administrative discretion when applying official secrets should be limited and guided by the principle of openness; third, safeguards should be put in place to reduce the subjectivity of the decision to establish official secrets; and lastly, the structural dependency of oversight actors on the secret-keepers for access to information should be addressed by ensuring some level of access independent from the power position of the secret-holder. The democratic constraints together with the elements that safeguard their realization should influence how the rules on official secrets are established and applied in practice.

[116] Dennis Thompson, *Restoring Responsibility: Ethics in Government, Business, and Healthcare* (CUP 2004).

Conclusions

This chapter explained the EU institutional framework and workings with a focus on security policies as a relevant background for setting out the debate on the more specific rules and practices of official secrets in the EU. For the evaluation of the latter, this chapter sets out a normative framework based on democratic foundations in order to provide specific democratic constraints to official secrets.

The chapter showed that the EU's powers have developed significantly and that the EU is responsible for numerous security measures addressing serious crime and terrorism, and has a broad set of security actors to coordinate these measures. Executive institutions drive the EU's security development, and particularly the Council leads in security cooperation and establishing systems of information exchange aimed at facilitating this cooperation. Security powers are somewhat fragmented between the EU and the national level as the MS retain a significant role in security. This legal context makes parliamentary, judicial, and administrative oversight more challenging since the prerogatives of oversight institutions do not always match the increased powers of executive institutions. Information asymmetries further increase this challenge.

Moving from the EU constitutional context in which official secrets are applied, to a theoretical discussion on how official secrets should be democratically constrained, the chapter set the theoretical framework of this book. This framework provides specific democratic limitations to official secrets based on the application of openness that enables the realization of both accountability and public deliberation. The aim of these conceptual clarifications is to be able to better point out how institutional arrangements should be established in order to meet the requirements for openness. The delineation of legitimate claims to official secrets as well as establishing processes of oversight and public deliberation are basic institutional arrangements in the efforts to align the exercise of official secrets with the democratic presumption in favour of openness. This chapter points to the relevance of the initial decision to establish official secrets as well as showing the importance of accessibility of oversight actors to official secrets without fully relying on the discretion of the secret-keepers. Moreover, it is salient to examine to what extent the legal framework of official secrets shows a presumption in favour of openness and how this presumption is rendered in institutional arrangements, both internally within administrative practice and through external processes of oversight. When these institutional arrangements are examined in practice they also reveal the extent of a culture of secrecy and whether indeed the practice promotes openness.

In the ensuing chapters, the book will examine in depth each of these aspects of official secrets and oversight within the legal context of the EU whilst building on the previous discussion on the specificities of the EU's evolving constitutional architecture, its institutional actors, and principles.

2

EU Regulation of Official Secrets

Abstracts
This chapter examines the establishment and the development of rules on official secrets in the EU. It identifies the key moments for the development of the regime as an independent set of rules from the Member States and its relevance for EU's efforts in increasing its security role. The chapter analyses the current legal framework and its complexities. It assesses whether and to what extent the presumption in favour of openness was taken into account during the establishment of official secrets dominated by executive EU institutions. It also questions the influence of security actors such as NATO on the possible introduction of a military-like secrecy culture in the EU.

Introduction

This chapter examines the establishment and the development of rules on official secrets in the European Union. It maps the legal framework applicable to European Union Classified Information (EUCI) and uncovers the complexities of this comprehensive regulatory regime. The chapter assesses whether and to what extent the presumption in favour of openness was taken into account when these rules were established mostly by executive EU institutions.

The principle of openness implies that the EU rules on official secrets should be publicly debated with due consideration on whether the limits to openness posed by official secrets are justified. Yet, rules on EUCI were quietly ushered in most prominently by the Council. Their establishment reflects the EU's dynamic evolution through formal and informal changes and shows the 'contest of powers' and disagreements among EU institutions as well as between the EU and Member States (MS) over the regulation of official secrets. The chapter also shows the influence of MS and NATO in the development of EUCI and examines the role of the regulation of official secrets in the EU's efforts to increase its autonomy in security policies.

The Legal Regime of 'European Union Classified Information'

Specific rules on classified information have existed in European law since 1958. On the basis of Article 24, the Treaty Establishing the European Atomic Energy Community, Regulation No 3 laid out the legal framework for *Euratom* Classified Information.[1] This *lex specialis* regime regarding classified information has a very narrow scope and it is established to safeguard sensitive information in the interests of the MS that pertain directly to the Euratom Treaty 'only to the extent strictly necessary'.[2]

The comprehensive and sophisticated regime on *European Union* Classified Information results from the more general rules initially introduced by the Council in 2001.[3] This was the first clear establishment of European Union classified information as separate from national rules on classified information and hence resulting in a separate legal protected category of information: European Union Classified Information.[4]

Unlike the Euratom Treaty, there is lack of a specific legal basis for the protection of classified information in the Treaty of the European Union (TEU) and the Treaty on the Functioning of the European Union (TFEU).[5] The 'pragmatic' choice of the EU institutions,[6] under the strong influence of the Council, has been to establish a system of classified information on

[1] This Regulation is still applicable. See Commission Regulation (Euratom) No 302/2005 of 8 February 2005 on the application of Euratom safeguards [2005] OJ L54/1, art 35(1).

[2] Regulation No 3 of 31 July 1958 implementing Article 24 of the Treaty establishing the European Atomic Energy Community [1958] OJ 17/406, art 9. See Opinion 1/78 regarding the Convention on the Physical Protection of Nuclear Materials, Facilities and Transports for peaceful purposes [1979] ECR 02871, on the relation betweeen Euratom and EU law.

[3] Council Decision 2001/264/EC of 19 March 2001 adopting the Council's security regulations [2001] OJ L 101/1.

[4] Previous rules of the institutions were focused on safeguarding measures for sensitive information but did not establish classified information as a separate category of information.

[5] The question of legal basis is particularly relevant in the context of the EU taking into account the nature of its conferred powers in line with art 4(1) TEU and art 5(1) TEU.

[6] David Galloway, 'Classifying Secrets in the EU' (2014) 52 Journal of Common Market Studies 668, 668.

the basis of rules of procedure. In the following subsections, the book addresses the regulation of EU official secrets focusing on the legal basis, the failed efforts to introduce a legislative act, and the current administrative rules as well as their expansion throughout EU institutions, agencies, and bodies.

Professional secrecy, official secrets, and EU primary law

Article 339 TFEU, the only provision referring explicitly to 'secrecy' in the Treaties,[7] stipulates the protection of *professional* secrecy.[8] Although professional secrecy implies that information would not be publicly available, it does not refer to classified information and it does not set procedures for the management of official secrets. Professional secrecy is a legal obligation of the official towards the EU institution not to disclose 'information about undertakings, their business relations or their cost components'.[9] This obligation of EU officials to professional secrecy is not intended to protect sensitive information about the EU's interests in security or international relations.[10] Professional secrecy encompasses information pertaining to the work of the institution and is used to protect the institutional workings and/or the interests of a third party. For example, a Commission official is under an obligation not to disclose any information regarding a cartel case she might be working on.[11] A significant difference between professional secrecy and EUCI, besides their rationale, is that the latter is strictly temporal; the information is always assumed to have a public character and that it will be declassified at some point. With professional secrecy, however, the obligation of the official is applicable even after she has terminated the working contract with the institution.[12] These differences imply that the establishment of administrative procedures for classified information

[7] But see Protocol (No 3) on the Statute of the Court of Justice of the European Union [2012] OJ C326/210, arts 2, 10, and 13; Protocol (No 4) on the Statute of the European System of Central Banks and of the European Central Bank [2012] C326/230, art 37 on professional secrecy.

[8] This provision stipulates professional secrecy more broadly in the EU, see Protocol No 4 (n 7) art 37 regarding professional secrecy for the ECB.

[9] See art 339 TFEU.

[10] Regulation (EC) No 1049/2001 of the European Parliament and of the Council of 30 May 2001 regarding public access to European Parliament, Council and Commission documents [2001] OJ L145/43, art 4(1)(a) and art 9.

[11] Respondent No 16.

[12] Art 339 TFEU. See second line: 'even after their duties have ceased'.

diverges from the legal arrangements necessary for professional secrecy.[13] In the EU, professional secrecy and official secrets are established separately, and whereas the legal basis for the former is unquestionable, official secrets are not explicitly stipulated in primary law.

This lack of mention of official secrets in the Treaties leads to questions about the legal possibility of establishing an EU legislative act on official secrets taking into account the principle of conferral, that is the EU has only those powers as assigned to it by the Treaties.[14] All residual powers belong to the MS. EU legislative powers result not from a general proposition but rather from different Treaty provisions vesting prerogatives for each of the areas of EU law.[15] The legal base matters both for the vertical divisions of powers between the EU and the MS, but also at the EU level due to differences in legal procedures for certain EU policies and as a result the different position of EU institutions therein.[16] EU measures can be based on one or more Treaty provisions. Where a measure can be validly based on one (or more) specific provision(s) of the Treaty, it may not be based on a nonspecific power.[17] Hence, the lack of an explicit mention of official secrets does not per se imply that the EU cannot legislate on the matter as long as other legal bases provide grounds for the EU to adopt a dedicated law on official secrets.

Arguably, Article 15 TFEU, pertaining to openness and the right of public access to documents, could be a legal basis for the establishment of rules on classified information. The limitations 'on grounds of public interest' stipulated therein could be linked with the system of classified information, in view of the latter's aim to protect sensitive information in the interests of the Union or one or more MS.[18] The current Regulation 1049/01

[13] See Sissela Bok, 'The Limits of Confidentiality' (1983) 13 The Hasting Center Report 24, who actually argues in favour of professional secrecy understood as confidentiality but is against the extent to which it can become secrecy as a shield of error that undermines and contradicts the bonds that confidentiality is supposed to protect.

[14] Art 5 TEU.

[15] Joined Cases 188-190/80 *France, Italy and United Kingdom v Commission* ECLI:EU:C:1982:257.

[16] Eg whether qualified majority voting or unanimity is required at the Council, whether the EP is a co-legislator or has merely powers of consent.

[17] Case 68/86 *United Kingdom v Council* ECLI:EU:C:1988:85; Case 45/86 *Commission v Council* ECLI:EU:C:1987:163. See also, Nicholas Emiliou, 'Opening Pandora's Box: the Legal Basis of Community Measures before the Court of Justice' (1994) 19 European Law Review 488.

[18] See art 15(3) TFEU, second subparagraph: 'General principles and limits on grounds of public or private interests governing this right of access to documents shall be determined by

on public access to documents, the only EU legislative act dealing with classified information, provides the security grading (classification category) in Article 9 and stipulates a special security management for this type of information when public access requests are handled. Yet, considering that the purpose of Regulation 1049/01 is to ensure *public access* to documents as opposed to security arrangements for not disclosing sensitive information, a separate legal act on a EUCI system would be necessary.

Article 15 TFEU is a less suitable legal basis for a more comprehensive and general legislative act on official secrets considering that some aspects of the EUCI system, for example the exchange with third states, do not strictly relate to the limitations of public access to documents. Nevertheless, a combination of provisions could facilitate the different aspects of the official secrets regime. It would be conceivable, for example, to rely on Article 4(3) TEU pertaining to sincere cooperation between the EU and the MS as they are supposed to 'assist each other' in fulfilling tasks derived from primary law as well as Article 13(2) TEU on horizontal mutual sincere cooperation.

Another possible option for a legal basis of EUCI rules could be Article 352 TFEU, the 'flexibility clause'.[19] When the EU does not have an explicit competence in primary law in order to act, this provision may be applied, under the condition that the act in question pertains to the achievement of the objectives set out in the Treaties. One can imagine different stipulations in the Treaty regarding the security of the EU,[20] or provisions pertaining to the workings of the EU,[21] to which the rules could relate. However, according to the relevant EU officials involved in the establishment of the regulation of EUCI, it was 'impossible' to match the rules on classified information with a specific objective or policy of the EU.[22] This position of EU officials that more specific objectives or policies about EUCI could not be found *at all* in primary law seems surprising considering that they have consistently defended the protection of EUCI as essential for the EU's

the European Parliament and the Council, by means of regulations, acting in accordance with the ordinary legislative procedure'.

[19] See Damian Chalmers, Gareth Davies, and Giorgio Monti, *European Union Law* (2nd edn, CUP 2010) 214. See also Theodore Konstadinides, 'Drawing the Line Between Circumvention and Gap Filling: An Exploration of the Conceptual Limits of the Treaty's Flexibility Clause' (2012) 31 Yearbook of European Law 227.

[20] See Title V TFEU.

[21] See art 13(2) TEU; art 7 TFEU.

[22] Galloway (n 6) 675.

security policy.[23] For example, the Council asserted that rules on official secrets are instrumental in the EU's security policy enhancement, beginning with the reforms of the Maastricht Treaty[24] and particularly after the EU's Helsinki Conclusions in 1999 when the Union faced the challenge of managing an 'increasingly complex external and internal agenda', including issues of military and civilian crisis management operations and sharing intelligence analysis.[25] The EU's cooperation with Member States as well as third parties is another aspect that is salient for establishing a system of classified information.

Although Article 352(4) TFEU provides a limitation for a general legislative act as it stipulates that the flexibility clause 'cannot serve as a basis for attaining objectives pertaining to the common foreign and security policy' (CFSP), it should be stressed that this is a limitation to establish a *single* legislative act on EUCI under the scope of which all types of classified information would be handled. Hence, it does not as such preclude the possibility of a legislative act on the EUCI system pertaining to all other fields with the exception of CFSP. In fact, the current legal framework too on some issues under CFSP, such as access to classified information by the European Parliament (EP), treats them separately from EUCI more generally.[26]

Yet, Article 352 TFEU was deemed unfitting by the Council. Its main concern, according to internal EU documents,[27] is that a legislative act on the basis of Article 352 TFEU would not encompass the *national* classified information exchanged among MS 'in the interest of the Union' or between

[23] See, eg, decisions prior to the Council Decision of 2001, which directly link the relevance of classified information with the developing of EU's security prerogatives and the EU's cooperation both with the MS and with third parties. A particular emphasis should be given to competences under CFSP, which under the pillar system did not fall under the prerogatives of the Commission and a legislative act on such issue was legally explicitly excluded.

[24] See Simon Nuttall, *European Political Cooperation* (OUP 1992).

[25] Helsinki European Council, 10 and 11 December 1999, Presidency Conclusions, Annex III.

[26] See the two separate agreements of the EP with the Council on access—Inter-institutional Agreement of 12 March 2014 between the European Parliament and the Council concerning the forwarding to and handling by the European Parliament of classified information held by the Council on matters other than those in the area of the common foreign and security policy [2014] OJ C95/1; and Draft Arrangement between the European Parliament, the Council and the External Action Service concerning access by the European Parliament to classified information in the area of the Common Foreign and Security Policy, Council Doc 15343/12.

[27] On file with the author. These documents were mostly made available to the author on the basis of public access to documents requests.

them and the EU institutions or agencies.[28] However, what is remarkable in this regard is that the legal basis of rules of procedure, favoured and applied by the Council, does not facilitate such exchange either and in fact a separate international agreement is signed by MS acting within the Council for exchanging this type of classified information.[29]

The reasons provided by the Council on why legislation is not possible seem unconvincing and to some extent contradictory with the stated aim of the current rules of the Council on official secrets. If indeed the Council aimed to establish rules that encompass *all* aspects of official secrets, this is still not the case with the current framework for the exchange of information. It also seems contradictory to defend the EUCI system as essential for EU security objectives and policies but concurrently to claim that the Treaties do not provide *any* legal basis for a legislative act. Therefore, the procedural rules for official secrets seem to result not merely from legal limitations imposed by the Treaties, but rather they seem to be an institutional preference by the Council. By contrast, the EP favours legislation on classified information that would specifically take into account the relevant case law on the wide applicability of public access to documents as well as the necessities of inter-institutional sincere cooperation. The following subsection delves into the institutional debates behind the failed efforts for legislation on EUCI.

[28] Security Committee, State of play of work on the review of the security rules governing EU classified information, 23 October 2008, Doc 14594/08. See specifically: 'The Committee recognised that it is not possible within the European Union to have a single legal instrument binding the institutions and the Member States for protecting all classified information exchanged in the interests of the EU. While the Commission representatives considered that the Treaties contain provisions enabling the adoption of rules on the protection of classified information for areas falling respectively within the TEC and the TEU, the Committee largely took the view that no obvious general legal bases appeared to exist for this purpose. However, it acknowledged that it may be possible to regulate in this way certain aspects of security, particularly relating to industry and the internal market. At any event, even if an appropriate legal basis could be identified for a Community instrument regarding such aspects, distinct instruments would still be needed to cover activities under Titles V and VI of the TEU. Moreover, none of these instruments can regulate the exchange of national classified information between Member States in the interests of the Union. This situation will not change in the near future.'

[29] Agreement between the Member States of the European Union, meeting within the Council, regarding the protection of classified information exchanged in the interests of the European Union [2011] OJ C202/13.

Institutional turf battles for legislation on EU official secrets

The EP has tried to draw attention to the need for legislation on official secrets that reflects the post-Lisbon constitutional architecture of parliamentary oversight and constitutional commitments to the principle of openness.[30] The EP is not the first EU institution to support a legislative act on official secrets. In 1988, the Commission and some MS already recognized the necessity of establishing a more general act on classified information as opposed to Regulation No 3 specifically pertaining to Euratom Classified Information. The German delegation presented a memorandum to the Council calling for Community rules on security measures applicable to classified information produced within, or transmitted between, the institutions or between the institutions and the MS in connection with Community activities.[31] This initiative led the Commission to present a proposal for a Council regulation on the security measures for official secrets produced or transmitted in connection with the European Economic Community or Euroatom activities.[32] Although the Commission's proposal acknowledged the lack of a specific Treaty provision allowing the adoption of a broad regulation on official secrets, it did not consider such limitations to be an obstacle for establishing a legislative act. On the basis of the Commission's proposal, the rationale for this regulation related to the development of the Community which had led to an increased flow of information, some of which was sensitive and required protection.[33] At the time, the EP was a fierce opponent of this proposal, although its legislative powers were limited and it had almost no significance in the

[30] The EP has paid attention to classified information even in a context where its powers have been more limited. In 1999, the EP adopted a Resolution on openness, which also called for better classification decisions. See European Parliament, Resolution of 12 January 1999 on Openness within the European Union, A4-0476/98, OJ C104/20 of 14/04/1999. See Deirdre Curtin, 'Official Secrets and the Negotiation of International Agreements. Is the EU Executive Unbound?' (2013) 50 Common Market Law Review 423.

[31] See Bart Driessen, 'The Council of the European Union and Access to Documents' (2005) 30 European Law Review 675.

[32] Commission, 'Proposal for a Council Regulation (EEC) on the security measures applicable to classified information produced or transmitted in connection with EEC or Euratom activities' COM(92) 56 final.

[33] At the time, the development of principles of democracy and transparency were not well-established or stipulated in primary law, yet it is noteworthy that the proposal for the regulation of classified information took due account of access to information as 'one of the fundamental principles of democracy' and explicitly stated that the classification of information must be limited to 'the absolute minimum'. See Preamble, para 4 of the proposal, ibid.

area of security, for which the rules on official secrets were drafted. The EP's opposition to the rules was allegedly motivated by the lack of rules on public access to information.[34] The Council officials publicly note that this opposition by the EP 'explains why the first post-Maastricht rules [of official secrets] were developed as internal decisions of the Commission in 1994 ... and the Secretary-General of the Council in 1995',[35] and why the Commission withdrew its legislative proposal under the justification of not fulfilling the principle of subsidiarity.

However, interviews with key senior EU officials, including from the Council, who partook in the debates regarding this proposal in the early 1990s, suggest an additional and different reason for the Commission's withdrawal of the legislative proposal.[36] The Council insisted on maintaining its own discretion over the establishment of the rules as the valid legal basis.[37] As explained by a senior Council official directly involved in the debates at the time:

> There was huge reaction from the Council because the Commission has nothing to do with [the regulation of official secrets] ... This was a prerogative of the Council. [The regulation of official secrets became a point of] competence and political opposition between the Council and the Commission.[38]

[34] Respondent No 13. See also Ulf Oberg, 'EU Citizen's Right to Know: The Improbable Adoption of a European Freedom of Information Act' (1999) 2 Cambridge Yearbook of European Legal Studies 303.

[35] Galloway (n 6) 674. See Commission Decision C (94) 3282 of 30 November 1994 on the security measures applicable to classified information produced or transmitted in connection with activities of the European Union and Council Decision No 24 of 30 January 1995 on measures to protect classified information applicable to the General Secretariat of the Council. It is noteworthy that six days after the withdrawal of the proposal for a regulation, the Commission adopted a decision on security measures applicable to classified information. *Two years later*, the Secretary General of the Council adopted for its part Decision No 24 of January 1995 on measures to protect classified information. The two-year delay has not been examined or elaborated in the literature and there are no legal documents from that period that might shed light on the matter. It could be pointed that at the time secrecy was rather the norm—there was no established access to information right—and competences did not include security and defence issues such as was the case later, a legal formal regime of classification was not deemed urgent.

[36] Respondents Nos 12, 13, 15, 16.

[37] This empirical finding of the insiders' views and debates at the time of the proposal does address to some extent the calls by academics who note that for outsiders it is not clear precisely why art 240(3) TFEU is chosen by the Council as a legal basis, considering also that by their nature the rules of procedure do not have any external binding effect.

[38] Respondent No 12.

This statement goes against current claims by the Council officials that the legal basis was a consensus matter for the institutions, including the Commission, and that rules of procedure provided a pathway to 'neatly avoid competence-based policy discussions'.[39] The Council's opposition to a legislative act on official secrets as proposed by the Commission contradicts the more recent claims by Council officials that the regulation of official secrets is an example of 'working pragmatically to integrate a new sector of activity involving national sensitivities and [avoiding] the potential for legal or institutional turf battles'.[40] In light of the institutional dynamics discussed above, it is less convincing that institutional turf battles were avoided, but it rather seems that the Council succeeded in protecting its discretion in establishing rules on official secrets.

The debate on a possible EU legislative act on official secrets has resurfaced. In 2009, the EP preferred including general provisions on the classification of documents in Regulation 1049/01, in the context of the long but failed efforts to revise the public access regime in line with the Lisbon Treaty.[41] In March 2014, through its Resolution on public access to documents, the EP asked the Commission to propose a separate regulation on the rules and the criteria for official secrets.[42] Besides more openness towards the citizens, the EP aims to stress 'the important role of proper classification rules for sincere inter-institutional cooperation'.[43] However, the EP does not have the legal prerogatives to change the nature and the establishment of the current executive engineered rules on official secrets.

[39] Galloway (n 6) 676.

[40] David Galloway, 'Classifying Secrets in the EU' Working Paper presented at Transparency and Access to the Records and Archives of the EU Institutions Seminar, the European University Institute (25 January 2013) 14.

[41] The EP calling for secrecy and transparency rules to be reconsidered—see European Parliament Resolution of 17 December 2009 on improvements needed to the legal framework for access to documents following the entry into force of the Lisbon Treaty, Regulation (EC) No 1049/2001—the Council has adopted its internal rules (Decision 2009/937/EU of 1 December 2009) and a revision of its security regulations (Document 13885/1/09) and the MS negotiated an agreement on the protection of classified information exchanged in the interests of the EU [2011] OJ C202/13.

[42] European Parliament Resolution of 11 March 2014 on public access to documents (Rule 104(7)) for the years 2011–2013 (2013/2155(INI)) point 31. The right to initiate legislation belongs almost exclusively to the European Commission, see art 17(2) TEU.

[43] The EP in its Resolution of 14 September 2011 on public access to documents (Rule 104(7)) for the years 2009–2010 (2010/2294(INI)) point 12.

EU rules on official secrets: Expanded across institutions, agencies, and bodies

The patchwork of EU rules on official secrets consists of rules of procedure,[44] on the basis of which each actor establishes more detailed provisions and guidelines.[45] The only directly relevant legislative act for EUCI, as noted above, is Regulation 1049/01 regarding the right of public access to documents in the EU.[46] Therein, Article 9 indicates the security grading of sensitive information and the special treatment of such information when it comes to managing requests due to its security sensitive nature. This is not, however, a regulation on official secrets and it does not stipulate measures for their protection.

The Commission had a basic internal protection regime in place from 1986,[47] whereas the current applicable framework was revised in March 2015.[48] The Council revised its rules in 2013, which the European Council also applies.[49] The Council's rules set a minimum standard for other EU actors, for example bodies such as the European External Action Service

[44] The following decisions are applicable: Council Decision 2013/488/EU of 23 September 2013 on the security rules for protecting EU classified information [2013] OJ L274/1; Decision of the High Representative of the Union for Foreign Affairs and Security Policy of 19 April 2013 on the security rules for the European External Action Service [2013] OJ C190/1; European Commission, Rules of Procedure [2000] OJ L308/26, as amended by Commission Decision 2011/737/EU, Euratom of 9 November 2011 [2011] OJ L 296/58.

[45] See art 240 TFEU about the Council and art 249 TFEU about the Commission. See inter alia Doc 10873/11 Guidelines on marking EU classified information; Doc 14125/02 Procedure for releasing EU classified information originating in the Council to third states and international organisations; Doc 14845/11 Council Security Committee (2011) Guidelines on downgrading and declassifying Council Documents; Doc 13140/11 High classified information exchange requirements for the European Council and the Council. See Doc13140/11 of 20 July 2011 about the need of the European Council and the Council to exchange information and how this is to be done. See Document Guidelines Doc 10873/11—The General Secretariat—Guidelines on marking EU classified information—previously approved by the Security Committee.

[46] Regulation No 1049/2001 of the European Parliament and of the Council of 30 May 2001 regarding Public Access to European Parliament, Council and Commission documents [2001] OJ L145/43.

[47] Commission Decision of 7 July 1986 on classified documents and security measures applicable to them SEC(86)1132 final.

[48] Commission Decision (EU, Euratom) 2015/444 of 13 March 2015 on the security rules for protecting EU classified information [2015] OJ L72/53.

[49] Council Decision 2013/488/EU (n 44). Apart from formal agreements, systems for electronic exchange of information have been set up such as between the European Council and the Council for high classified information, Confidential and Secret (Doc 13140/11).

(EEAS),[50] although in the case of the latter it is the High Representative that adopts the applicable decision. Regarding agencies such as Europol, Regulation 2016/794 as the new foundational act for this EU law enforcement agency clearly provides in the preamble that Europol's rules on official secrets should be consistent with those of the Council.[51] The EUCI regime extends to other EU bodies and agencies such as the EU Satellite Centre, the European Defence Agency, and Eurojust.[52] In addition, agreements and memorandums of understanding facilitate the exchange of classified information among the EU institutions and bodies as well as between them and third parties.[53] These rules are not only fragmented horizontally at the EU level, but also vertically between the EU and the national level since each MS has its own rules on state secrets, their protection, and exchange.[54] Standards for the protection of classified information are similar, but they are not fully unified. This may lead to challenges in practice when sharing classified information, as the next chapter explains in more detail.

[50] Decision of the High Representative of 19 April 2013 (n 44).

[51] Paragraph 65, Regulation 2016/794 of the European Parliament and the Council of 11 May 2016 on the European Union Agency for Law Enforcement Cooperation (Europol) and replacing and repealing Council Decisions 2009/371/JHA, 2009/934/JHA, 2009/935/JHA, 2009/936/JHA, and 2009/968/JHA OJ L 135. See for a critique of new parliamentary oversight arrangements regarding classified information, Vigjilenca Abazi, 'The Future of Europol's Parliamentary Oversight: A Great Leap Forward?' (2014) 15 German Law Journal 1121.

[52] Council Regulation (EC) No 2007/2004 of 26 October 2004 establishing a European Agency for the Management of Operational Cooperation at the External Borders of the Member States of the European Union [2004] OJ L349/1, as amended by Regulation (EC) No 863/2007 of the European Parliament and of the Council [2007] OJ L199/30 and by Regulation (EU) No 1168/2011 of the European Parliament and of the Council [2011] OJ L304/1; Council Decision 2014/401/CFSP of 26 June 2014 on the European Union Satellite Centre and repealing Joint Action 2001/555/CFSP on the establishment of a European Union Satellite Centre [2014] OJ L188/73, art 15; Council Joint Action 2004/551/CFSP of 12 July 2004 on the establishment of the European Defence Agency [2004] OJ L245/17, as amended by Council Joint Action 2008/299/CFSP [2008] OJ L102/34, art 30; Council Decision 2002/187/JHA of 28 February 2002 setting up Eurojust with a view to reinforcing the fight against serious crime [2002] OJ L63/1, as amended by Council Decision 2003/659/JHA [2003] OJ L245/44 and by Council Decision 2009/426/JHA [2009] OJ L138/14, art 39a.

[53] Inter-institutional Agreement between the European Parliament and the Council (n 26). For exchange between administrative bodies, see the Agreement between Eurojust and Europol, 1 October 2009, The Hague. Some of these arrangements are technical modalities, which despite a non-binding nature of the EU overall, have problematic effects on the exchange and access of classified information.

[54] Each MS has its own rules on classified information, most of which are stipulated in a legislative act. See table of equivalence for classification grading between the EU level and national level for the applicable laws: Council Decision 2013/488/EU (n 44) Appendix B.

The EP and the Court of Justice of the European Union (CJEU) have adopted their rules on official secrets in much the same fashion as the Council and the Commission: under internal discretion through revision of rules of procedure with no public debate.[55] Prior to the current rules on official secrets, the EP's first mention of 'confidentiality' is based on its Rules of Procedure in 1989.[56] Annex VII on classified information of the EP's Rules of Procedure constituted the general rules, which were amended in November 2001 due to legislation on public access to documents.[57] At the time, the EP did not have specific rules on official secrets nor agreements for their exchange. With the enactment of Regulation 1049/01 on public access to information, the EP revised its Rules of Procedure and removed confidentiality as a reason to restrict access to documents. The EP aligned its system with Article 4 of Regulation 1049/01 as the only basis for the possible rejection of public access to documents. According to the new changes, documents were only excluded from public access by virtue of Article 4 of Regulation (EC) 1049/2001 and the EP's confidentiality provision in Annex VII could not as such be the basis for non-disclosure of documents.

The rules specifically addressing EUCI are a result of the necessity of the EP to exchange classified information with the executive institutions, starting with the first Agreement in 2002 concluded with the Council regarding classified information in the area of security and defence policy.[58] Almost a decade later, the Bureau of the EP, which is composed of the

[55] Decision of the Bureau of the European Parliament of 6 June 2011 concerning the rules governing the treatment of confidential information by the European Parliament [2011] OJ C190/2; Rules of Procedure of the General Court [2015] OJ L105/1, art 105(11). Decision (EU) 2016/2386 of the Court of Justice of 20 September 2016 concerning the security rules applicable to information or material produced before the General Court in accordance with Article 105 of its Rules of Procedure [2016] OJ L355.

[56] As noted earlier, confidentiality is a broader notion referring to professional secrecy and not as such directly encompassing classified information.

[57] This was done on the basis of the report by MEP Hanja Maij-Weggen: Report of 15 October 2001 on the adaptation of the Rules of Procedure to the Regulation (EC) No 1049/2001 of the European Parliament and of the Council regarding public access to documents (2001/2135(REG)).

[58] Inter-institutional Agreement of 20 November 2002 between the European Parliament and the Council concerning access by the European Parliament to sensitive information of the Council in the field of security and defence policy [2002] OJ C298/1. See also the EP decision of 23 October 2002 implementing the Inter-institutional Agreement with the Council, which laid down basic principles and the necessary measures to be able to exchange information in the area of security and defence policy.

President and the fourteen Vice-Presidents of Parliament, established the internal rules for EP classified information,[59] taking into account the inter-institutional agreements of the EP with the Council and the Commission for the exchange of classified documents.[60] The Bureau did not have an open deliberation or involve a broader public discussion on the EP's internal rules on EUCI.[61] This lack of openness in how the EP developed its own rules makes its position of demanding an open debate about EU rules on secrecy to some extent less credible.

The General Court (GC), as part of the broader revision of its Rules of Procedure, is the latest institution to adopt provisions regarding information and material that is confidential in nature. According to the GC's documents, the rationale of having specific provisions on confidentiality is to address a legislative gap.[62] Chapter 7 of the Rules of Procedure, particularly Article 105, deals with the handling of confidential information and material 'pertaining to the security of the Union or that of one or more of its Member States in the conduct of their international relations'. The scope of confidential information is important since, on the basis of a textual reading of the provision, it seems to be specifically limited to international relations. This differs from the Council's rules on EUCI, which do not limit the scope of EUCI to security or international relations.[63]

The Court revised the rules behind closed doors and perhaps this lack of openness of the Court should not be surprising.[64] Lawyers and experts from varied organizations sent a letter to the then President of the CJEU offering an opinion on the legal implications for due process rights arising

[59] See Rule 24, EP Rules of Procedure, January 2017.

[60] See Rule 25, EP Rules of Procedure, January 2017.

[61] EP Rules of Procedure, January 2017, Rule 25(12): 'The Bureau shall lay down rules concerning the treatment of confidential information by Parliament and its bodies, office-holders and other Members, taking into account any inter-institutional agreement concluded on such matters. Those rules shall be published in the Official Journal of the European Union and annexed to these Rules of Procedure.'

[62] See draft Rules of Procedure of the General Court, 14 March 2014, at 103 <http://curia.europa.eu/jcms/upload/docs/application/pdf/2014-06/tra-doc-en-div-t-0000-2013-201311050-05_00.pdf>. It is noteworthy that AG Bot in the *ZZ* case had alluded to the lack of possibilities for the Court to deal with classified information especially in terms of receiving it and whether or not this is shared with the applicant due to the lack of specific rules on this: Case C-300/11 *ZZ v Secretary of State for the Home Department*, Opinion of AG Bot EU:C:2012:563.

[63] Council Decision 2013/488/EU (n 44) art 1.

[64] See Alberto Alemanno and Oana Stefan, 'Openness at the Court of Justice of the European Union: Toppling a Taboo' (2014) 51 Common Market Law Review 97. Also Deirdre Curtin, 'Judging EU Secrecy' [2012] Cahiers de Droit Européen 459.

from the changes of the GC's procedure with regard to classified information. The concerned lawyers suggested that the Court hold an open deliberation on these issues considering the critical impact on the fundamental right of access to justice.[65] However, the Court rejected an open discussion on the basis that it was under no legal obligation to discuss publicly or with third parties the revision of its rules of procedure.[66] This direct rejection is remarkable considering that the changes to the rules of procedure affect fundamental rights in the EU and profoundly change the manner in which the adversarial principle is practised in the EU.[67] By contrast, the opinion of the Council's Security Committee on the draft Security Rules was taken into account both by the Council's Working Party on Court of Justice as well as by the GC itself.[68] On the basis of Articles 253(6) and 254(5) TFEU, Rules of Procedure of the General Court and the European Court of Justice are proposed by them and approved by the Council. In March 2014, the President of the General Court submitted the proposed rules to the Council, which it approved and the rules have been in force since April 2015. The revised rules give rise to serious concerns about the implications for the fundamental right of access to justice and whether they are compatible with the established case law of the European Court of Human Rights on access to justice, as analysed in more detail in Chapter 5.

The European Ombudsman (EO), unlike the EP and the GC, does not have a separate set of rules or dedicated security arrangements for official secrets.[69] Article 3(2) of the Statue addresses classified information as a category that requires special handling by the EO when such information is requested from the EU administration in line with its prerogatives to

[65] Maya Lester, 'Organisations Call on European Court to Consult on Classified Evidence Rule Change' (*European Sanctions*, 27 July 2013) <http://europeansanctions.com/2013/07/27/organisations-call-on-european-court-to-consult-on-classified-evidence-rule-change/>

[66] Maya Lester, 'Draft European Court Rules Propose Secret Hearings' (*European Sanctions*, 6 April 2014) <http://europeansanctions.com/2014/04/06/draft-european-court-rules-for-secret-hearings/>.

[67] An issue that the Court acknowledges in its elaboration of the draft rules since the adversarial principle clearly required that all information and material must be fully communicated between the parties. See Draft Rules of Procedure of the General Court (n 62) 104.

[68] General Secretariat of the Council, Rules of Procedure of the General Court of the European Union: Approval by the Council Doc 5007/15, Point 3.

[69] Note however that the Statute of the EO mentions the following in the preamble: 'the Ombudsman should have agreed in advance with the institution or body concerned regarding the conditions for treatment of classified information or documents and other information covered by the obligation of professional secrecy'.

initiate an inquiry or address a complaint received by individuals. Quite exceptionally in comparison with other EU institutions, the EO's rules on official secrets have been subject to public debate as the EP approves the Statute of the EO. Looking at the negotiations, the issue of official secrets is a significant point of disagreement between the Council and Commission vis-à-vis the EP's proposal.[70] The executive institutions insisted on more rigid rules regarding (non)accessibility to classified information, whereas the EP aimed to ensure that the work of the EO is not hindered by secrecy and an executive discretion to prevent access. The final text is a 'scheme where the Ombudsman's investigative prerogatives largely retained the scope put forward by the MEPs but clearly lost a considerable part of their intensity'.[71]

Overall, this discussion shows that the adoption of rules on official secrets in the EU has been a contested issue among EU institutions. It may be understood in what has been referred to as a 'contest of powers' between EU institutions in light of the multiplicity of EU actors and the varied competences. The latter dynamics may result in institutional efforts to protect or advance certain (institutional) interests. To some extent, this type of contest between the institutions and protection of interests was a factor in the Council's adamant position against a legislative act on official secrets led by the Commission. The Council insisted on maintaining its discretion over the establishment of the rules, an issue that might also explain its strong insistence on rules of procedure now stipulated in Article 240 TFEU. Rules of official secrets are a sensitive issue also for the Member States as the prerogatives for 'state secrets' is viewed as fundamental to the capacity of states to act in the security realm. The importance to MS of preserving 'national security' as a 'sole responsibility' is also evident in Article 4(2) TEU. Yet, EU rules on official secrets provide the EU with more autonomy in receiving and sharing sensitive information, especially in security issues, and hence affect its role as a more informed security actor. Hence, these rules are not merely necessary for secret sharing but become an instrument with which the EU may gain more autonomy from the MS in security. The following section maps the actors and events that help to pinpoint and understand the relevance of rules on official secrets for the EU's security role.

[70] Alexandros Tsadiras, 'Unravelling Ariadne's Thread: The European Ombudsman's Investigative Powers' (2008) 45 Common Market Law Review 757, 758–59.

[71] ibid 759–60.

Mapping the Executive Engineering of EU Official Secrets

This section identifies the main actors and developments in the legal regime of official secrets behind the piecemeal approach of the establishment of EUCI. It points to the key moments of change from a coordination role to a more independent role of the EU brought about by the legal design of independent EU rules of official secrets. Understanding the background of the EUCI is particularly salient in light of the fact that it provides a deeper knowledge of the current design and its implications, as well as a clearer sense of who the main actors are behind the regime on official secrets, why and what changes were deemed desirable by them.

Actors behind the design of EUCI

The Council has led the development and expansion of the EUCI rules as well as established the minimum standards for the security and exchange of classified information.[72] The Council's influence on the overall legal arrangements of EUCI stems from its institutional role in the field of security but also from its position to control access to official secrets. For example, in the case of EEAS, the Council is in a structural position to influence the rules through adopting the constituting Decision,[73] but in the case of the EP, the Council used its leverage over access to official secrets to

[72] Note the difference with Regulation No 3 Euratom (n 2) where the Commission takes the lead, as well as the initial stages of the development of the rules, as we saw above on a possible legislative act proposed by the Commission.

[73] It further becomes the 'task' of the body in question to establish a system: organize security and the overall management of classified information, its implication and whom it is shared with. Hence, the Council, through its prerogative as an EU executive and having the prerogative to establish these other bodies, has also managed to set the rules on classified information. See Council Decision adopting the implementing rules governing Europol's relation with partners, including the exchange of personal data and classified information [2009] OJ L325/6. Unlike the previous experience with Europol, whereby the Council established both the Decision to create it as an agency and its system for classified information, for the EEAS the Council Decision merely stipulates in the preamble that rules should be 'laid down covering the activities of the EEAS … for the protection of classified information' and art 10 provides the legal basis to do so. In the case of the EEAS, it is the High Representative who should actually adopt the rules once they have been agreed by the Security Committee of the EEAS and CSC has given its opinion. This position is understandable considering that the EEAS is accountable to the High Representative and is autonomous from the Council.

negotiate the terms under which the EP would gain access to the classified information.[74]

The actual 'engineering' of EUCI, in the sense of discussions and drafting rules, took place at the Council Security Committee (CSC), a working body established by the Council Decision on classified information in 2001. The Council at the ministerial level mostly gave formal approval of rules already agreed upon at the CSC. The latter is composed of representatives from the Council and each MS as well as the Commission and the EEAS.[75] Representatives of Europol and Eurojust also attend when discussions concern these agencies.[76] The direct participation of national authorities illustrates the national sensitivity about protection of official secrets. The power of MS over their 'State Secrets' is of core significance to their sovereignty and in EU law it pertains to their prerogatives in 'national security'.[77]

In the past decade, the CSC has been key in the development of the EUCI rules.[78] This Committee holds the most salient discussions about EU rules on official secrets.[79] For example, rules on cooperation and exchange

[74] See Vigjilenca Abazi, 'European Parliamentary Oversight Behind Closed Doors' (2016) 5 Cambridge International Law Journal 31.

[75] The novelty in regard to the composition is the inclusion of EEAS. During the negations for the EUCI Decision II, the CSC considered that cooperation with EEAS would result in a better protection of classified information if permanent presence of the EEAS is warranted (Doc 14475/1/10 REV 1, Amendment of Article 16(2) of the draft Council security rules for protecting EU classified information): 'At its meeting on 29 September 2010, the Council Security Committee considered that close cooperation with the EEAS on matters relating to the protection of EUCI could be facilitated in practice by ensuring a permanent presence of the EEAS in CSC meetings to shape discussions on the basic principles and minimum standards for protecting EUCI. The Committee agreed to report this change to the Antici Group, which is finalising work on the Council security rules.'

[76] Council Decision 2013/488/EU (n 44) art 17(2) second subparagraph.

[77] See art 4(1) last sentence, TEU.

[78] By comparison, in Regulation No 3 regarding Euratom classified information (n 2), it is the Commission that has a more dominating role and specifically the Security Bureau, which was established under the authority of the Commission. Similarly to the Council's Security Committee, the Commission Security Bureau had supervisory prerogatives for the application of the Regulation not only with the Commission but also with 'institutions, committees, services and installations of the Community'. Art 6(b) Regulation No 3 (n 2) includes empowerment for the Commission Security Bureau to verify national procedures and it could propose amendments if it considered them necessary to the Regulation.

[79] Policy on creating EU classified information, 30 May 2011, Doc 10872/11; State of play of work on the review of the security rules governing EU classified information, 23 October 2008, Report Doc 14594/08; Draft Council Decision on the security rules for protecting EU classified information—Declarations for the Council minutes, 16 July 2013, Doc 12433/13 ADD 1; Guidelines on downgrading and declassifying Council documents, 3 September 2011,

of official secrets with third countries were initially established at this level and were, in principle, merely approved by the Council.[80] Most importantly, the CSC through its opinions and recommendations has directly influenced the rules on official secrets of the EP and the GC.[81] The CSC was directly involved in the processes of evaluating the legal arrangements and advising on the necessary revisions during the establishment of the Interinstitutional Agreement between the Council and the EP on the exchange of classified information as well as the process of the GC's revision of its Statute in 2015, which for the first time in the Court's history, explicitly provides a provision on confidential information and material.

External security actors who exerted significant influence on official secrets are also relevant in mapping relevant actors for the development of the EUCI system. The necessary steps taken for cooperation with NATO have also opened the way for a direct influence by NATO in how the EU regime of official secrets would develop. This influence is evident in the immediate and rapid changes that were made to the rules on official secrets.[82] In the Helsinki Presidency meeting in 1999 the need for cooperation between the EU and NATO was emphasized.[83] Four ad hoc NATO–EU working groups were established to facilitate the development of EU–NATO relations and in this respect the working groups covered issues pertaining to the EU's military capabilities, the EU access to NATO assets and capabilities, and the definitive arrangements to be concluded between the EU and NATO.[84] It is well documented that NATO asserted its influence on its members' secrecy regulation through NATO agreements for the security

Doc 36/11; Opinion of the Council Security Committee on the draft Security Rules of the General Court, 7 October 2014, Doc 14024/14.

[80] General Secretariat of the Council, Exchange of EU classified information (EUCI) with third States and international organisations, 7 July 2011, Doc 12619/11.

[81] Documents derived from public access request filed by the author: ST 13086 2003 INIT, ST 11395 2012 INIT, ST 12737 2010 INIT, ST 9518 2009 ADD 1, ST 6770 2000 INIT, ST 7756 2013 INIT, ST 11036 2011 INIT, ST 13885 2009 INIT, ST 13096 2007 INIT, ST 6230 2013 INIT, ST 15104 2010 INIT, ST 13646 2009 INIT, ST 7592 2003 INIT.

[82] See Alasdair S Roberts, 'Entangling Alliances: NATO's Security Policy and the Entrenchment of State Secrecy' (2003) 26 Cornell International Law Journal 329; Guri Rosén, 'Can You Keep a Secret? How the European Parliament got Access to Sensitive Documents in the Area of Security and Defence' (2011) RECON Working Paper 22; Martin Reichard, *The EU-NATO Relationship: A Legal and Political Perspective* (Ashgate Publishing 2006).

[83] Richard G Whitman, 'NATO, the EU and ESDP: An Emerging Division of Labour?' (2004) 25 Contemporary Security Policy 430, 438.

[84] ibid 450. At Ambassador level, the group responsible for permanent EU–NATO arrangements met for the first time in September 2000.

of information. For example, the agreement between NATO and Austria shows that the 'operative provisions of this agreement replicate, with some formal adaptations, the exact text ... down to the article numbers' of the NATO rules.[85] This type of influence was even more clearly asserted towards the states in Central and Eastern Europe during their accession period in NATO.[86] In light of these developments, the following subsections continue to examine whether and to what extent a NATO culture of military secrecy pervaded in the establishment of EU rules on official secrets.

What can become a secret? From NATO 'Cosmic Top Secret' to 'EU Top Secret'

Whether certain information becomes an official secret is not merely a technical question. Rather, officials make choices on the basis of the sensitivity of the information while following guidelines to apply a 'security grading' or 'classification category'. Different categories of official secrets limit the accessibility of information with varying consequences. Whether the legal provisions are stipulated in a vague or precise wording on what may become an official secret is extremely important for two main reasons. Firstly, it indicates to what extent concerns regarding openness are taken into account and secondly, whether secrecy is applied only to the extent that is strictly necessary considering that security justifications may be 'uncertain or probabilistic, setting the stage for disagreements over its necessity' of keeping information undisclosed.[87] In the EU, Regulation 1049/01 does not provide a specific definition for each grading, but Article 9(1) only enumerates the categories starting from the highest level to the lowest: Top Secret, Secret, and Confidential. The definitions are stipulated in the classification rules of each institution.[88]

The EU categories of official secrets draw from the practices of the MS but also from security actors such as NATO. Scholars argue that the

[85] Reichard (n 82) 318. [86] Roberts (n 82); Reichard (n 82).

[87] Steven Aftergood, 'An Inquiry into the Dynamics of Government Secrecy' (2013) 48 Harvard Civil Rights—Civil Liberties Law Review 511, 513.

[88] Council Decision 2013/488/EU (n 39) art. 2; Decision of the Bureau of the European Parliament of 15 April 2013 concerning the rules governing the treatment of confidential information by the European Parliament [2013] OJ C96/1, art 2; Decision of the High Representative of 19 April 2013 (n 39) art 2 of Annex A; Commission Decision (EU, Euratom) 2015/444, art 3.

inclusion of the EU '*Top Secret*' category as the highest level in the EU framework, is an equivalent category of NATO's highest marking '*Cosmic Top Secret*'.[89] The category of '*Top Secret*' already existed in the *lex specialis* regime of Euratom Classified Information, although it was not stipulated in the Council's classification rules of 1995. Prior to the Council, the Commission rules of 1993 stipulated the category of '*Top Secret*'. The Commission also had specific provisions authorizing the exchange of classified information with the West European Union and NATO, hence before the revised rules of the Council in 2000,[90] and the legal definitions of the categories were similar to those of NATO.[91]

The main significant revisions in light of NATO are the *definitions* of the classification levels. Regulation No 3 on Euroatom Classified Information stipulates four categories in Article 10, as noted in the table below. Applying one of the categories requires more than a vague probability that the risk of disclosure is present. All categories use the wording '*would have*' and refer to '*consequences*' as opposed to a chance or likelihood. However, as we noted, Regulation No 3 is only applicable to Euratom. The Council's Decision on its classification rules of 1995, applicable only to the Council's General Secretariat, and the Commission's rules of 1993 are more significant. The Council Decision of 1995 stipulates only three categories of classification: '*Secret*', '*Confidential*', and '*Restricted*'. Although this Council Decision does not include the '*Top Secret*' grading, it is noticeable that the wording is less strict than Regulation No 3. For example, there is a lack of referencing the consequences of disclosure but only a rather broad stipulation of '*interests*', which offers more leeway for classifying information. More importantly, the category of '*Restricted*' is revised to a more open-ended and vague definition by broadly referring to '*inappropriate*' and '*premature*' disclosure.

Most pertinent regarding the NATO influence are the 'Solana Decisions', that is the Decisions by the former Council's Secretary General who revised the system in 2000. The Secretary General made most of the changes in a rapid manner and in secret.[92] The plans for the changes were laid out in a secret 'Note for the Committee of Permanent Representatives regarding Security Plan for the Council'. In this Note, Secretary General Solana

[89] Kaljia E Schilde, 'Cosmic Top Secret Europe? The Legacy of NATO and Cold War US Policy on European Union Information Policy' (2015) 24 European Security 167.

[90] See also Reichard (n 82).

[91] ibid.

[92] General Secretariat of the Council, Council Guide, Part III, 'Delegates' Handbook' (2000) <http://aei.pitt.edu/8825/1/8825.pdf>.

stated that the 'higher level of security required to protect information under the [European Security and Defence Policy] makes it necessary to amend existing legislation or to adopt new texts'.[93] Moreover, the Council had refused to provide copies of drafts to NGOs because this 'could *fuel public discussion* on the subject and raise questions among the Council's partners as to the latter's reliability as regards its obligations under the security arrangements'.[94]

The Decision of the Secretary General on measures for the protection of classified information applicable to the General Secretariat of the Council was adopted in July 2000.[95] This Decision abolished the possibility for officials to change a document's specific classification marking.[96] Additionally, nineteen days after the new decision on classification rules, the Secretary General also amended previous Council Decisions regarding public access to the Council's documents as well as the improvement of information on the Council's legislative activities and the public register of documents.[97] With these revisions, the Secretary General widened the scope of the notion of public security, including military and *non*-military crisis management, which in turn meant a higher margin for classification and rejection of public access to documents.[98]

These changes seem to be a 'one-way influence from NATO to the EU'[99] and that in building its classified information policy, the EU 'had to come to terms with a significant part of NATO's internal culture of military secrecy'.[100] However, before the 'Solana Decisions' and the agreement with NATO,[101] in 1999 the EU concluded 'arrangements for enhanced

[93] General Secretariat of the Council, Note for the Permanent Representatives Committee on the Council Security Plan, 30 June 2000, Doc SN 3328/1/00 REV 1, 4.

[94] See Council letter to NGO Statewatch, as a response to a request for access to the document setting out the options for changing the 1993 Decision put before the COREPER meeting of 26 July 2000, 14 August 2000. See further Reichard (n 82) 331. Emphasis added.

[95] Decision of the Secretary-General of the Council/High Representative for the Common Foreign and Security Policy of 27 July 2000 on measures for the protection of classified information applicable to the General Secretariat of the Council [2000] OJ C239/1.

[96] See Council Decision No 24 (n 35) art 3(3).

[97] Council Decision 2000/527/EC of 14 August 2000 amending Decision 93/731/EC on public access to Council documents and Council Decision 2000/23/EC on the improvement of information on the Council's legislative activities and the public register of Council's documents [2000] OJ L212/9.

[98] See Council Decision 2000/527/EC (n 98).

[99] Reichard (n 82) 311.

[100] ibid 20.

[101] General Secretariat of the Council, Council Guide, Part III, 'Delegates' Handbook' (n 92).

cooperation' with the Western European Union (WEU).[102] In the Annex of the arrangements, two separate letters were included for the exchange of classified information with the Council and the Commission. This aspect in the development of the EU rules has been overlooked, despite the fact that the EU rules followed the wording of the WEU security regulations.[103] Nevertheless, the differences between NATO and WEU are not significant considering that the former had an impact on the latter regarding security of information.[104]

Originator control: From 'soft' to 'hard' gatekeeping of secrets

Rules on official secrets imply a level of control that the secret-keeper can exercise over the dissemination of the information. The principle of originator control embodies this aspect of official secrets rules. 'Originator control' means that the actor who provides the classified information retains complete control over its dissemination by other actors, with whom such information has been initially shared. The originator of secrets through this rule aims to safeguard its discretion of whether, if at all, the party with whom this information is shared may disclose its secrets. This logic of ownership derives from the exclusivity the secret-keeper has over disclosure or sharing of its secrets. Article 25(2) of the Euratom Treaty stipulated this principle, which was further established in Regulation No 3. Hence, this principle did not emerge during the NATO influenced revisions, but it was significantly made more rigid during the revisions of rules by the Secretary General in the 1999–2001 period.

Prior to the Solana Decisions, the EU had practised a soft form of originator control, the 'authorship rule', where MS could request non-disclosure of a document.[105] In Declaration No 35 of the Amsterdam Treaty, the MS reserved an explicit right to 'request the Commission or the Council not to communicate a document from that state to third parties without its prior agreement'. The authorship rule became relevant for MS considering the reforms of the Amsterdam Treaty and the inclusion of openness and access to information in the EU, as a consequence of which the EU's documents

[102] Council Decision of 10 May 1999 concerning the arrangements for enhanced cooperation between the European Union and the Western European Union [1999] OJ L153/1.

[103] Reichard (n 82) 323. Interviews with EU officials also reveal that the WEU had a significant impact on EU rules. Respondent No 11.

[104] Respondents Nos 8, 10,11.

[105] Reichard (n 82) 323; Rosén (n 82).

became directly accessible to European citizens. The MS sought to preserve their discretion in deciding whether that would indeed be the case for documents originating from them. The authorship rule was a 'soft' form of control because the MS had to expressly request the non-disclosure of the documents. On the contrary, the originator rule is considered 'hard' because it places the onus on the requesting party to obtain a written consent from the originator before being able to receive any document and the consent of the originator is (almost) absolute. Remarkably, in NATO the originator consent even applies to documents that are not classified when they are shared outside the organization.[106]

The hard form of originator rule existed between the EU and the WEU prior to the former's security arrangements with NATO. Article 1(d) of Annex V of the Agreement between the Council and the WEU stipulates the control of the originator. The rule was included in the Council Decision on classified information in 2001, and also stipulated in Article 9 of Regulation 1049/01 on public access to documents. In fact, Article 4 of the Regulation 1049/01 also foresees the possibility for MS to give their opinion on the disclosure of documents, however the CJEU has drawn a distinction between the originator rule in Article 9 and MS' prerogatives stipulated in Article 4, as the case of *Sweden v Commission* illustrates. According to the Court, unlike Article 9(3) of Regulation 1049/01 that stipulates originator control, Article 4(5) of the same regulation does not 'make the prior agreement of the Member State an absolute condition for the disclosure of a document, but makes the possible need for such agreement subject to a prior expression of will by the Member State concerned'.[107] In relation to Article 4(5), the Court further clarifies that the author of the document is irrelevant because the right to access documents extends not only to the EU level but also to 'documents received from third parties, including the Member States, as expressly stated by Article 3(b) of the regulation'.[108] However, in the case of *Sison* II specifically regarding classified information within the meaning of Article 9, the Court recognizes the application of the originator control. Furthermore, the Court affirms the

[106] NATO C-M(55) 15 Final, p 11, para 3.

[107] Case C-64/05 P *Sweden v Commission* EU:C:2007:802, para 47. The Court applies the same understanding of the article, by making it further clear in Case T-59/09 *Germany v Commission* EU:T:2012:75. Art 4(5) of Regulation No 1049/2001 entitles the MS concerned to object to the disclosure of documents originating from it only on the basis of the exceptions listed in art 4(1), (2), and (3) of the Regulation and if it gives proper reasons for its position.

[108] Case C-64/05 P *Sweden v Commission* (n 107) para 55.

discretion of the originator to decide on not merely the disclosure of the substance of the document but also its very existence.[109]

The relevance of the originator rule from a security perspective is presented as indispensable.[110] The Council consistently defends the originator rule as instrumental to the EU to gain the trust of other security actors by assuring them that they retain absolute control over their State secrets and sensitive information. The originator control is seen as a relevant security factor in forming autonomous relations with MS and third parties and to enhance the EU's perception as a serious security actor. For example, the Solana Decision clearly provides that:

> [T]he exchange of information ... *will work only if the originator of such information can be confident* that no information put out by him will be disclosed against his will. It is therefore necessary to provide that a Council document from which conclusions may be drawn regarding content of classified information put out by a natural or legal person, a MS, another community institution or body or any other national or international body may be made available to the public *only* with the *prior written consent* of the author of the information in question.

The originator rule creates a high margin of discretion and one that seems difficult to reconcile with the presumption in favour of openness even if it may be a relevant factor for the exchange of classified information among the community of executive secret-keepers. The originator rule in the EU is stipulated across the board and not only with the Council and the Commission. The rule is incorporated in the EU bodies and agencies as well as oversight institutions.[111] To some extent the rule of the originator expands through what may be portrayed as a domino effect: once an institution establishes this rule for how classified documents will be exchanged, in order for any other body to receive these classified documents, similar rules and arrangements must be adopted. Yet, oversight institutions have incorporated this rule due to the fact that it was an explicit condition by executive actors in order for them to share classified information.[112] Rules on official secrets provide a level of autonomy for the secret-keeper to decide with whom secrets would be shared and how. The final subsection below

[109] Case C-266/05 P *Sison v Council* EU:C:2007:75 (known as Sison II), paras 101–02.

[110] Respondents Nos 1, 3, 5, 6, 11, 18, 19, 22.

[111] See Decision of the Bureau of the European Parliament of 15 April 2013 (n 88) Annex II, para 24.

[112] See Galloway (n 40) for a more detailed explanation of these conditions of access and exchange of classified information with regard to the EP.

examines the consequences of this aspect of secrecy with regard to EU as a security actor.

Independence from Member States and external security cooperation

Secrecy ensures the independence of the secret-keeper to selectively disclose information, to receive and share secrets with only trusted actors.[113] Gaining more independence through secrecy was an opportunity recognized by the EU security actors, specifically by Secretary General Solana during his time in office, for the establishment of the EUCI system and developing an independent EU network for the exchange of official secrets. Once the EU system of sharing classified information was in place, it was easier for the EU to establish its own contact points with third parties and other relevant security actors,[114] as we saw, starting with NATO. Important in this regard is that MS too recognized the need for EU-level security action and information exchange as a valuable resource in this regard.[115] This sense was not equally appreciated by all MS, especially those who saw the security rationale of the classified information as too limiting for the principle of openness in the EU. This is most evident with the Solana changes of EUCI. Namely, the action filed by the Netherlands against the legality of the Council Decision of 14 August 2000, with the argument that this legislation could only have been adopted and based on the then Article 255 TEC and not on Article 207 TEC, and that by doing this the Council had infringed the prerogatives of the Commission and the EP since with the latter provision the Council legally did not need to involve the other institutions.[116] The case was withdrawn from the register of the Court in June 2002, as Regulation 1049/01 was already agreed and adopted at that stage, and there was an Inter-institutional Agreement between the EP and the Council for the exchange of classified information in 2002. However, the support of the MS for the independent EU regime on official secrets is not only a question of legal contestation, but even more important is whether in practice they share national State secrets with EU institutions under the

[113] See generally Sissela Bok, *Secrets: On the Ethics of Concealment and Revelation* (Pantheon Books 1982).

[114] Respondents Nos 5, 7, 8, 9.

[115] See generally Simon Nuttall, *European Political Cooperation* (OUP 1992).

[116] See Case C-369/00 *Netherlands v Council* OJ C316/19 of 4/11/2000 subsequently removed from the register OJ C144/30 of 15/6/2002.

newly EU established system. This is an aspect of the EU regime of official secrets examined in depth in the ensuing Chapter 3.

The EUCI regime is significant for the security responsibilities of the EU as it enables the EU to establish information as resources for action in security matters. Looking at the current legal situation counterfactually, that is the EU not having an autonomous regime of official secrets, it would imply that the EU would lack its own sources of information and abilities to deal with sensitive information. With the classification system in place the EU is able to assure international actors and MS that it can safeguard their secrets.[117] Reciprocal trust in sharing official secrets is of paramount importance for the system to actually work and enable a continuous flow of information.

The legal basis for an exchange of information with third parties, Article 37 TEU, enabling the EU to conclude agreements in the area of foreign and security policy has been used since 2002. At the outset the Commission had challenged this legal basis yet the Commission was faced with the unanimous decision of the members of the Council in which it emphasized that this particular proviso and the area of CFSP covered all questions relating to the Union's security. Information in the field of Common Security and Defence Policy (CSDP) may be through a so called framework 'participation agreement' or 'ad hoc participation' or if either of these is yet lacking then the Council adopts an ad hoc administrative arrangement.

Since the establishment of the Council Decision on EUCI in 2001, a three-level cooperation system has been set to exchange classified information with third parties regarding security. The first level deals with third parties whose security policy and regulations are very close to EU's. The second level consists of a group where these are 'markedly different'. The third level deals with occasional cooperation with third parties whose policy and security regulations cannot be assessed. Presently, there are four different ways in which the EU shares information with third parties. There are permanent security of information agreements with third states or international organizations; permanent administrative arrangements; framework agreements with third states for their participation in CSDP crisis management operations; and last there are the ad hoc agreements with third states for their participation in CSDP crisis management.

[117] Respondents Nos 9, 10, 11.

The EU shares classified information in various manners that depend on the type of security collaboration the EU has with these actors. With most parties the highest level of sharing classified information includes '*Top Secret*' classification such as Australia, Norway, USA, NATO, but there are also cases where only '*Restricted*' information is shared such as with Bosnia and Herzegovina, Montenegro, Ukraine. Moreover, there is a difference in the level of sharing electronically which is at the level of restricted with most partners but can also be confidential (USA) or secret (NATO) but also not possible at all to share electronically (Israel, Ukraine, Internal Criminal Court).[118]

The Council is slowly moving beyond the exchange of classified information in the area of security and defence, although in accordance with the Decision on EUCI these two fields were *the* main reason and areas where the justification for classified information exists. The broad notion of 'different area of EU business' created an open door for the Council to give and receive classified information and this was discussed at a level of Committee Decision behind closed doors.

Conclusions

The establishment of EU rules on official secrets was driven by administrative pragmatism, influenced by NATO military secrecy, and is predominately security oriented. In the context of the EU, openness considerations are missing both during the establishment of the rules and for the applicable rules on classification categories and ownership principles. Despite the EP's efforts, its opinion and call have been ignored regarding a classification system that takes into account the case law on public access to documents and the new constitutional oversight architecture. Setting up rules of official secrets aimed to balance between interests in openness and secrecy would be better facilitated if there were a discussion with parties with different interests. The lack of a legislative act or any involvement by an external (democratic) body and the executive nature of the rules raise questions regarding the extent of the margin of discretion in the manner the classification process takes place. In addition, any involvement of oversight

[118] Council of the EU, Policy orientation for negotiating security arrangements with third parties for the protection of EU Classified Information, 7 July 2003, Doc 11255/03.

bodies (parliament, court, ombudsperson) takes place within already established contours of classification, which could be disproportionally focused on executive necessity and executive interpretation of the margin of discretion.

NATO and WEU rules have influenced the regulation of official secrets in the EU. Even the wording of the rules is to a large extent the same, which has led scholars to point out that we can even gain an understanding of the NATO rules, which unlike the EU's, are not public. NATO has a different organizational culture and follows a presumption of security as the primary purpose. It is difficult to talk about a presumption in favour of openness for NATO, considering that even the documents for the regulation of classified information are not publicly available.[119] However, military security is not the EU's rationale as an organization and hence adopting secrecy rules that follow that logic seems misplaced in a legal setting that is bound by democratic principles.

Adhering to openness does not strictly mean that the EU rules on official secrets should have a legislative character, as this could take place through administrative rules if these rules were to incorporate the presumption in favour of openness. Yet, the legal categories of what may constitute a secret in the EU remain mostly vague and, more importantly, rules that ensure full executive discretion over disclosure are incorporated throughout the EUCI, both with executive and oversight actors. Even more striking regarding the oversight actors is the manner in which they have established the rules, following the closed-door style meetings in the same fashion as the executive actors.

In this shadowy background, the CSC is the body actually giving shape to the regulation of official secrets in the EU. Remarkably, this Committee is not only deciding issues pertaining to the Council, but it influences how the Court and the EP will deal with classified information, especially when it concerns the executive actors' discretion of disclosure, making sure that the hard originator rule is well spread out in the EU legal system. Significantly, this Committee makes decisions mostly behind closed doors and its opinions and recommendations become public at a later stage with mostly blacked-out passages.

The EUCI regulation in the eyes of the Council is very simple: something fully within its prerogative, mostly technical, that facilitates its

[119] Roberts (n 82) 332.

position in the security discussion with other security actors, becoming a trusted institution to exchange information with ever-growing numbers of third countries and international organizations. The fact that this regulation is fragmented into so many layers of internal rules, with each EU actor having its own internal regulation, seems of secondary importance since the CSC aims to ensure coherence through laying out common standards for all EU actors.

The fragmented nature of the EUCI rules might imply that there is not one coherent EU practice on the application of classified information which may be evaluated as effective, secure, or accountable, but rather many practice*s* varying per actor, and with different variables. The following chapter aims to uncover these insights looking at the practices of different EU actors.

3

EU Practices of Official Secrets: Administrative Discretion in Action

Abstracts

This chapter examines the practices of official secrets in the European Union. It provides 'real life' perspectives from Eurocrats based on interviews but also draws attention to patterns in the EU practices of official secrets and their special characteristics. The chapter enquires into how the discretion to create official secrets is applied and whether internal administrative review mechanisms exist, either *ex durante* or *ex post*, to address possible unwarranted official secrets. In addition, the chapter provides an account of the central principles of managing official secrets and questions the role of national rules and national authorities in this regard.

Introduction

> On basis of what criteria are you going to say that I overclassify? [Creating official secrets] is no exact science and that means before a court it would be an interpretation and you would lose. You will lose your case as a disciplinary authority or even as a criminal authority.[1]

This candid statement by a high EU official points to the basis of creating official secrets: administrative discretion. Precisely due to this discretion, this chapter aims to expose the institutional workings behind the scenes in EU administration in order to analyse the legal implications of

[1] Respondent No 15.

official secrets. The discretion to classify documents commences a complex administrative procedure as a result of which information is publicly inaccessible, sometimes for more than thirty years. This poses significant limits to public access to information, but also makes access for oversight institutions such as the European Parliament (EP) or the Court of Justice of the European Union (CJEU) more challenging. Documents that are marked as official secrets may remain outside the public register, which adds a further layer to secrecy in EU administration. Since openness and public access to documents are directly affected by the regime of official secrets, it is of high relevance to determine how official secrets are created in the EU. Official secrets pose challenges also within the EU administration. Access to official secrets is restricted internally leading to a group of 'inside-insiders' that is a limited number of officials who have access to official secrets. It is therefore pertinent to enquire how officials apply their discretion and how insiders' access to classified information works. Considering all these implications of the classification system, the purpose of this chapter is to critically assess administrative review mechanisms, both *ex durante* or *ex post*, that should exist to keep official secrets in check. The chapter therefore looks at the differences and similarities in the application of official secrets rules and observes the complexities in practice due to the EU's specificities as a compound administration where national rules and national authorities retain a significant role.

Administrative Discretion to Create Secrets

In his study of bureaucracies, Max Weber emphasized that secrecy enables bureaucracies to increase their influence.[2] EU officials acknowledge this aspect of secrecy and point out that 'some people simply want to show that they are important. They use the classification system to stamp documents in order to give importance to their work.'[3] Official secrets may also be used to conceal incriminating or embarrassing information or cover errors

[2] See 'The Power Position of Bureaucracy' in Max Weber, *Economy and Society* (Guenther Roth and Claus Wittich eds, Bedminster Press 1968) 990. For a different view see Richard A Hilbert, *The Classical Roots of Ethnomethodology* (University of North Carolina Press 1992) 142 noting directly that 'bureaucracies do not work the way Weber said they do'.

[3] Respondent No 10.

and inefficiency.[4] Hence, the discretion to create official secrets is key as it empowers the official to selectively hide or disclose information favourable to her self-interest.

Discretion, as understood and applied in this book, implies an official's appreciation of facts when they are put in relation with the norms to determine which course of action may be taken in view of the factual and legal reasons.[5] In the context of official secrets, discretion implies that an official uses personal judgment to decide whether and what security grading will be applied to a document and for how long. The drafter of classified documents has a certain view and expertise on the subject matter and she is also guided by experience.[6] These elements are combined with examples of documents that require security protection and a variety of guidelines and manuals.[7] Yet, as EU officials acknowledge, it 'is not black and white' clear which documents should be classified and the 'ability to assume personal responsibility plays a huge role' when it comes to making a decision whether to classify a document or not.[8] Classifying documents is assumed to be 'an art based on experience' and a process that is based on officials' *subjective* perception of potential risk if the document were to become public.[9]

The discretion to conceal information creates the potential for abuse of power and hence justifies oversight even when we are fully convinced

[4] Stephen Schulhofer, 'Oversight of National Security Secrecy in the United States' in David Cole, Federico Fabbrini, and Arianna Vedaschi (eds), *Secrecy, National Security and the Vindication of Constitutional Law* (Edward Elgar 2013) 40.

[5] This definition of discretion is identified as a 'classical discretion' in the literature, see Paul Craig, 'Law, Fact, and Discretion' in Paul Craig (ed), *EU Administrative Law* (OUP 2012) 433. See also Joana Mendes, 'Discretion, Care and Public Interests in the EU Administration: Probing The Limits of Law' (2016) 53 Common Market Law Review 419; Ronald M Dworkin, 'The Model of Rules' (1967) *Faculty Scholarship Series*, Paper 3609, 32 <http://digitalcommons.law.yale.edu/fss_papers/3609>.

[6] There are also so-called 'born classified' documents. This concept assumes that newly discovered information might be so significant with respect to security that it requires immediate and absolute control. A unique example of this concept is to be found in the US Atomic Energy Act of 1945, where there is an assumption that the newly discovered atomic-energy information is important for security reasons and that it requires instant and utter control. See Richard G Hewlett, 'Born Classified in the AEC—A Historian's View' (1981) 37 Bulletin of the Atomic Scientists 20; and Harold P Green, 'Born Classified in the AEC—A Legal Perspective' (1981) 37 Bulletin of the Atomic Scientists 28.

[7] The more specific manuals for EUCI are classified and inaccessible. Some older versions of documents, with blacked out passages, have been released.

[8] Respondent No 8. [9] Respondent No 6.

of officials' good faith in doing their work.[10] The starting premise of this chapter is *not* that EU officials use secrecy as a means of advancing their personal interests or hiding maladministration. However, administrative oversight of official secrets is salient due to the potential for the EU institutions to conceal error or embarrassment through the system of European Union Classified Information (EUCI).

Whilst some level of discretion is inevitable, this does not imply that the discretion is open-ended. EU primary law provides a clear legal obligation for all institutions, agencies, and bodies to conduct their work as openly as possible.[11] Secondary law also stipulates obligations for institutions to balance the necessity for some level of secrecy with the constitutional commitment and public interest in openness.[12] Hence, the discretion to classify documents is restricted by the legal obligations in favour of openness. The presumption in favour of openness in the administration of official secrets should be implemented in all stages starting with the decision to classify a document and until the document is declassified. Whether a document should be classified at all, who has the authority to make this decision, and what considerations justify keeping information undisclosed are all aspects of official secrets to be scrutinized. This scrutiny should not be driven merely by security concerns about the sensitive information but also with respect to how and to what extent openness is limited as a result of this process.

Who decides? Mapping actors with discretion to create official secrets

Every EU official can *potentially* classify documents. This is particularly the case with the executive and administrative actors in the EU, such as the Council or Europol or the European External Action Service (EEAS). At the EP, the discretion to classify documents is limited to officials with certain functions. In accordance with Article 4 of the EP's Bureau Decision

[10] See Steven Aftergood, 'An Inquiry into the Dynamics of Government Secrecy' (2013) Harvard Civil Rights—Civil Liberties Law Review 48, 511.

[11] Art 1 TEU.

[12] Regulation (EC) No 1049/2001 of the European Parliament and of the Council of 30 May 2001 regarding public access to European Parliament, Council and Commission documents [2001] OJ L145/43. See also Deirdre Curtin, 'Official Secrets and the Negotiation of International Agreements. Is the EU Executive Unbound?' (2013) 50 Common Market Law Review 423, 441.

on classified information,[13] the President of the EP, the chairs of the parliamentary committee, the Secretary General, and 'any person duly authorised' by the Secretary General have discretion to 'originate confidential information', that is to create new classified information.

EU officials may generate new documents and materials based upon original classified information. In this case, the EU official in the technical expressions of the classification system would be known as a 'derivative' classifier.[14] These officials reproduce, extract, or summarize classified information, and apply classification markings derived from source material.

The distinction between 'original' and 'derivative' classification is relevant due to the margin of discretion that an official has in each case. For the derivative classifier, the margin of discretion is largely limited and her role is to use the classified information in strict accordance with the originator's will.[15] An EU official frankly points out that 'you will not agree with [the decision of the originator] but you still have to put the [same security] marking [on the newly created document]'.[16] This in turn may result in over-classification, which is attributing a higher security level to the information than necessary,[17] because 'if the [official from the national] Capital over-classifies, you are stuck' a Council official explains[18] Over-classification also means that a document is classified when it should have been made public instead,[19] and EU officials point out that 'some Member States do over-classify'.[20]

Derivative classification is particularly prevalent at the EU institutions and bodies that have a more intergovernmental character because they rely mostly on Member States (MS) to receive classified information. Information gathering and sharing with the MS is a significant

[13] Decision of the Bureau of the European Parliament of 15 April 2013 concerning the rules governing the treatment of confidential information by the European Parliament [2013] OJ C96/1.

[14] Respondent No 1; see also Council Decision 2013/488/EU of 23 September 2013 on the security rules for protecting EU classified information [2013] OJ L274/1, art 3.

[15] Council Decision 2013/488/EU of 23 September 2013 on the security rules for protecting EU classified information [2013] OJ L274/1, art 3(2).

[16] Respondent No 15.

[17] Council, Guidelines on marking EU classified information Doc 10873/11.

[18] Respondent No 8.

[19] Liza Goitein, *Reducing Over-classification Through Accountability* (New York University School of Law 2011).

[20] Respondent No 3.

task of many EU actors in security policy. For example, Europol as a law enforcement cooperation agency or the EU Intelligence Analysis Centre (INTCEN) functioning within the EEAS, are fully reliant on the MS and their classified information.[21] EU officials working in these agencies and bodies explain that they rarely originally classify documents and most of their documents have a direct link with national information, which in turn means that the national authority makes the classification decision.[22] Discretion at EU level is minimal in such cases, since the newly created document cannot be personally assessed for a different classification marking by the EU official than the one deriving from the national authorities. For example, a Council official describes his experience:

> So far in my own practice, which includes 5 years, I have only classified 1 or 2 documents on my own initiative. The rest are all from the position of the derivative classifier.[23]

The hierarchical position of an official is another factor that determines the discretion to classify documents. A junior official for example would be under an obligation to consult her superiors in the official ranks because 'a junior official would not [decide to classify] things "*EU Secret*" without the agreement of a manager'.[24] In practice, it is mostly the Head of the Unit that decides on whether a document would be classified and if so at which security level.[25] Hence, often a decision to classify documents is not taken by one official individually, but it is rather done in consultation with the Director or the Director General. The consultation between an official and his superior in turn implies that the superior will de facto decide the security marking of the document. EU officials explain that one 'would send the document [classified] as "*Restricted*" and it comes back as [public] or "*Secret*"'.[26] Hence, in EU practice classification decisions are more often based on a consultation, which raises questions about locating responsibility of officials involved, but concurrently, this provides an opportunity to exchange different opinions about the sensitivity of the information and could potentially avoid over-classification.

[21] Respondents Nos 1, 2, 3, 4, 18,19, 20, 21.
[22] Respondents Nos 1, 2, 5, 7, 11, 12, 22.
[23] Respondent No 5.
[24] Respondent No 6.
[25] Respondent No 9.
[26] Respondent No 12.

Justifying official secrets

The discretion to create official secrets implies making a two-fold decision: the security grading to be applied and the period of time for which the document will be concealed. Article 9 of Regulation 1049/01 stipulates three security categories: '*Confidential*', '*Secret*', and '*Top Secret*'. However, the internal rules of the EU institutions and bodies foresee '*Restricted*' as an additional security category.[27] Determining the duration of classification, which may be defined in terms of a future date or a future event, is very important as it directly affects the public accessibility of the document. EU officials are not obliged to set a specific duration for the applicability of secrecy at the time of classifying a document. The default duration of security marking is five years. Some rules, as in the case of Europol, foresee a maximum of thirty years and longer if necessary. The rules of the EP provide for a review for possible declassification and archiving after twenty-five years.[28]

The institutional working culture is highly relevant in whether and how official secrets are justified. Firstly, the institutional working culture relates to whether discussions and meetings are documented at all and if so to what extent these documents are perceived to be security sensitive. For example, Europol information is undisclosed unless it is specifically designated as public. Due to law enforcement cooperation, the working premise of the agency is 'information is secret, unless' as opposed to 'information is public, unless'.[29] The EU's High Representative and its diplomatic helping hand, the EEAS, are another example of how the nature of a body affects the practice of official secrets. The practice of EU diplomacy has shown some inclination for more informal meetings and informal communications, which do not lead to formal documents and hence classification per se is also redundant.[30] The European Council also shares such tendency of informality in its meetings when crucial policies are discussed.[31] Secondly,

[27] Eg Council Decision 2013/488/EU of 23 September 2013 on the security rules for protecting EU classified information [2013] OJ L274/1, art 2.

[28] EP Bureau decision (n 13) art 13(3); Council Decision 2009/968/JHA of 30 November 2009 adopting the rules on the confidentiality of Europol information [2009] OJ L332/17.

[29] Respondent No 1.

[30] Eg, see former High Representative's opinion on formality, Catherine Ashton, 'Quiet Diplomacy Will Get our Voice Heard' *The Times* (17 December 2009).

[31] Wolfgang Wessels et al, 'Democratic Control in the Member States of the European Council and the Euro zone Summits' (2013) study requested by the European Parliament's Committee on Constitutional Affairs. See also Uwe Puetter, *The European Council and the Council. New Intergovernmentalism and Institutional Change* (OUP 2004).

the institutional working culture is also reflected in the considerations for classifying documents. For example, officials at the Council have a high sense of security of information, as a senior EU official explains:

> If you're dealing with operational information related to a military crisis management situation that the EU is running somewhere in Africa or whatever, some of that information could be very sensitive. *You could be affecting the lives of the people on the ground.* You have to be aware of that. If that information falls in the wrong hands that could have a lot of consequences.[32]

The Commission officials acknowledge that the sensitivity of the issues might keep the information undisclosed but would not lead to a classification decision and protection within the meaning of EUCI, as the following statement illustrates:

> You can imagine that when the Commission is preparing its decision on Microsoft, if we going to fine them at all, how much are we going to fine them, this is Top Secret information. I would say Top Secret in the normal common sense. But do we classify it? Perhaps we don't because we are working in a different environment.[33]

However, this does not mean that the Commission makes the information publicly available. Although documents may not be classified within the legal regime of EUCI, other markings and internal rules on non-disclosure could apply. In the current framework, besides the classification markings, the Commission has twenty-two categories of protected information with specific distribution and handling instructions, which are not made public.[34] These categorizations address the different Directorates in the Commission and the Units.[35] Commission officials acknowledge that there is 'internally a confusion regarding what happens and what is classification'.[36] This confusion is not only about the categories of security, but also relates to the legal terminology that is supposed to be guiding the decisions to classify documents.

An additional aspect to examining how official secrets are justified is to look at the terminology of security categories and the stated interests that are protected therein. The EU legal terminology of the classification markings may be described as 'very vague'.[37] The terminology is broad in

[32] Respondent No 6. [33] Respondent No 15. [34] Respondent No 15.
[35] Respondent No 16. [36] Respondent No 10.
[37] Henri Labayle, 'Principles and Procedures for dealing with European Union Classified Information in Light of the Lisbon Treaty' (2010) note requested by the European Parliament's Committee on Civil Liberties, Justice and Home Affairs.

order to encompass a variety of issues, however this makes the categories open-ended and possibly inclusive of issues that should not be classified at all. When the legal terminology is not precise or only provides broad interests that should be protected, it offers more leeway for classifying documents. Officials explain that 'high levels of generality may provide some needed flexibility, but it heightens the inherent subjectivity of the classification process and introduces an element of unchecked arbitrariness'.[38] Notions such as 'disadvantages' or 'inappropriate' applicable in the current EUCI system are too open-ended. For example, 'inappropriate' in practice may mean: 'a statement of a politician or head of state that would undermine the EU position on diplomacy: embarrassing by providing a frank opinion about a person or a situation'.[39] But it can also mean 'application for tenders: these types of information are not necessarily sensitive from a security point of view, but it would be inappropriate for the party involved if the information is known publicly'.[40] Under the wording of 'disadvantageous', the security marking could refer to issues pertaining to the 'internal cooking' of decision-making or to a 'mandate to negotiate'.[41] Sometimes it is not a question of sensitivity or damage, 'but it can create problems' even if it is 'background facts'.[42] These types of interpretations of legal categories show that information in the EU may be over-classified if the wording of even the lowest marking is broadly applied.

EU officials mostly consider 'damage' or 'identifiable damage' when classifying information.[43] One way to specifically address the damage question is by considering 'what if a journalist publishes this?' or 'what happens if the document is made immediately public'.[44] For former practitioners these questions were irrelevant because it 'used to be very simple: "*Restricted*" was a normal classification for all [documents], *everything*'.[45] Besides the interests of the MS or the EU, officials could have their own personal interests in mind when labelling documents secret or not.[46]

EU officials point out the disproportionality between usability and protection of information. For example, a document marked as '*Secret*', will be stored only physically and not electronically; it may only be accessed and used within a designated highly secured area; the document cannot be

[38] Aftergood, 'An Inquiry into the Dynamics of Government Secrecy' (n 10) 514.

[39] Respondent No 10.

[40] Respondents Nos 21, 22.

[41] Respondent No 12.

[42] Respondent No 12.

[43] Respondents Nos 2, 5, 6, 11, 20, 22, 23, 24.

[44] Respondents No 21, 22.

[45] Respondent No 12, emphasis added.

[46] Respondents Nos 4, 10.

copied and taken outside the secure area.[47] In contrast, a document classified as '*Restricted*' is accessible in electronic form and is generally made more easy to use. In practice, this leads the officials to favour lower marking levels, while making sure that the security of the information is ensured.[48] Omitting information from a document that would render the classification higher is one manner to create documents classified as '*Restricted*'.

The vague language of the classification markings coupled with the fact that there is no clear legal stipulation to require the official *not* to classify a document in case of doubt regarding the sensitivity of the issues covered by that document make it fairly easy for an official to classify documents. Therefore, review procedures to address unwarranted secrecy claims are highly pertinent to prevent over-classification.

Administrative oversight of official secrets

Internal administrative review mechanisms are necessary to address either *ex durante* or *ex post* possible unwarranted official secrets and to minimize, if not fully eliminate, the possibility of abuse of discretion to classify documents. The internal review mechanisms are of varied nature and scope, such as the Register of classified information and review procedures, administrative briefings as well as requirements of written justifications when classifying documents. The review of application of EUCI rules is particularly salient taking into account that all institutions, agencies, and bodies in the EU have powers to classify documents and even for those bodies that might not be originators of classification decisions, they still produce and share 'derivative' classification documents. The growth of EU administration, for example if we look at the constant increase of numbers of EU agencies,[49] make the review procedures of classification of documents even more pertinent in order to assess possible over-classification.

The registration and public records of the number of classified documents are significant indicators of whether the classification system takes due account of openness obligations and whether unnecessary secrecy dominates in the administration, as for example, studies have shown with

[47] See Council Decision 2013/488/EU of 23 September 2013 on the security rules for protecting EU classified information [2013] OJ L274/1, Annex II, para 26.

[48] Respondents Nos 4, 22.

[49] See Madalina Busuioc, '*European Agencies: Law and Practices of Accountability*' (OUP 2013).

regard to the US practice.[50] Keeping track of classified information is relevant for the usability of the information but even more so for possible declassification purposes.[51] Yet, in the EU context, as established with the Council Decision in August 2000, there is a possibility for classified documents not to be referenced at all in the public register of documents of the Council.[52] Consequently, classified documents become further invisible, not merely in substance—the text of the document—but also in form—the procedural number of the document.

EU numbers of classified information are not systematic, fully accurate, and/or public. Internal review mechanisms that focus on the number classified documents are often missing or do not offer a systematic tracking of numbers, which would make the overall analysis of numbers more reliable. For example, the Council's Report on the number of documents classified as '*Confidential*' produced in 2012 was found to be incorrect due to a 'technical error' and this was only clarified in a footnote in a different report a year later.[53] In the case of some EU actors, such as Europol, the amount of classified information is itself classified information.[54] MS and third parties may veto the public registration of documents they have shared with the EU institutions, leading to incomplete numbers for classified information at EU level.[55]

Furthermore, the EU practices with regard to registers are not unified. Europol's Register is classified as '*Restricted*', with access only to confidentiality desk officers. Heads of Unit have access to their 'own part of the Register' but no official has an overall view other than confidentiality desk officials.[56] The Register is centralized. At the Commission, there is a centralized register, at the level of Secretary General, but there are also local

[50] Eg Steven Aftergood, 'Reducing Government Secrecy: Finding What Works' (2009) Yale Law & Policy Review 27, 399.

[51] Goitein (n 19).

[52] Council Decision 2000/527/EC of 14 August 2000 amending Decision 93/731/EC on public access to Council documents and Council Decision 2000/23/EC on the improvement of information on the Council's legislative activities and the public register of Council documents [2000] OJ L212/9.

[53] See Council Annual Report on Access to Documents 2013, footnote 3.

[54] Respondents Nos 1, 3.

[55] See Council Decision 2000/527/EC of 14 August 2000 amending Decision 93/731/EC on public access to Council documents. See also Tony Bunyan, 'Constructing the Secret EU State: 'Restricted' and 'Limite' Documents Hidden from View by the Council' <http://www.statewatch.org/analyses/no-240-restricted-documents.pdf>

[56] Respondent No 1.

registries. Not every Directorate General has a local register since some do not have many classified documents, such as in areas of education and culture. The practice of registers is not unified even within institutions, but it is established based on necessity and the number of classified documents. For the EEAS, the register is classified as '*Restricted*' as well. But they do not 'keep figures systematically'[57] and it lacks an overview of the amount of classified information or possibly declassified information. The Council is similar to the Commission in the sense that there is a central and a sub-registry. For both institutions, the organization of the Register takes place on basis of the institutions' size and functions.

Among practitioners there is consensus that 'the register is in a significant position of possible power; it controls access in and out'.[58] However, the registry is not set up for the purpose of maintaining an overall track of classified information, to facilitate the declassification, to report on numbers of documents, or to in any way facilitate a review of the security basis or the transparency of the figures. For example, for classified documents there is no strict legal obligation for the Council to identify the originator, which would facilitate tracking who was responsible for the classification and noting whether officials within the Council originally classified the document.[59] The latter would be relevant in cases when access is requested from third parties, such as the CJEU.[60] Moreover, the officials in these settings do not have access to the overall Register or to an overview of numbers. This also eliminates the possibility of reports or reviews and it seems that there is a complete lack of any binding requirement to facilitate consistent annual reviews and measures to prevent over-classification. Some EU officials consider that it is not necessary to follow up on declassification and numbers of documents.[61] A review of the technical and security issues of the systems takes place, but there is no review driven by the idea of internal oversight of the EUCI system. Besides security-focused internal reviews, an inter-administrative review between EU actors, also exist to check the applicable security measures and whether the actors share similar technical facilities for safeguarding EUCI.[62] However, these reviews are not focused

[57] Respondents Nos 21, 22. [58] Respondent No 4.

[59] Council Decision 2013/488/EU, Annex III on Management of Classified Information, para 10(a).

[60] See eg Case T-284/08 *People's Mojahedin Organization of Iran v Council* EU:T:2008:550.

[61] Respondent No 3.

[62] See Council Decision 2013/488/EU of 23 September 2013 on the security rules for protecting EU classified information [2013] OJ L274/1, art 13(5).

on oversight that would facilitate openness or question the balance an official makes between openness and the classification of documents.

Openness in the official secrets system often is ensured most easily through obligations to apply the presumption in favour of openness during the process of classifying a document. However, EU officials point out that an entire document may be classified even if the information therein is only to some extent sensitive:

> What is confidential? Imagine a document stamped 'Confidential', a large document, about 30 pages. All pages are stamped confidential. But the question is: within these 30 pages, what is actually confidential? Names? Locations? Actions? Very little information is confidential actually.[63]

Classified information hence becomes a cost both from an openness perspective and in terms of usability of the information for the EU administration. The lack of considerations for openness during the classification decision could be mitigated for example via administrative briefings or written justifications. Considerations of openness in EUCI could be part of the briefing process that every EU official undergoes at the start of his/her employment contract. Yet, the briefing as it is currently structured in the EU is only focused on security measures and there is no mention of openness or public access to information.[64] The current purpose of the briefing is to make EU officials aware of the security risks and protection measures but it does not expand to discuss the implications of classified information, especially from an openness perspective.[65] Some practitioners are very direct that:

> There is no link to openness. We do not really look at that side. Our job is the security of the document. [Official's] job is to classify ... No need to know about access and transparency. [Officials] have to start thinking like 'what if the document is going to be in the newspaper'. This is the logic we want them to have, to be prudent.[66]

Another possibility of implementing the presumption of openness within the classification process would be to include a written justification for the decision to classify a specific document. This could be an incentive to rethink the specific harm and it would facilitate the process of declassification

[63] Respondent No 4.

[64] Eg Council Decision 2013/488/EU of 23 September 2013 on the security rules for protecting EU classified information [2013] OJ L274/1, art 7(5).

[65] Respondents Nos 21, 22, 23.

[66] Respondent No 22.

or disclosure.[67] For example, if a request for public access to information that concerns a classified document is received, the justification regarding the harm disclosure would cause is already stated in the document. This written justification would enable an EU official to immediately assess whether the reasons for classification of the document are still applicable, that is whether the disclosure of the document would specifically and actually harm EU interests, or whether the document should be disclosed. However, this aspect is also lacking in EU practice. In fact, as we noted above, EU officials confess that sometimes security grading is used not to give protection to the documents but more to provide a personal enhancement of interest in what they call 'stamps-of-importance'.[68] The issue with this aspect of classifying documents is that there is neither an *ex post* mechanism of review of the classification decision nor a system that would try to allocate 'wrong' classification decisions or track responsibility. Quite the contrary, practitioners insist that such a system of review of classification decisions is not feasible precisely because the 'classification decision is always subjective'.[69] By contrast, in the US, the Executive Order of President Clinton had a specifically dedicated and clear provision in favour of openness and stipulated that in case of doubt whether to classify a document, the official is obliged to disclose the document, hence leading to a clear incentive for less classified information.[70]

Overall, the internal organizational setting for classified information in the EU is focused on the security of information, but it lacks mechanisms to address oversight and openness concerns. One notable example is classification for personal gains or systematic misconceptions by officials. Exiting administrative instruments, such as the registry, are established mostly (if not only) on the basis of security concerns, although these instruments have the potential to be utilized also for purposes of administrative oversight.

[67] Open Society Justice Initiative, *The Global Principles on National Security and the Right to Information* (Open Society Foundations 2013) <https://www.opensocietyfoundations.org/sites/default/files/global-principles-national-security-10232013.pdf>.

[68] Respondent No 10. [69] Respondent No 6.

[70] Executive Order 12958, 'Classified National Security Information', 17 April 1995, Section 1.2(b). See also Harold C Relyea, 'Opening Government to Public Scrutiny: A Decade of Federal Efforts' (1975) 35 Public Administration Review 3. Note however that this remains an exception and the next Executive Act revised this rule, as each President has the authority to establish new rules on classified information.

Insiders' Access to Official Secrets

Limiting internal access to official secrets creates a cluster of inside-insiders, that is only a limited number of officials know the information, leading to asymmetries and compartmentalization in the administration.[71] It is the insiders, those who know the secret information, that are in a position to determine which other officials may gain access to classified information and when such access may be granted.[72] The issue of compartmentalization becomes even more pressing to examine if we follow the reasoning that agencies and institutions are involved in an incessant competition.[73] In the following subsection, the book maps internal access to official secrets by examining institutional structures and administrative principles.

EU institutional structure

Internal privileges to access official secrets are determined in line with whether and to what extent the administration of official secrets is centralized. For example, the Commission is more decentralized, unlike Europol, where most decisions regarding official secrets are taken in consultation with the Confidentiality Desk Office. At the Commission, many of the issues regarding classified documents are decided at the level of the Director General. A two-layered institutional set-up is in charge of official secrets within the Commission: first, at the institutional level of the Commission there is a Commission Security Directorate,[74] second, at the level of the Commission departments, responsibility lies with one or more Local Security Officers. The Commission Security Policy Advisory Group[75] and the Commission Security Board are the two other relevant

[71] George Stigler, 'The Economics of Information' (1963) 69 Journal of Political Economy 213.

[72] Such asymmetries are not strictly limited to executive actors, see Vijay Krishna and John Morgan, 'Asymmetric Information and Legislative Rules: Some Amendments' (2001) 95 American Political Science Review 435.

[73] Eg David C Kozak and James M Keagle, *Bureaucratic Politics and National Security: Theory and Practice* (Lynne Rienner Publishers 1988) 7.

[74] This Directorate consists of different Authorities, which are in charge of various security aspects of the information. Examples include the Security Accreditation Authority also acting as Crypto Authority.

[75] Consists of the Member of the Commission responsible for security matters, representatives of the NSA of each Member State. Representatives of other European institutions may

bodies that are specifically related to official secrets. The Directorate on Human Resources and Security is the only structural body that can mark documents when they are reviewed under the security policy. Issues of physical security, mostly contracted to third (private) parties, are organized at the central level of the Commission.[76]

The EEAS shares features with the Commission regarding the level of complexity and the broad structures involved for the management of classified information. The institutional structure of EEAS is divided into the Headquarters, Delegations, and position of the Military Unit. As a diplomatic body related to more than 140 EU missions (civil or otherwise) in the world, the level of information flows at the EEAS is paramount.[77] The institutional aspect of the classification system structure encompasses many directorates that have a specific focus on security and exchange of information. The internal institutional structure of the EEAS that is important for the classification system involves: Managing Directorate, Security Directorate, Security Committee, and EU INTCEN.

The Council's institutional set-up for classified information is split between issues decided at the ministerial level and the different organs, some of which are especially created to manage the classification system. At the ministerial level, the Council only acts when it is necessary to approve security agreements with third parties, to authorize the release of EUCI to third states and international organizations, and to consent to an annual inspection programme proposed by the Secretary General concerning inspections of MS' and EU's agencies services and premises. The Secretary General has the role of the Security Authority in the Council and exercises a few key responsibilities in this capacity. The Secretary General is responsible for implementing the security policy and ensuring its review in addition to having a coordinating role. The Secretary General coordinates with the MS' national security authorities on *all* security matters relating to the protection of classified information relevant for the Council's activities. Throughout these tasks, the Security Office that was formally established in 2001 assists the Secretary General with the coordination, supervision, and implementation of security measures. Importantly, accessibility to classified information at the EU level directly depends on the

also be invited. Representatives of relevant EC and EU decentralized agencies may also be invited to attend when issues concerning them are discussed.

[76] Respondent No 15.

[77] See EEAS, Ongoing Missions <http://eeas.europa.eu/eueom/missions/index_en.htm>.

national rules, whereas national authorities enable the technical and security functioning of the EUCI system. National authorities conduct the screening of officials who will be working at EU institutions and bodies to assess whether a security clearance should be granted. National rules apply to the screening process resulting in differences between the MS as to how these procedures are carried out. Similarly, the process of determining the application of the principle of 'need-to-know', which means establishing whether an EU official will be granted access to a specific classified document, depends on national rules.

Administrative principles: Security clearance and the need-to-know

Internal access to classified information, especially information classified with a higher security marking, is impossible without a security clearance. The procedure for the issuance of a security clearance is similar in all institutions and bodies of the EU. It is actually one of the few elements in the system of the EUCI that is more commonly shared. It is similar in two very important respects: at the national level, the vetting procedure takes place in accordance with applicable national regulations, which is thereafter followed by a decision regarding approval at EU level. Questions arise regarding the implications of the first layer of decisions, which take place at the national level. To what extent does the vetting process of national authorities bind the EU? How do EU institutions respond if a MS does not approve the vetting of a prospective EU official? Based on the practice thus far, EU officials could not report a case in which the MS would not approve of the person and that person would get the job.[78] This does not mean that the institution in question has no discretion whatsoever to at least address the MS in question and raise concerns that the vetting result might not be correct. However, the EU body would have no legal authority to overturn the national decision. Everyone is vetted by the MS and EU officials admit that they are 'bound to accept' the national vetting decision.[79] This situation of the national vetting process having final implications at EU level could lead to a strange situation for the elected Members of the EP. A MEP who has a direct mandate from European citizens would be limited in her functions due to the vetting process for classified information. This, according to MEPs, 'makes no sense'.[80]

[78] Respondents Nos 3, 6, 22.

[79] Respondents Nos 1, 6.

[80] Respondent No 26.

The vetting process is even more complex in the external missions of the EU. At EULEX, for example, three different types of security clearance procedures exist: seconded staff must have a security clearance before they arrive; contracted staff will receive a security clearance from the MS of which the person is a national; and then there are officials who are part of the 'contributing third states' and are vetted by their own states in accordance with their regulations.[81] From a practical viewpoint, the two-step process of vetting at national level and approval at EU level is sensible considering that the state would have most information on the person concerned. Yet, there are different regulations and practices between MS and some MS have more robust examinations while others have more privacy protection oriented measures.[82] The EU institution de facto acts on the basis of the national decision. Hence, differentiation exists within each institution or body regarding how the official's background is checked.

The security clearance is not necessarily linked to the hierarchical level of the official. A security technician can get clearance up to '*Top Secret*' classified information as can a Director General. In practice, most officials are not cleared for '*Top Secret*' access; their access rights remain valid for the level of security grading '*Secret*' or (mostly) '*Confidential*'. A security clearance is the first level of filter to determine which officials could have access to official secrets. But thereafter, it is not the prevalent factor regarding whether or not an official actually receives access to official secrets. Whether indeed such official would gain access to classified information in a concrete case is determined by another key administrative principle of official secrets, that is the need-to-know principle.

The principle of 'need-to-know' implies that an official must have some necessity in order to be acquainted with the classified information. This principle did not always exist in the EU rules regarding classified information and was introduced by the Council in 1998.[83] Throughout the EU the principle of the need-to-know is designed in a similar fashion. Although each administrative actor establishes it separately, the logic of its functionality is similar. How broad or narrow is the application of the principle

[81] For EULEX eg it is inter alia the US, Canada, Turkey; Respondents Nos 23, 24.

[82] Respondent No 1 and see eg, Germany, Law on Prerequisites and Procedures for Security Clearance Checks Undertaken by the Federal Government of 20 April 1994 as amended by Act to Fight International Terrorism of 9 January 2002.

[83] Council Decision 98/319/EC of 27 April 1998 relating to the procedures whereby officials and employees of the General Secretariat of the Council may be allowed access to classified information held by the Council [1998] OJ L140/12, art 1(1).

of 'need-to-know' and who decides or determines its scope? The distinction between the originator classifier and the derivative classifier explained above matters in this respect. The originator of the classified information has the primary discretion to decide with whom the document will be shared and practically this may be arranged in several manners. For example, in Europol, a clear system exists to enable a MS to share only with Europol, or with another MS, or many others, through a system of 'handling codes'.[84] The originator of the information may also be an outsider actor of the EU, such as a third state or organization. The latter have the potential to create different circles of who gets to see what classified information in the EU when they share this information with an EU actor. The authority of the 'outsider' extends both *within* the institution and (crucially) *between* the institution and other actors. It is a similar case with the MS when they are in the position of the originator.

For the lower level of classification, '*Restricted*' documents, the 'need-to-know' principle does not apply. For example, everyone working in Europol, which adds up to almost 900 individuals could gain access to '*Restricted*' documents.[85] With more than 160 officials in Brussels and an office in Luxembourg directly linked to issues of classified information,[86] the Commission too has many individuals who can access documents. The usability of the information is at times more relevant in EU practice than strictly abiding to the security requirements for classified information. In this regard, practitioners acknowledge that

> When you have a colleague with you and you are working together on a topic you show a page or a paragraph so in that case you do not give the whole file but yet they see something even though you have not checked all the need-to-know and other conditions. You could say then that access is tailor made. It needs to fit the purpose and fit the occasion.[87]

When the classified information is indeed shared in good faith and on the basis of progressing with a particular policy, perhaps these exceptions to security principles are understandable or even desirable. However, at the

[84] See generally Vigjilenca Abazi, Unveiling the Power over Europol's Secrets (25 April 2013). Amsterdam Law School Research Paper No 2013-26; Amsterdam Centre for European Law and Governance Research Paper No 2013-04 <http://papers.ssrn.com/sol3/papers.cfm?abstract_id=2256317>.

[85] See Europol public website with indicated number of staff <https://www.europol.europa.eu/content/page/our-people-19>.

[86] Respondent No 15. [87] Respondent No 22.

same time, the example shows that documents may be shared in practice, even in circumstances when they should not be. Informally sharing documents could be beneficial to a policy as well as to advance some particular interest of the official. These situations go unnoticed and are considered as part of the 'everyday practice' of classification.[88]

What emerges from the discussion of these administrative principles on access to official secrets is that *internal* access to classified information is regulated and leads to layers of inside-insiders and inside-outsiders are created. These layers are not always determined by EU rules and officials, but often depend on the national level rules and decisions that are made by national authorities. In a direct way, the latter shape who gets to see official secrets in the EU. Hence, the level of secrecy at the EU level also depends on decisions taken at the *national* level. As the discussion thus far has shown, an intrinsic link with the national administrations exists on varied issues regarding classified documents, such as decisions to classify documents, security vetting procedures, or registration of documents. MS' rules and authorities have a significant role in the functioning of the EUCI system. The extent of their involvement and relevance depends on the specific institutional set-up and nature of each EU actor. In the area of security, most EU actors rely on national authorities in several respects, as elaborated below.

Compound EU Administration: The Role of National Rules and Authorities

National rules and authorities

The initial decision of whether to classify a document at all often takes place at the national level since most of the information originates from the MS and carries with it national markings. Bodies and agencies, such as INTCEN and Europol, receive the classified information from MS and work on analysis and reports that are sent back to the MS. National rules, in this regard, follow the document in terms of classification and declassification markings. In addition, for some EU actors, a more direct involvement of the national authorities is possible, although not through

[88] Respondent No 4.

specific decisions regarding EUCI but through the institutional organization and the tasks foreseen at the EU and national level. Within Europol distinctions may be drawn between actors involved at the MS level and those that function within Europol's structures. At the level of the MS, it is their national regulations that apply when deciding which bodies are entrusted with handling classified information. This can vary from the State Commission on Information Security, the Ministry of Justice and Home Affairs, or possibly to the Ministry of Defence.[89]

A significant number of EU classified documents derive from the MS. For all these documents, the balance between secrecy and openness is already established by the national administration, which then is only extended at the EU level. The applicable EU rules on classified information only grant authority of consultation to EU institutions and bodies when the information is already classified at the national level. The EU official might disagree with the security marking but she would have to apply it to the newly EU created document. To do otherwise, for example, could imply that the EU official makes an independent decision to lower the classification marking or indeed to make the document public. Doing so however, would directly risk the trust of MS to continue sharing information. Such issues are particularly sensitive with agencies such as Europol that already note the lack of trust and information sharing by the MS.[90] Hence, in the view of Europol officials, of key priority is the trust of MS, which relies on their ability to retain national control over classification markings and dissemination of the information.[91] Therefore, despite the fact that the EUCI regime is an independent EU established policy on the regulation of classified information, key aspects of its application rely and depend on the MS. This feature of the EUCI regime is a reflection of EU institutional structure with its compound and interdependent layers and hence de facto makes the EUCI policy deeply reliant on the cooperation between MS.

In addition to the decision to classify documents, security clearance is also largely dependent on national rules and authorities. A two-step procedure is a common feature of issuing a security clearance in the EU. This implies that it is always the national authorities that conduct the vetting process (sometimes in cooperation with authorities from other states where

[89] See Council Decision 2013/488/EU, Appendix C.

[90] See eg House of Lords (2008) 'Europol: Co-ordinating the Fight Against Serious and Organised Crime' Select Committee on the European Union, Session 2007-08, 29th Report.

[91] Respondents Nos 1, 3.

the official has been a resident), and only thereafter does the EU level administration make a decision regarding the approval. However, approval should be seen in a soft sense, considering that the level of discretion not to follow the results of the vetting procedure of the MS is minimal. In addition, different national regulations apply during the issuance of the security clearance despite the fact that all these officials upon admission become part of the EU administration that is independent of the MS. EU missions face the biggest mix of vetting procedures due to the diversity of backgrounds of officials. The concern here is that there are no mechanisms at the EU level to ensure some sense of consistency in the multiple procedures applicable both to MS and third parties. The variety of rules results in EU officials undergoing a different scrutiny treatment, with direct consequences for the security of information. EU practitioners are the first to admit that the human element is the weakest link in the chain of security of classified information,[92] hence the vetting process is quite significant in ensuring the credibility and trustworthiness of an official who will handle sensitive material. Beyond the security of information, another relevant consequence for the EU is that officials could face responsibility at their national level. The national authorities, however, do not have prerogatives for any oversight mechanism at the EU level. This duality creates a situation for the official that her clearance and responsibility remains at the national level for matters that are of EU-level concern and her actions take place within the EU working environment.

Particularly significant is the fact that national rules apply if there is a breach of security of EUCI and if criminal charges were to be initiated against an EU official suspected of violation of EUCI security, the prosecution would take place at the national level. The application of national rules to classified information that originates from MS has direct consequences for the access of EU oversight actors to classified information.

Lastly, national representatives participate in EU bodies that make relevant decisions for the application and development of EUCI rules at EU level. More specifically, the Security Committees consist of EU and national officials who make key decisions and provide guidelines on how documents are classified in the EU and set procedures and determine partners for the exchange of classified information. For example, Europol's Security Committee is comprised of representatives from MS and is in

[92] Respondents Nos 3, 4, 6, 15.

charge of setting broader policies when it comes to classified information. The Council Security Committee is also a very prominent body that is involved in setting guidelines and providing opinions that are applicable to all security actors but also including EU oversight actors. The EEAS also has a Security Committee comprised of similar members to those in the Council, which in turn leads EU officials to remark at times on the duplication of efforts.[93]

Differences and similarities in EU practices of secrecy

The complexity of the EUCI regime in practice does not only derive from to the interdependence with the MS regimes on official secrets, but is partly the case due to the fragmentation of the EU rules regarding classified information and how they are applied in practice. Hence, differences could arise also at the EU level regarding how secrets are created and managed. Indeed, some differences in the EUCI system exist. Firstly, the administrative organization of bodies varies and depends on the actor. The larger institutions work on a two-tier level, central and local. Secondly, in cases where the legal or technical principles regarding EUCI are the same, differences could be noted in their application: some actors are more focused on the usability of the information. However, these differences in the rules and their application are not vast nor of such a nature to signify problems with the management and exchange of classified information.

Many similarities derive from our discussion, particularly when EUCI is more closely examined in respect of who actually has classification authority and the process of classification. The following applies to all actors. Firstly, regarding the actors behind the scenes, at a micro level, the structure of individuals is guided by the same principles of security clearance and need-to-know. These principles function in a similar procedural sense. For the structure of the 'inside-insiders', the security clearance is less relevant; it is the need-to-know principle that actually limits internal access to classified information. However, practice is focused on 'tailor made access', ignoring the strict access rules if the official considers her colleague should see the information as well. Each official has classification authority and it is more a question of seniority and rank in the administration that is relevant to distinguish the level of classification someone can mark. Secondly, the relevance of the MS is a common denominator for all EU actors, albeit

[93] Respondent No 22.

to different extents. The relation of EU actors to the MS regarding the classification system is of particular relevance and bares consequences in EU procedures. The position of the MS is important in two respects: the dependency of EU actors on national information and national rules applicable to procedures that are of EU character. In this manner, national rules and national working methods together with the EU rules and practices create a compound EUCI regulation.

Conclusions

Administrative discretion, broad interpretation of legal terminology, and the lack of review mechanisms are key features of the EU practice of official secrets. The practice shows a pragmatic approach on the side of EU officials for the use of information and, more importantly, a neglect of internal oversight considerations fostering openness. A salient aspect to the legal framework of official secrets, especially in light of their application, is the centre role that national rules and national authorities play. This role is evident in two important factors of internal access to official secrets: security clearance and the need-to-know principle. Although the EU has its own independent set of rules on official secrets, the significance of MS in practice remains central because the main administrative principles in the creation and management of official secrets are based on national discretion, rules, and authorities.

Discretion is inherent in the decision to create official secrets. This is the starting point to understanding the workings behind the system of official secrets. It should be emphasized, however, that EU officials' discretion and autonomy regarding classifying documents are significantly minor. Derivative classification predominates in the EU. Derivative classification means following the original classification marking in a strict manner, leaving EU-level discretion as minimal. In the EU's work on security, the originators of the information are mostly the MS, as can be seen in the examples of Europol or the EU Intelligence Analysis Centre, or third states and organizations. The derivative classification operates strictly from a security perspective and enforces a more rigid secrecy culture as it makes the highest classification marking applicable to the entire document when, for example, a variety of documents with different security markings are used. Furthermore, it creates space free from responsibility for the EU official as she merely needs to reproduce the classification stamp without challenging it. From a security perspective, maintaining the originator's security marking is seen as positive because it provides the necessary assurances of a rigid security culture and trustworthiness by control. The national administrative culture of how secrets are managed affects EU-level decisions and processes due to the extensive applicability of derivative classification of EUCI.

From the perspective of openness, it is relevant that this inherent discretion in the establishment of official secrets is addressed by review mechanisms. In EU practice, specific security guidelines and manuals as well as security briefings are a common feature for making sure that officials classify with prudence. However, this prudence is directed fully at the security of the information whilst considerations for openness are lacking. Not only are they lacking but also there is a sense from EU officials, as some of their statements quoted in this chapter illustrate, that considerations of openness and public access to information are not relevant when it comes to classifying documents. In addition, the legal definitions of the security markings are broad and vague leaving space for interpretations of what could constitute a damage or security risk and hence potentially lead to classifying more documents, even if EU officials apply EUCI in good faith.

EU officials are aware that categories are broad and of the impossibility of administrative review proving that a specific classification decision is wrong, unless it is a 'clear case' of negligence or abuse.[94] This in turn implies the lack of perspective for disciplinary measures as a possible disincentive for over-classification. It is noteworthy that in practice the EU security markings are applied to cover information that officials would not want to read in the press, that could be embarrassing for a political figure, or even if some background facts are considered 'inappropriate' as they would reveal the internal 'cooking' of EU decision-making. These aspects of the practice of official secrets lead to questions on whether there are internal oversight mechanisms, such as registers or reviews. Although institutions and bodies have internal registers, they do not facilitate reviews for over-classification checks. These registers are not public nor is the number of official secrets in the EU overall. Some institutions such as the Council report on the number of official secrets, but these numbers are not always fully accurate, and more importantly, documents from originating parties

[94] Respondents No 3.

such as the MS may be blocked from the register and hence they would be publicly untraceable. Overall and similar to the establishment and regulation of official secrets discussed in the previous chapter, the practice of official secrets lacks considerations of openness.

Internal access to classified information is the second main aspect examined in this chapter. Limitations on internal access are maintained through two key security arrangements, mentioned above, the security clearance and the principle of 'need-to-know'. The EU is dependent on the national rules and national authorities: whether an EU official or a MEP is granted a security clearance and to which level of classification marking, are contingent upon the varied national procedures, some of which are more intrusive to privacy. The need-to-know principle may significantly limit internal access if we were to examine it strictly from a legal perspective. Yet, in practice, EU officials informally share information if they personally consider the information to be valuable to their colleagues.

This 'flexibility' with internal access to official secrets is in contrast with the rigid rules and limitations for institutional access by the oversight institutions, such as the EP or the Court. One of the main problems indeed with official secrets in the EU has been their inaccessibility by these institutions, which in turn led to serious limitations in parliamentary oversight and judicial review. Hence, not only the rules but also their application give rise to questions whether they adhere to the EU's constitutional obligations to openness and oversight. These later aspects of official secrets are examined in detail in the next chapter.

4

Access to Official Secrets and Reviewing Executive Secrecy

Abstracts

This chapter examines access to official secrets for the three branches of oversight in the EU: the Court of Justice of the European Union, the European Parliament, and the European Ombudsman. A joint analysis of these institutions provides a comprehensive insight and a comparative understanding of the tensions between EU executive secrecy and oversight. The chapter also examines the legal framework for oversight institutions to review executive power in establishing official secrets. It provides an in-depth analysis of judicial review of secrecy especially as it affects EU fundamental rights. It is argued that the current rules on official secrets provide executive institutions with a wide discretion on the establishment and access to official secrets. Whilst this discretion challenges oversight, the issue is further exacerbated by the complexity of compound administrative procedures in the EU. The latter imply that official secrets often derive from national authorities, which in turn can block access for EU oversight institutions. The challenge of access to classified documents runs both ways as national oversight institutions, in particular parliaments, also face limited access to EU official secrets. Against this background, the chapter questions whether the current rules and the resulting limitations for oversight institutions in gaining access to and the review of official secrets lead to an 'executive privilege' in secrecy in the EU.

Introduction

Access to information is a pre-condition for oversight. Informed oversight is complex and depends on many factors, some of a practical importance, such as sufficient resources,[1] and others of a political nature, such as the

[1] Eg sufficient time and assisting staff at oversight institutions for the conduct of a systematic information analysis are relevant aspects.

parliamentary representatives' selectivity of issues to oversee in accordance with the perceived interests of their electorate. This chapter focuses on whether EU oversight institutions have the legal prerogatives to access classified information fully and timely, and whether they are able to obtain this information without any reliance on the discretion of executive institutions. The chapter maps the 'insiders' of oversight institutions by identifying who precisely gains access to classified information.

Review of executive decisions establishing official secrets and their ramifications is equally relevant for a holistic oversight. The chapter examines the legal framework of the Court of Justice of the European Union (CJEU), the European Parliament (EP), and the European Ombudsman (EO) directed at reviewing executive claims for the necessity of secrecy. Parliamentary, judicial, and administrative[2] oversight are often treated separately in the literature as they concern different types of institutions that have a varied nature and position towards executive actors in the overall EU constitutional architecture. Yet, there is nothing unique about the challenges each institution faces regarding classified information, since the difficulties are rooted in the same rules of official secrets. In addition, oversight institutions have a comparable role in reviewing executive discretion in order to determine the necessity of secrecy. A joint analysis of oversight institutions offers a comprehensive insight and a better comparative understanding of the tensions between executive secrecy and oversight.

The chapter shows that access to official secrets is a continuous challenge in practice and reviewing secrecy in the EU is complex partly due to the compound nature of the EU's administrative procedures combined with rigid security rules for official secrets. EU classified information derives from multiple national sources and many (national) actors are involved in its management. This often leads to challenges for EU oversight institutions to gain access to classified information. However, access to information deriving from EU institutions is also a challenge for national oversight actors, in particular national parliaments. This chapter shows these dynamics, drawing examples from the EU and national context. Against this background, the chapter questions whether the current rules and the resulting limitations for oversight institution in gaining access to and the

[2] The ombudsman is treated as semi-judicial as well, which also applies in the case of the EO, see Paul Craig, *EU Administrative Law* (OUP 2012) 739–62. The EO has an administrative role for the review of official secrets.

review of official secrets lead to an 'executive privilege' in secrecy in the EU. It argues that a wide scope of discretion in official secrets on the side of executive institutions would be incompatible with the EU's constitutional commitment to principles of democracy and openness.

Access to Official Secrets

EU oversight institutions have 'privileged' access to European Union Classified Information (EUCI). Their access to classified documents is privileged for two main reasons. First, access is strictly related to the institution's oversight prerogatives and its role as set out in EU primary law. The understanding of this access as privileged denotes its difference from public access to documents available to any individual within the scope of Article 2 of the Regulation 1049/01 on public access to documents. Second, privileged access to classified information means that the information does not become publicly accessible. It is accessible only to the oversight institution. This is in contrast to public access to documents under Regulation 1049/01, considering that if access is granted the information becomes available not only to the requesting party but also to the public at large.

EU Treaties do not provide specific provisions for access to classified information. However, different provisions apply as a basis for privileged access, considering that this type of access is related to the institutions' prerogatives in oversight. For the EP, Article 14(1) Treaty on European Union (TEU) provides a basis for its oversight role. Other provisions enumerate its powers of consent or consultation and set out obligations on executive institutions to share information. Article 36 TEU stipulates that the High Representative will regularly consult the EP, whereas Article 71 Treaty on the Functioning of the European Union (TFEU) provides that the Council's standing committee on operational cooperation for internal security informs the EP. The clearest obligation for the executive institutions to inform the EP is stipulated in Article 218(10) TFEU regarding international agreements. For the CJEU and EO, primary law provides only a broad basis for privileged access, taking into account that on the basis of Article 19(1) TEU the CJEU is to ensure that EU law is observed, whereas Article 228 TFEU lays out the EO's prerogative of administrative review through inquiries.

Rules of procedure of institutions are generally the basis for access to classified information. For example, the General Court's (GC) access rights are stipulated in Article 91(b-c) Rules of Procedure regarding measures of inquiry in conjunction with Articles 103–105 Rules of Procedure specifically pertaining to confidential information and material. In a similar fashion, the EO and the EP provide specific rules on access to classified information. Article 3(2) of the EO Statue provides for an obligation for EU institutions and bodies to provide information, whereas the EP has a separate Annex VII on classified information in its Rules of Procedure. In accordance with Article 220 of the EP Rules of Procedure, the EO is also obliged to inform the EP. Unlike the other oversight institutions, the EP through Inter-institutional Agreements has specific arrangements with the Council and the Commission regarding access to classified information.[3] The EP's prerogative to access classified information however does not apply across the board to all bodies and institutions. For example, until the legal revisions under the Lisbon Treaty, agencies such as Europol and Eurojust were not under a legal obligation to grant access to classified information to the EP. Access to classified information for the EP has been directly linked with the level of its oversight powers.

The existing legal framework for access to classified information for oversight institutions hence is mostly stipulated in procedural rules, although they do find an indirect basis in the Treaties. The procedural nature of the rules has given power to institutions, especially executive institutions, to set their own arrangements on how wide the scope of access would be and who exactly gets to access such information within the oversight institution. The chapter turns to the key aspects of access: the scope, time, and the people behind the practice of access to classified information.

[3] Inter-institutional Agreement of 12 March 2014 between the European Parliament and the Council concerning the forwarding to and handling by the European Parliament of classified information held by the Council on matters other than those in the area of the common foreign and security policy [2014] OJ C95/1; Inter-institutional Agreement of 20 November 2002 between the European Parliament and the Council concerning access by the European Parliament to sensitive information of the Council in the field of security and defence policy [2002] OJ C298/1. Framework Agreement on relations between the European Parliament and the European Commission [2010] OJ L304/47.

Scope and time of access to official secrets

The scope of privileged access to EUCI in practice may be examined through the number of documents exchanged as well as the categories of classification. In the EU, no set of public data exists for the amount of shared classified information. Systematic overview of classified information received by the EP from the Council or the Commission is lacking. Interviews with many of the EU officials involved in the EUCI did not shed light on this matter either. Consistently, interviewed officials have refused to give an approximate number for the documents shared with the EP.[4] It remains speculative whether such hesitation is motivated by security concerns or whether there is simply no specific systematic overview of the information shared overall, although in accordance with Article 3(1) second sentence of Annex II, the EP and the Commission are obliged to ensure the registration and traceability of classified information.[5] There is a register of documents exchanged between the Commission and the EP, which is not specifically for classified information, but information more generally.[6] Similarly regarding the Council, Article 6 of the Inter-institutional Agreement on exchange of classified information in Common Foreign and Security Policy (CFSP), provides that documents classified as *Confidential*, *Secret*, and *Top Secret*, will be registered for security purposes and ensure traceability at all times. Despite these provisions however, a registry for classified information is not accessible and numbers are publicly unknown.

Examining the categories of official secrets is another way to reveal how access for oversight institutions works in practice. For example, the scope of 2014 Agreement between the EP and the Council does not include the category of *Limité* documents, which is not strictly foreseen as a classification category, although this marking too makes information publicly inaccessible. The Council considers *Limité* documents as 'internal to the Council',[7] and not to be shared externally, although in practice this is

[4] Respondents Nos 1, 3, 6, 8, 13.

[5] Eg, the documents classified as 'CONFIDENTIAL UE' and 'SECRET UE,' are supposed to be forwarded from the Commission's Secretariat General central registry to the equivalent competent Parliament.

[6] Agreement between the European Parliament and the Commission on procedures for implementing Council Decision 1999/468/EC laying down the procedures for the exercise of implementing powers conferred on the Commission, as amended by Decision 2006/512/EC [2008] OJ C143/1.

[7] Council, Handling of documents marked LIMITE, 16 March 2006, Doc 5847/06.

one of the biggest categories of information that the Council produces.[8] *Limité* documents are also not fully shared with all national parliaments. An internal document of the Council that is based on an assessment of the number of delegations that provide access to national parliaments reveals that only twenty national delegations share these documents.[9] Some of these national parliaments have specific agreements with their governments to not disclose these documents to the public and the practice is very varied in terms of who actually gets access within national parliaments and under what further conditions. An equally relevant issue regarding access for national parliaments is that only eight chambers have access to *EU Confidential* documents, whilst only the Austrian *Nationalrat* and *Bundesrat* receive *EU Secret* and *EU Top Secret* documents, as per legal arrangements between the Austrian parliament and government.[10] Legally, the Swedish Riksdag is also guaranteed full access to these levels of classified documents, but in practice reports show that the Swedish parliament has not received documents higher than *EU Restricted*. The position of the EP is similar to national parliaments in this sense, as the EP is also legally obliged not to publicize Council's *Limité* documents. By contrast to the Council, in the framework agreement between the EP and the Commission, it is explicitly stated that the broader notion of confidentiality is applicable, which includes both EUCI and documents that are not public due to other reasons, such as internal documents or documents related to professional secrecy.[11] Hence, the EP has a clearer legal scope in terms of access to classified but also sensitive unclassified documents with the Commission.

Information that is classified due to security concerns has separate institutional and legal arrangements for access. The EP's access to classified information in issues of CFSP is stipulated both through the

[8] Council Annual Reports on access to documents 2012, 2013, and 2014 <http://www.consilium.europa.eu/en/documents-publications/publications/>. Also Deirdre Curtin, 'Overseeing Secrets in the EU: A Democratic Perspective' (2014) 52 Journal of Common Market Studies 684, 685–86.

[9] Council, Survey on the distribution of the Council documents to National Parliaments in Member States, 20 May 2014, Doc 9699/14.

[10] Secretariat of the Conference of Parliamentary Committees for Union Affairs of Parliaments of the European Union, Seventeenth Bi-annual Report: Developments in European Union Procedures and Practices Relevant to Parliamentary Scrutiny, April 2012, 5.

[11] Framework Agreement between the European Parliament and the Commission (n 3) Annex II, art 1(2) second sentence states that 'confidential information' will include both the classified information in the strict sense (EUCI) but also 'non-classified' other confidential information'.

Inter-institutional Agreement of the Council concluded in 2002 and the Council Decision establishing the European External Action Service (EEAS) in 2010.[12] The initial proposal for the EEAS Decision did not make any mention of the EP's access to classified information. It kept the text of primary law very strictly that the 'the High Representative will regularly consult the European Parliament on the main aspects and the basic choices of the CFSP' and that the views of the EP are taken into consideration. The EP insisted on access rights to the EEAS classified information by applying the existing provisions under the 2002 Inter-institutional Agreement with the Council.[13] The final Council Decision does stipulate in the preamble (paragraph 6) that the EP will have access to classified information in accordance with this Inter-institutional Agreement.[14]

The time of receiving access to classified information is salient to ensure timely oversight of executive decisions. In principle, the Agreements between the EP and the executive institutions provide that information should be shared 'regularly', 'without delay', and 'immediately'.[15] Article 108(1) of the EP Rules of Procedure stipulates that access should be to 'immediate, regular and full information'. Another similar example is Article 110(4) on the obligation of the appointed Special Representative to keep the EP 'fully and regularly informed'. In practice, lack of timely access is especially with regard to the EP. For example, regarding the preparation of the Schengen Borders Code, the EP wanted to obtain copies of classified documents, yet this was rejected and only a special meeting behind closed doors took place.[16] In another instance, regarding the Schengen

[12] Inter-institutional Agreement of 20 November 2002 between the European Parliament and the Council (n 3); Council Decision 2010/427/EU of 26 July 2010 establishing the organisation and functioning of the European External Action Service [2010] OJ L201/30.

[13] Inter-institutional Agreement of 20 November 2002 between the European Parliament and the Council (n 3).

[14] Political scientists argue that the final arrangement highlights that 'the Council decided against its own rational cost-benefit calculation'. Elisabeth Wisniewski, 'The Influence of the European Parliament on the European External Action Service' (2013) 18 European Foreign Affairs Review 81, 94.

[15] Inter-institutional Agreement of 12 March 2014 between the European Parliament and the Council (n 3); Inter-institutional Agreement of 20 November 2002 between the European Parliament and the Council (n 3); Framework Agreement between the European Parliament and the Commission (n 3). These notions refer to the exchange of information more broadly and do not strictly concern EUCI.

[16] General Secretariat of the Council, Draft Interinstitutional Agreement concerning access by the European Parliament to classified information of the Council [and of the Commission] in the field of Freedom, Security and Justice—List of documents sent to the European Parliament

Information System for Bulgaria and Romania, the EP received important classified information through diplomatic channels of exchange with the Romanian Ambassador as opposed to getting information directly from the Council.[17] Lack of timely access to information has also been noted regarding the EP and Commission relations.[18]

Important developments regarding the EP's rights to access information result from case law in the context of international negotiations in line with Article 218(10) TFEU. The right to be informed for the EP in international negotiations is clarified by the Court to include also agreements in the CFSP, an area of EU policy where the EP has limited oversight powers. For example, in the *Mauritius* case,[19] the Council did not adhere to the requirements of regularity and immediacy but delayed sharing information with the EP for more than three months.[20] The Court held that the EP has a right of scrutiny, albeit limited, and that Artcle 218(10) refers to 'any procedure for concluding an international agreement, including agreements relating exclusively to the CFSP'.[21] Whilst this case does not per se refer to classified documents, it is particularly relevant as CFSP is an area with more classified documents for security protection purposes.

Both the Court and the EO have broad stipulations about receiving access to *any* information that they require for their review.[22] For instance, regarding the EO, Article 3 of the Statute stipulates that the EU institutions and bodies are obliged to provide access to 'any information' and files

in the field of Freedom, Security and Justice during the following period: 1/07/2004–30/06/2005, 20 March 2006, Council Doc 7542/06.

[17] ibid.

[18] Sergio Carrera, Nicholas Hernanz, and Joanna Parkin, 'The "Lisbonisation" of the European Parliament: Assessing Progress, Shortcomings and Challenges for Democratic Accountability in the Area of Freedom, Security and Justice' (2013) CEPS Paper in Liberty and Security in Europe No 58.

[19] Case C-658/11 *European Parliament v Council of the European Union* EU:C:2014:2025.

[20] Another similar instance of the Council not sharing information with the EP is the Pirate-Transfer Agreement with Tanzania, Case C-263/14 *Parliament v Council* EU:C:2016:435. See SR Sánchez-Tabernero, 'The Choice of Legal Basis and the Principle of Consistency in the Procedure for Conclusion of International Agreements in CFSP Contexts: *Parliament v. Council*' (2017) 54 Common Market Law Review 899, explaining how the CJEU utilized the principle of consistency as a supporting argument to the duty to inform the EP specifically in the context of the CFSP where oversight powers of the EP are limited.

[21] Case C-658/11 *European Parliament v Council of the European Union* (n 19) para 85.

[22] Rules of Procedure of the General Court [2015] OJ L105/1, art 65.

requested.[23] There is no enumeration of types of information, as the EO in line with her inquiries must determine what information is specifically relevant. The EO is entitled to inspect and copy the files.[24] In addition to powers at EU level, the EO has 'direct vertical' investigative powers that pertain to the relations between the Ombudsman and the national authorities.[25] National authorities too are obliged to provide the EO with any information that may help to clarify instances of maladministration by Union institutions.[26] The EO has also 'indirect vertical' investigative powers, which are concerned with access to documents that originate in a Member State (MS), but are in the possession of a Union institution or body.[27]

Specific timeframes are not stipulated with regarding to the Court or the EO. Neither the Statute of the EO nor the Implementing Measures refer to a specific time regarding access to EUCI. Arguably, in line with Article 3 of the Statute, in order for the EO to conduct an inquiry, access to information should be granted without delay. However, the EO announces the inquiry and visit to the institution being examined, which means there is a lack of immediate and unannounced access to documents. This in turn 'gravely undermines the efficacy of the Ombudsman's investigative efforts as it provides the targeted institution or body with ample time to go through the file in question and suppress written evidence of any administrative irregularity'.[28] For example, in some cases the files inspected were found to be incomplete and crucial documents were missing under unspecified circumstances.[29]

[23] Decision of the European Parliament of 9 March 1994 on the regulations and general conditions governing the performance of the Ombudsman's duties [1994] OJ L113/15, as amended by decision of 14 March 2002, OJ L92/13 and decision of 18 June 2008, OJ L189/25 (the Statute of the European Ombudsman), recital 6 and art 3(2); Decision of the European Ombudsman adopting implementing provisions of 8 July 2002 as amended by decisions of the Ombudsman of 5 April 2004 and 3 December 2008, art 5(1) <http://www.ombudsman.europa.eu/en/resources/provisions.faces>.

[24] Statute of the European Ombudsman (n 23) recital 6 and art 3(2); Decision of the European Ombudsman on implementing provisions (n 23) art 5(2).

[25] Craig (n 2) 739-62.

[26] Statute of the European Ombudsman (n 23) art 3(3).

[27] This type of power was the most debated issue in the discussions of the Ombudsman's Statute in the Luxembourg Inter-institutional Conference, Richard Corbett, 'Governance and Institutional Developments' (1994) 23 Journal of Common Market Studies 27, 33.

[28] Alexandros Tsadiras, 'Unravelling Ariadne's Thread: The European Ombudsman's Investigative Powers' (2008) 45 Common Market Law Review 757, 765.

[29] See Complaint 466/97/PD [1999] EOAR 135; and Complaint 548/2002GG [2003] EOAR 115.

Insiders of oversight institutions

Access to classified information is in principle limited within oversight institutions. By looking deeper than the bird-eye view of the institutional level, findings emerge that access to EUCI internally within oversight institutions is constrained to certain individuals or committees, but by no means open to the entire institution. This raises questions as to who are the 'insiders' of oversight institutions who actually have the prerogatives to access classified information, on the basis of what rules are such lines between insiders and outsiders of oversight institutions drawn as well as how are those decisions and arrangements made? These aspects of access to classified information point to the complexity of access and also to the possible information asymmetries that arise within oversight institutions. The question of access to classified information is most complex with regard to the EP considering it is the largest oversight institution and not a unified actor, like the EO, or several individuals, like the Court. Only certain committees of the EP deal with access to classified information on a regular basis as a result of their functions, although any committee may request from the President of the EP that access to classified information be provided. The Committee on Foreign Affairs is one of the key committees dealing with classified information. This Committee is responsible for the promotion, implementation, and monitoring of the EU's foreign policy. The other key committee to deal with issues of oversight and classified information within the EP is the Committee on Civil Liberties, Justice and Home Affairs (LIBE), first established in 1992. The LIBE Committee is responsible for legislation in the areas of transparency and the protection of personal data. The Treaties and the EP's Rules of Procedure expressly confer upon LIBE the responsibility to hold the Council and Commission accountable in the area of freedom, security, and justice.

A distinction also exists between individuals who have the prerogatives to request access to classified information and those that actually gain access to the material at the EP. In addition, access varies and is determined in accordance with the level of the classified information.[30] Regarding the Council, on the basis of Article 3(1) of the 2002 Agreement, the following have a right to request access to classified information: the President of

[30] See Inter-institutional Agreement of 12 March 2014 between the European Parliament and the Council (n 3) art 4.

the EP and the Chairman of the Committee on Foreign Affairs (CFA).[31] These requests are addressed to the Presidency of the Council or the High Representative. When requests are approved due to the prerogatives of the EP in this field, access to information in the area of CFSP is given at the premises of the Council to the President of the EP and by what the Inter-institutional Agreement calls 'special committee', which is in fact composed of only *five* individuals, that is the Chairman of the CFA and four members designated by the Conference of Presidents.[32] Furthermore, when access is granted, the President of the EP may decide that information is intended for the Chairman of the CFA or access to information is restricted to the members of the CFA only. Access to EUCI on the basis of the 2014 Agreement with the Council is of wider scope *ratione personae*. Access is also granted to rapporteurs and shadow rapporteurs provided that they have security clearance or 'for whom notification has been made by a competent national authority that they are duly authorised by virtue of their functions in accordance with national laws and regulations'.[33]

Similarly with regard to the Commission, there is a difference between individuals who are authorized to request access to EUCI and those that are granted access. The scope of authorized individuals in the latter category is bigger.[34] On the basis of Annex II, Article 1(3), the Commission may forward any information on its own initiative. In line with Article 1(4) Annex II, the following may request access to the EUCI: the President

[31] Note that since the agreement dates from before the Lisbon changes, the Inter-institutional Agreement refers to the committee as it was structured in 2002, ie Chairman of the Committee on Foreign Affairs, Human Rights, Common Security and Defence Policy.

[32] See Inter-institutional Agreement of 20 November 2002 between the European Parliament and the Council (n 3) art 3(3): 'The President of the European Parliament and a special committee chaired by the Chairman of the Committee on Foreign Affairs, Human Rights, Common Security and Defence Policy and composed of four members designated by the Conference of Presidents shall be informed by the Presidency of the Council or the Secretary-General/High Representative of the content of the sensitive information where it is required for the exercise of the powers conferred on the European Parliament by the Treaty on European Union in the field covered by the present Interinstitutional Agreement. The President of the European Parliament and the special committee may ask to consult the documents in question on the premises of the Council.'

[33] Inter-institutional Agreement of 12 March 2014 between the European Parliament and the Council (n 3) art 4(2)(b).

[34] When the EP requests classified information from the Commission: 'Details of the category or categories of persons who are to have access to the confidential information shall be communicated simultaneously with the request.' See Framework Agreement between the European Parliament and the Commission (n 3) Annex II, art 2(5)(3) second sentence.

of Parliament, the chairs of the parliamentary committees concerned, the Bureau and the Conference of Presidents, the head of Parliament's delegation included in the Union delegation at an international conference.[35] Access to classified information, in line with Article 2(5) first sentence, Annex II, is determined by the level of the classification and access may only be granted to Parliament officials and those employees of Parliament working for political groups to whom it is strictly necessary, and who have been designated in advance by the parliamentary body as having a 'need-to-know' and who have been given an appropriate security clearance. Hence, the security principles of 'need-to-know' and the security clearance are not only applicable for determining inside-insiders within the executive institutions, as discussed in the previous chapter, but also apply to the EP. Access to classified information by the officials working at the EP is equally important for an effective oversight considering that they conduct the preparations for meetings, reports, and other relevant issues within the administration.[36] Based on Article 2(5) second sentence, due to the prerogatives of the Parliament, MEPs who have not been given a personal security clearance could be granted access to documents classified as *Confidential* under practical arrangements defined by common accord, 'including signature of a solemn declaration that they will not disclose the contents of those documents to any third person'. Such arrangements are not applicable for access to documents classified at the level of *Secret*.

Against this background, it becomes apparent that classified information is not generally shared but is strictly limited to those internally in the EP the President deems relevant to know and have access to the information. It may be concluded that access to EUCI is concentrated among certain MEPs and relevant committees as opposed to discussing access at a level of the EP as an institution. It is equally important to note that the requests for access to classified information are not of strict obligatory nature since the executive institutions have the option to refuse such requests.

With regard to the Court, access to classified information under the Rules of Procedure adopted in 2015 will apply to the judges deciding on the case. The GC has access to classified information that the institution

[35] The Commission may forward any confidential information on its own initiative to Parliament: Framework Agreement between the European Parliament and the Commission (n 3) Annex II, art 1(3).

[36] Inter-institutional Agreement of 12 March 2014 between the European Parliament and the Council (n 3) art 4.

chooses to submit to the Court to support its arguments. The institution retains discretion in deciding which classified documents it would submit to the Court that could be taken into account by the Court for its judgment. If the Court agrees with the classification marking as assigned to the document for security purposes, it will also use those documents to base its judgment, whilst this information is not shared with the applicant and her lawyer. Hence, such evidence is closed for the applicant. This important aspect of classified documents and their ramifications for access to justice are further discussed below and in the following chapter.

Limited access: The biggest challenge

Lack of or limited access to classified information has been a repeated issue for all EU oversight institutions. The originator control is the most pressing limitation to access to EUCI. Under this rule, the classified document is treated as a property of the actor that initially created the document and established its classification marking. This logic of ownership is safeguarded by allowing the originator of that document to have the major, if not final, say in whether the document is shared and with whom. The originator rule has become very rigid in the EU because firstly, both executive and oversight actors have fully incorporated it in their EUCI regimes, and secondly, externally this rule is included in all EU agreements or technical arrangements with third parties for the exchange of classified information. Whilst the previous chapter discussed in more detail the manner in which this rule was established and how it is expanded in the EU institutions, this section of the book examines how specifically the discretion of the executive institutions to conceal plays out against the oversights institutions' right to privileged access to classified information.

The originator rule is predominantly invoked by MS under the justification of national security. In the case of *OMPI*, France refused to disclose classified information to the Court on the grounds of national security rules and procedures for the protection and disclosure of classified information. Remarkably, these objections were raised by France towards the Courts despite the fact that such information had been shared with the governments of all MS.[37] The UK too in the case of *Fulmen v Council* refused to grant the Court access to the classified information on the basis

[37] Case C-27/09 P *France v People's Mojahedin Organization of Iran*, Opinion of AG Sharpston, EU:C:2011:482, para 72.

of national security.[38] Both cases pertain to counter-terrorist sanctions against individuals and in both cases the refusal resulted in an annulment of the challenged sanctions measures for the very reason that without the confidential information the Court was unable to review the merits of the case. In fact, this has been a repeated issue: the Court annulling decisions of the Council due to the lack of access to the underlying information.[39] The Court could not take into account evidence that was not disclosed to it, since the Court needs to take a fully informed decision. Yet, the Council, as an EU institution, was in a difficult position since MS hesitated to share sensitive information with the Court. The Council was unable, because of the composite listing procedure in which *national* authorities take the relevant decision,[40] to share the relevant information with the Court. The resulting repeated annulments in turn raised serious concerns, especially when the annulments were followed by a re-adoption of sanctions with minor procedural adaptations.[41]

Third countries and organizations that have agreements with the EU for the exchange of classified information, also invoke security concerns to limit sharing documents with EU oversight institutions. For example, the US Treasury Department refused authorization to Europol to share the classified report regarding the Terrorist Finance Tracking Programme (TFTP) programme with the EO on justifications of national security. The EP's access to such documents was also denied. Current rules of the originator rule raise concerns especially because some of their key aspects are unclear such as the applicability and scope of consequences in the EU. First, it is not fully clear upon which specific legal basis this limitation is

[38] Case C-280/12 P *Council v Fulmen and Mahmoudian* EU:C:2013:775, para 77.

[39] Joined Cases C-584/10 P, C-593/10 P and C-595/10 P *European Commission and Others v Yassin Abdullah Kadi* ECLI:EU:C:2013:518; Case T-85/09 *Kadi v Commission* ECLI:EU:T:2010:418; Joined Cases C-402/05 P and C-415/05 P *Kadi and Al Barakaat v Council* ECLI:EU:C:2008:461; Case C-27/09 P *France v People's Mojahedin Organization of Iran* ECLI:EU:C:2011:853; Case T-284/08 *People's Mojahedin Organization of Iran v Council* ECLI:EU:T:2008:550; Case T-256/07 *People's Mojahedin Organization of Iran v Council* ECLI:EU:T:2008:461; Case T-228/02 *Organisation des Modjahedines du peuple d'Iran v Council* ECLI:EU:T:2006:384. See also Christina Eckes, *EU Counter-Terrorist Policies and Fundamental Rights: The Case of Individual Sanctions* (OUP 2009); Christina Eckes, 'EU Restrictive Measures against Natural and Legal Persons: From Counterterrorist to Third Country Sanctions' (2014) 51 Common Market Law Review 869.

[40] Christina Eckes and Joana Mendes, 'The Right to be Heard in Composite Administrative Procedures: Lost in between Protection?' (2011) 36 European Law Review 651.

[41] Vigjilenca Abazi and Christina Eckes, 'Closed Evidence in EU Courts: Security, Secrets and Access to Justice' (2018) 55 Common Market Law Review 753.

applicable within the EU legal order. Disagreements persist between the oversight institutions on whether the originator rule blocks access to classified information as a matter of arrangements for exchange of classified information agreed between the executive institutions. For example, in the TFTP case, the Legal Service of the EP opined that the discretion of the originator is final vis-à-vis the EO, not on the basis of the technical arrangements between the EU agency and the US, which are not of a nature of an international agreement and cannot constitute a binding effect on the EU institutions, but on the basis of the Statute of the EO, which itself accepts that privileged access to classified information is not absolute.[42] It is indeed hard to specifically decipher whether the applicability of the originator rule means a final limit for access and if so upon what legal basis this is the case, since the originator consent is included in the rules of each institution, both executive and oversight, and also in all agreements and Council Decisions, such as for Europol and the EEAS. Yet, it must be stressed that the oversight institutions have incorporated the originator condition. Hence, this rule currently forms part of their regimes. It may be argued therefore that the applicability of the rule and the resulting limitation of access are due to the oversight institutions' acceptance of limited privilege access. This relates to the second aspect of oversight and the originator rule in need of clarification: Why would the oversight institutions accept limitations to privileged access to classified information?

Partly, EU oversight institutions have incorporated the originator control because they had no choice to do otherwise at the time of making the legal arrangements for access to EU executive classified information. For example, the Council conditioned access by the EP clearly with the adoption of the originator rule,[43] and in some cases the Council refused to grant access to classified information to the Court precisely noting the lack of confidentially rules for the Court,[44] until the latter was recently the last oversight institution to incorporate it. It is quite remarkable that the Council, through arrangements for access to EUCI, de facto conditions and affects the constitutionally set prerogatives of oversight institutions.

[42] European Parliament Legal Service, Legal Opinion regarding the European Ombudsman's access to documents concerning Europol's activities under the TFTP Agreement, 2 February 2015, Doc SJ-1058/14, D(2015)1986.

[43] See David Galloway, 'Classifying Secrets in the EU', paper presented at Transparency and Access to the Records and Archives of the EU Institutions Seminar, European University Institute, 25 January 2013.

[44] *Council v Fulmen and Mahmoudian* (n 38).

As argued in this book, the secret-keeper through secrecy has the power to alter the actions of the outsider institution. The outsider is reliant on the secret-keeper, giving the latter discretion to affect the relationship in line with its interests. It seems that this misbalanced relation between the secret-keeper and the outsider is not prevented in the institutional setting of the EU, as would be expected from an openness perspective.

To some extent however, the oversight institutions accepted the originator rule without fully realizing its limitations. Accepting what is presented as 'confidentiality' is seen as a *sine qua non* for conducting oversight in issues pertaining to security and secrecy. However, confidentiality in this case does not imply merely having access to classified information behind closed doors and not sharing with the public. It goes further and limits privileged access fully. For example, it is worthwhile to note the surprise of the EO regarding the lack of access to the TFTP report. The rules of the Statute of the EO were changed long ago and have incorporated the originator rule, yet it is only after the opinion of the EP's Legal Service in 2015 with regard to the rigidity of originator consent that the EO actually realized the consequences and understandably disagreed with them.[45] The originator rule limits privileged access to classified information and does so based on the rules internalized by the oversight institutions, regardless of whether the latter had no choice in doing so or were not fully aware of the profound resulting consequences. The question then becomes whether EU oversight institutions have any powers to review and influence what information can become a secret in the first place. Do EU oversight institutions have powers to keep official secrets in check by reviewing executive discretion in their creation? The book turns to answer this question in the following section.

Reviewing Executive Secrecy: Keeping Official Secrets in Check

To what extent do EU executive institutions and bodies have sole discretion to determine the *necessity* of secrecy? The first and key step of oversight

[45] Letter from the Ombudsman to the European Parliament LIBE Committee in relation to case 1148/2013/TN, 27 February 2015.

is to decipher legitimate and necessary secrets from unnecessary executive claims to secrecy. This external review is particularly salient in the EU considering that, as Chapter 3 showed, internal administrative reviews are either completely lacking or not geared towards ensuring a balance with openness, and indeed in the view of many EU officials such balance is not necessary.[46]

The Courts and fundamental rights

The CJEU has the authority to make the final assessment on whether and to what extent the *failure to disclose* classified information affects the realization of fundamental rights in the EU.[47] This implies that the Court does not evaluate the decision to classify a document in terms of the assigned grading (i.e. whether it should be *Restricted*, *Confidential*, *Secret*, or *Top Secret*) or the time of declassification.[48] However, within the revised Rules of Procedure in 2015, Article 105(3) to (5) provide that the Court has the authority to assess the confidentiality of the submitted information in the sense that the Court may decide that the party's decision of non-disclosure is unjustified in light of all information and disregard the information in its review of the case.[49] This type of review is limited to cases where individual's right of access to justice is in question due to the executive use and reliance on classified information. More specifically, case law brings two main strands of instances where executive secrecy claims are counterbalanced by fundamental rights.[50] Firstly, secrecy is balanced

[46] Respondents Nos 1, 4, 6, 21, 22.

[47] See Joined Cases C-584/10 P, C-593/10 P, and C-595/10 P *Commission and Others v Kadi* (known as *Kadi II*) EU:C:2013:518, para 129; Case C-300/11 *ZZ v Secretary of State for the Home Department* EU:C:2013:363, para 67.

[48] See however that in the US, courts do evaluate whether the document should have been classified at all. DC District Judge Richard W Roberts ordered the US Trade Representative to disclose a classified document to a FOIA requester because the classification of the document was not properly supported. See *Center for International Environmental Law v Office of the United States Trade Representative* <http://fas.org/sgp/jud/ciel/042612-notice.pdf Civil Action No. 01-CV-498 (RWR/JMF)>. The number of cases involving security remains small, since courts, especially in the post-9/11 context, hesitate to override executive evaluations on the need for secrecy. But see *Gulet Mohamed v Eric Holder* Civil Action No. 1:11-cv-50 (AJT/TRJ) <http://fas.org/sgp/jud/statesec/gulet-091514.pdf>.

[49] Abazi and Eckes (n 41).

[50] It is worthwhile recalling the distinction made for cases of professional secrecy, which differ from official secrets due to their specific nature. The scope of cases that we are interested in therefore relates specifically to classified information, which is understood as sensitive information as provided in Regulation (EC) No 1049/2001 of the European Parliament and

against the public interest in disclosure pertaining to the right of public access to documents under Regulation 1049/01, stipulated as a fundamental right under Article 42 of the Charter of Fundamental Rights.[51] The Court has continuously emphasized the democratic nature and necessity of public access to documents.[52] However, this is not an absolute right, and exceptions to public access are foreseen under Article 4 of Regulation 1049/01.[53] The mandatory exceptions under Article 4(1)(a) are most relevant because they concern documents that may be classified due to their sensitivity with respect to the EU's security or international relations interests.[54] Secondly, secrecy is measured against the individual's right to information pertaining to the right of defence and of a fair trial, guaranteed under Article 47 of the Charter of Fundamental Rights. The principle of effective judicial protection is a general principle of EU law 'stemming from the constitutional traditions common to the Member States'.[55] The right to defence includes both the right to be heard and the right to have access to one's file.[56] However, similarly to the right of public access to documents, this

of the Council of 30 May 2001 regarding public access to European Parliament, Council and Commission documents [2001] OJ L145/43, art 9. Regarding professional secrecy, see Case T-462/12 R *Pilkington Group Ltd v Commission* EU:T:2013:119, where certain passages have been redacted from the judgment—the information is missing and is stated only as [confidential]. See Case T-371/94 *British Airways and Others v Commission* EU:T:1998:140, para 63; Case T-353/94 *Postbank v Commission* EU:T:1996:119, para 87; information regarding the costs and organization of public services may constitute a business secret if it relates to a business which has actual or potential economic value and the disclosure or use of the information could result in economic benefits for other companies—Joined Cases T-109/05 and T-444/05 *Navigazione Libera del Golfo Srl v European Commission* EU:T:2011:235, para 144.

51 Also art 15(3) TFEU; see Chapter 2.

52 See Case C-280/11 P *Council v Access Info Europe* EU:C:2013:671; Case C-350/12 P *Council v Sophie in 't Veld* EU:C:2014:2039.

53 Regulation 1049/2001 (n 50) art 4(1)–(3) enumerates the exception grounds to the public right of access to documents. Art 4(1) lists all mandatory exceptions, including public security, defence and military matters, international relations, and financial, monetary, or economic policy.

54 See Regulation 1049/2001 (n 50) art 4(1)(a) in relation with art 9(1).

55 On the basis of the European Convention for the Protection of Human Rights and Fundamental Freedoms. See also Deirdre Curtin, 'The Right to Fair Procedures in Administrative law' in James O'Reilly (ed), *Human Rights and Constitutional Law: Essays in Honour of Brian Walsh* (Round Hall Press 1992).

56 Access must be granted either to the decision or the file where the reasons for the decision are stated because the individual concerned must be able to ascertain the reasons of the decision against her. This in turn enables the person to defend her rights in the 'best possible conditions and to decide, with full knowledge of the relevant facts, whether there is any point' to applying for a judicial review of the lawfulness of the decision. *Kadi II* (n 47) para 100. Some

right is not absolute and derogations are foreseen, particularly on the basis of public security. A variety of security policies in the Area of Freedom, Security and Justice and Common Foreign and Security Policies give rise to a tension between secrecy and the right to a fair trial. For example, cases relate to anti-terrorism measures such as individual sanctions[57] or expulsion measures under grounds of public security.[58] The Court's review of executive claims to secrecy in these cases differs in terms of the scope of the review and the extent that executive secrecy is justified vis-à-vis the invoked right. The book analyses more closely these aspects of judicial review of secrecy.

Scope of review: Wide margin of executive discretion?

The Court exercises a 'marginal' review in cases regarding the right of public access to information in international relations and security and allows a higher margin of executive discretion in the assessment of non-disclosure of documents.[59] The Court assesses whether the procedural rules and duty to state reasons have been complied with, whether the facts have been accurately stated, and whether there has been a manifest error of assessment of the facts or misuse of power. The *Sison II* case is a key example of a restricted review on the basis of exceptions laid down in Article 4(1)(a) of Regulation 1049/01. Mr Sison, a resident in the Netherlands, filed a public access to information request at the Council in view of the fact that in 2007, the Council adopted a decision which it then confirmed on several occasions to include the name of Mr Sison in the list of persons whose assets are frozen pursuant to the EU regime of counter-terrorist sanctions.[60] Mr Sison's request was motivated by the need to gain access

scholars argue that the Court has been 'activist' and 'imposed' a right be heard as a general rule of Union law. See Craig (n 2) 290.

57 Council Common Position 2001/931/CFSP of 27 December 2001 on the application of specific measures to combat terrorism [2001] OJ L344/93; Council Regulation (EC) No 2580/2001 of 27 December 2001 on specific restrictive measures directed against certain persons and entities with a view to combating terrorism [2001] OJ L344/70.

58 Derogation from free movement of persons on the basis of art 45(3) TFEU and art 52 TFEU. MS may derogate from EU law on the basis of security and also in the areas of the free movement of goods (art 36 TFEU) and capital (art 65 TFEU).

59 Regarding exceptions under Regulation 1049/2001 (n 50) art 4(1)(a), the Court uses the terminology of 'marginal' for its review. See Case C-266/05 P *Sison v Council* (known as *Sison II*) EU:C:2007:75, paras 34–35.

60 See Common Position 2001/931/CFSP (n 57); Council Regulation (EC) No 2580/2001 (n 57).

to information that had been used to include him on the sanctions list. However, his request was rejected and the Court explicitly restricted itself to what it called a 'marginal' review focusing on the procedural aspects of the non-disclosure decision of the Council.[61] The Court did not ascertain any procedural errors in the Council's assessment and dismissed the claims of Mr Sison, also on the grounds that he had failed to show the *public* interest of disclosure for applying Regulation 1049/01 as opposed to merely a personal interest.

Yet, the Court does not accept broad and general references to security by executive institutions aiming to maintain secrecy and apply restrictions to public access to documents.[62] Rather, refusal of access must be founded on an analysis of the *specific* factors to the contents or context of the document that make it evident why disclosure of documents would impair the EU's interests, as the case of *Kuijer v Council* illustrates.[63] In addition, the Court's review follows the broader established principle on the overall application of Regulation 1049/01, that is giving the widest possible public access to documents held by the institutions.[64] In line with *Hautala v Council*, derogations from public access to documents must remain within the limits of what is appropriate and necessary for achieving the intended aim.[65] In the case of *Council v In 't Veld*, the European Court of Justice (ECJ) for the first time explicitly affirmed that even in international relations the institutions are obliged to explain whether disclosure could 'specifically and actually' undermine a protected interest.[66] Although the ECJ does not require the institution to show actual prejudice, the institution cannot automatically invoke the exceptions if it fails to demonstrate specifically and

[61] *Sison II* (n 59) para 34.

[62] See also Regulation 1049/2001 (n 50) Preamble para 7, which explicitly foresees that the right of access also applies to documents relating to the CFSP and to police and judicial cooperation in criminal matters.

[63] Case T-211/00 *Kuijer v Council* EU:T:2002:30, paras 60–61. Also, Case T-264/04 *WWF European Policy Programme v Council* EU:T:2007:114, para 39.

[64] Art 1 of the Regulation 1049/01 dealing with its 'purpose'. Case T-174/95 *Svenska Journalistförbundet v Council* EU:T:1998:127, para 66; *Kuijer v Council* (n 63) para 55; *Sison II* (n 59) para 61.

[65] Case T-14/98 *Hautala v Council* EU:T:1999:157, para 28.

[66] This requirement has been established before for the other exceptions under Regulation 1049/2001 (n 50) art 4, but not for the mandatory exceptions under art 4(1)(a) of that regulation. Before *Council v in 't Veld* (n 52), the GC in Case T-331/11 *Besselink v Council* EU:T:2013:419 also referred to the requirement of specifically and actually undermining an interest as opposed to a broad reference to a protected interest.

actually how granting access to the requested document gives rise to a risk that undermines public security or international relations.[67] Nevertheless, these developments in case law do not override marginal review established in *Sison II*, as the Court explicitly asserted in *Council v In 't Veld*.[68] Yet, the Court seems to gradually establish a differentiation on the applicability of the exceptions under Article 4(1)(a). If the undisclosed document concerns public interests and relates to possible future legislative changes and in particular fundamental rights,[69] the Court seems to favour disclosure even under security and international relations exceptions and hence limits the extent of executive secrecy in these fields.[70]

By contrast to case law on public access requests under Article 4(1) (a) of Regulation 1049/01, the Court makes a strict assessment in cases regarding the right to defence and fair trial and substantively assesses whether the executive claim to secrecy is well founded. If the Court finds that the reasons provided by the executive institution do not preclude partial disclosure 'at the very best', the Court 'gives the opportunity' to executive institutions to disclose the information.[71] If the executive institution does not grant disclosure, the Court only conducts an examination of the contested measure on the basis of the material that has been disclosed. However, if the Court finds that the executive claim to secrecy is well founded, the Court validates the claim that secrecy is necessary. In such instances, the Court explicitly affirms its authority to conduct the *final* assessment as to whether and to what extent the failure to disclose classified information to the individual concerned affects her ability to defend her rights and takes this into consideration in the final judgment.[72]

Cases such as *OMPI* and *Kadi II* are the most important among a growing number of cases where executive secrecy in the context of counter-terrorism measures challenges essential procedural rights to a fair trial and effective

[67] See also Case C-350/12 P *Council v in 't Veld*, Opinion of AG Sharpston EU:C:2014:88.

[68] *Council v in 't Veld* (n 52) para 63.

[69] In the case of *Besselink v Council* (n 66)—the ECHR; in the case of *Council v in 't Veld* (n 52)—privacy rights.

[70] See Vigjilenca Abazi and Maarten Hillebrandt, 'The Legal Limits to Confidential Negotiations: Recent Case Law Developments in Council Transparency: *Access Info Europe* and *in 't Veld*' (2015) 52 Common Market Law *Review* 1.

[71] See Rules of Procedure of the General Court [2015] OJ L105/1Rules of Procedure of the Court of Justice of 25 September 2012 [2012] OJ L265/1, as amended on 18 June 2013 [2013] OJ L173/65; Rules of Procedure of the General Court [2015] OJ L105/1; *Kadi II* (n 47).

[72] *Kadi II* (n 47) para 129; *ZZ v Secretary of State for the Home Department* (n 47) para 67.

judicial review. These measures concern individual sanctions of freezing assets on the basis of lists of suspects for terrorism. The *OMPI* was sanctioned on the basis of the EU lists of terrorists, contrary to the *Kadi II* case, subject to the EU sanctions giving effect to the United Nations lists of terrorists suspects.[73] The relevance of this distinction of the basis for the listing has to do with the Court's scope of review, which is broader if the sanctions are based on the EU lists, since they are established by the Council.[74]

Secrecy is also invoked in cases of expulsion and limitations of freedom of movement. The Court applies the same strict scope of review and requires some level of disclosure to the person subject to expulsion, as clarified in the *ZZ* case. This case regards an EU citizen who was subject to an expulsion measure on grounds of public security without having been informed of the grounds justifying that measure, either in detail or in summary form, because the UK authorities claimed that disclosure would be contrary to the interests of state security.[75] This aspect of the case raises questions regarding the extent of non-disclosure of information that could be deemed acceptable to the Court, which the following subsection explains.

Levels of secrecy: Justified 'deep secrecy' and closed evidence

What is the extent of acceptable secrecy in view of the EU courts? An important type of secrecy is 'deep secrecy', which refers to information or documents whose very existence is unknown.[76] This is the opposite of what are called 'shallow secrets', where the content of the document is undisclosed but its existence is public or could be disclosed.

In the case of *Sison II*, the Court affirmed that the originator of sensitive information, which could be an EU institution or agency, MS, or a third party,[77] is justified in refusing not only the disclosure of the document's

[73] On 28 September 2001, the United Nations Security Council adopted Resolution 1373 (2001) laying down strategies to combat terrorism by all means, in particular their financing. Para 1(c) of that resolution provides that all states must freeze without delay funds and other financial assets or economic resources of persons who commit, or attempt to commit, terrorist acts or participate in or facilitate the commission of terrorist acts; of entities owned or controlled by such persons; and of persons and entities acting on behalf of, or at the direction of, such persons and entities.

[74] Common Position 2001/931/CFSP (n 57); Council Regulation (EC) No 2580/2001 (n 57).

[75] *ZZ v Secretary of State for the Home Department* (n 47).

[76] David Pozen, 'Deep Secrecy' (2010) 62 Stanford Law Review 257.

[77] *Sison II* (n 59) para 75; Case C-266/05 P *Sison v Council* (known as *Sison II*), AG Geelhoed noted in points 58 and 59 of his Opinion EU:C:2006:427.

content but also its *very existence* on the basis of Article 9(3) of Regulation 1049/01.[78] Moreover, the identity of the originator of the document could also remain undisclosed.[79] The *Sison II* case gives rise to the need to further clarify Article 9(1) of Regulation 1049/01 as a basis for classified information and its relation to Article 4(1)(a) as the only legal basis for exceptions to public access, more recently reiterated by the Court in the judgment *Jurašinović v Council.*[80] Article 9 of Regulation 1049/01 is intended to provide special treatment for sensitive information, especially in relation to the officials responsible for processing the public access request and as such this provision is not a basis for refusal of access to documents and it cannot be seen as limiting access in any way.[81] The mere fact that a document is classified as 'sensitive' within the meaning of Article 9(1) of Regulation 1049/2001 cannot prevent the application of the exceptions provided in Article 4(1)(a). To hold otherwise, would deprive Article 4 of 'all practical effect'.[82] Hence, the relation between Article 4 and Article 9, clarified further by the GC in *Corporate Europe Observatory v Commission*,[83] means that the presence or absence of one of the designations referred to in Article 9(1) of Regulation No 1049/2001 or of the 'EU Restricted' classification on a document does not constitute a conclusive factor in the assessment of whether or not the document must be protected.[84] However, if the originator of the sensitive information refuses disclosure on the basis of discretion as stipulated in Article 9(3) of Regulation No 1049/2001, the Court in *Sison II* held that: 'the originating authority of a sensitive document is empowered to oppose disclosure not only of that document's content but even of its existence'.[85] In this respect, although the sensitivity of the information or the fact that it is classified in any of the categories is only relevant with regard to the internal 'special treatment' or internal management of the document,[86] under Article 9(3) the originator retains authority to refuse disclosure of the document in a request for public access. This manner of applying Article 9 leads effectively to a situation of deep secrecy for the

[78] *Sison II* (n 59) para 101.

[79] *Sison II* (n 59) para 102. There is a difference if legislation is concerned, as derived from *Council v Access Info Europe* (n 52) para 40 where the Court clearly established that when it comes to legislative processes the identity of the decision-makers (thus not originators of documents as such) must be publicly disclosed due to democratic accountability concerns.

[80] Case C-576/12 P *Jurašinović v Council* EU:C:2013:777.

[81] ibid paras 43 and 46.

[82] ibid para 47.

[83] Case T-93/11 *Stichting Corporate Europe Observatory v Commission* EU:T:2013:308.

[84] ibid para 55.

[85] *Sison II* (n 59) para 101.

[86] ibid para 103.

individual requesting public access as she would not be able to know neither whether the document indeed exists nor its originating authority.

Contrary to such level of secrecy in cases of public access requests, a minimum level of disclosure was necessary in the cases pertaining to the right to defence and a fair trial. However, the revised Rules of Procedure of the General Court, specifically Article 105(8), allow for the first time in the history of the EU Courts the use of closed evidence, that is reliance on evidence that is not disclosed to the applicant. This new level of secrecy is not in line with the Court's own case law on minimum requirement for disclosure prior to the revision of the Rules of Procedure, as shown below, and it also goes against the case law of the European Court of Human Rights (ECtHR), which requires that some minimum level of information must be disclosed to the defendant.[87] For example, in cases of sanctions such as counter-terrorist measures or expulsion on the basis of public security, the Court has consistently held that information must be available, despite the low threshold, and that the Court would only base its judgment on disclosed information.[88] In the case of *OMPI*, a case that marks the first decision by the Court to annul a designated Union list for freezing the assets of terrorist suspects,[89] the Court held clearly that without the relevant information the person affected adversely by the measure would not be in a position to submit her observations to correct an error or produce information in favour to her position and crucially, that the Court itself must be able to take a fully informed decision.[90] Furthermore, as evident in the *ZZ* case, for the expulsion of an EU citizen on the basis of security, the individual must be given a precise and comprehensive statement of the grounds of the decision.[91] Although a statement could be qualified in cases of security considerations, the disclosure of a summary must be considered. The person

[87] Abazi and Eckes(n 41).

[88] See Case T-284/08 *People's Mojahedin Organization of Iran v Council* (OMPI/PMOI III) EU:T:2008:550, paras 71–73; Case C-27/09 P *France v People's Mojahedin Organization of Iran* EU:C:2011:853. See also Christina Eckes, 'Decision-making in the Dark? Autonomous EU Sanctions and National Classification' Amsterdam Centre for European Law and Governance Working Paper Series 2012-02, 12–13.

[89] See also Eckes (n 39) 306.

[90] As Eckes points out, the 'Court could hardly have expressed criticism more clearly' towards the executive institution regarding the secret nature of the procedure that led to the listing of OMPI and resulted in the Court not being in a position to take an informed decision. ibid 307.

[91] *ZZ v Secretary of State for the Home Department* (n 47).

must have 'full knowledge of relevant facts'.[92] However, this threshold of minimum disclosure towards the individual is no longer applicable for cases involving classified information under Article 105(8) of the Rules of Procedure of the General Court. The EU closed evidence procedure is mostly motivated by the necessity to allow EU Courts access to official secrets which, as discussed above, has been a challenge for the Court. Whilst the revised procedure might facilitate access to classified documents for the Court, it undoubtedly does so in a manner that limits the individual's right to access to justice. The level of this limitation, as noted above, is not in line with the Court's own case law prior to the revised rules of procedure and it also goes against the minimum requirements of information disclosure (i.e. requirement of the gist of information) as established by the case law of the ECtHR. The book questions whether other procedural requirements in the judicial review provide sufficient safeguards to the fundamental rights of access to documents and access to justice.

Duty to state reasons: A sufficient safeguard?

The duty to state reasons is a crucial procedural criterion in both sets of reviews as it is relevant for the individual to defend her rights, for the institution to be reflective and self-restrained, and for the Court to be able to be fully informed in order to review the decision.[93] In principle, the statement of reasons must be 'appropriate to the act at issue and must disclose in a clear and unequivocal fashion the reasoning followed by the institution which adopted the measure in question'.[94] However, in both set of cases it seems that the Court allows for a brief statement of reasons, where the extent it allows the individual to defend her essential procedural rights can be questioned. Regarding the exceptions under Article 4(1)(a) of Regulation 1049/01, the Court leaves a margin for institutional discretion by only requiring a short statement of reasons. The Court held that abstaining from reference to issues that would *indirectly* undermine the protected interest is justified when Article 9 of Regulation 1049/01 is taken into account. The Court justifies such brevity by:

[92] *Kadi II* (n 47) para 100.

[93] Case C-269/90 *Technische Universität München v Hauptzollamt München-Mitte* EU:C:1991:438.

[94] *Sison II* (n 59) para 80; Case T-92/98 *Interporc v Commission* EU:T:1999:308, para 55.

The need not to undermine the sensitive interests protected by the exceptions ... through disclosure of the very information which those exceptions are designed to protect.[95]

Similarly, in cases in the sanctions regime, the Court accepts a short statement of reasons. For example, in the case of *Council v Fulmen*,[96] the Court held that the statement of reasons may be brief *if* the individual is able to first, understand what the person is accused of and second, on the basis of such information the person is able to dispute either the accuracy or the relevance of the information. The evidence does not need to be detailed, as the Court held in *Al-Aqsa v Council*.[97] In sanctions cases, it is further relevant whether the individual is listed for the first time or whether it is a recurring measure. When the individual is initially listed, the statement of reasons does not need to be issued before the measure is applied so as to preserve the element of surprise that secrecy offers. In the application of security measures, secrecy may be used to create a situation where the intended target is left unprepared to take counter-action. In sanctions cases, in order for the measure to be successful, the individual should not be aware that her assets will be frozen. In specific circumstances it is also possible that 'restrictions on access may concern the specific content of or particular reasoning of [the restrictive] decision, or even the identity of the authority that took it'.[98] Regarding the subsequent listing, considering that the element of surprise is no longer necessary, the institution must provide the 'actual and specific reasons' for the justification of the continuation of the measure.[99] This level of justification on the side of executive institutions seems thin and not offering sufficient or concrete information to the application for the course of action the institution has taken. Since these cases pertain to issues of security, it is not uncommon not only in the EU context but also in the MS and other practices in the world that security interests are strongly protected. However, it is questionable to what extent the level of safeguards for allowing such level of protection of security interests is proportionate to the fundamental rights which are supposed to be protected. The following Chapter 5 offers an analysis of the ramifications of secrecy for oversight and fundamental rights in the EU. In the next

[95] *Sison II* (n 59) para 82; Case T-110/03 *Sison v Council* EU:T:2005:143, paras 62 and 63.

[96] Case C-280/12 P *Council v Fulmen and Mahmoudian* EU:C:2013:775, paras 61, 62, 68.

[97] Joined Cases C-539/10 P and C-550/10 P *Al-Aqsa v Council* and *The Netherlands v Al-Aqsa* EU:C:2012:711.

[98] Case T-228/02 *OMPI* EU:T:2006:384, para 148.

[99] ibid para 143.

section, the discussion is focused on the powers and the review of secrecy by the EP and the EO.

Parliamentary review and disclosure of secrets

The EP has limited powers to evaluate decisions regarding official secrets made by executive institutions, such as whether a document should be classified or disclosed to the public. Parliamentary review of executive claims to secrecy does not include institutional mechanisms through which the EP could review the executive decisions on whether to classify a document. On the contrary, executive actors have the potential to alert each other about the possible wrong classification label or make their views known when they disagree with the classification label, such as '*Confidential*', '*Secret*', or '*Top Secret*'. For example, Europol can address a MS if it considers that a document should be classified in a lower or higher security level or should not be classified at all.[100] Exceptionally, only with regard to the Commission, the EP has a similar prerogative to draw attention to its disagreement regarding the classification decision. If the EP doubts the confidential nature of the information or its appropriate level of classification, it may consult the Commission to make the necessary changes.[101] At the consultation, the chair of the parliamentary body concerned represents the EP whereas a Member of the Commission with responsibility for that area represents the Commission, after internally having agreed with the Commission official responsible for security matters. If the two institutions have divergent views regarding the classification status of the document despite consultations, the issue is referred to the Presidents of the two institutions so that they may resolve the dispute.[102] If an agreement is not reached at the end of the procedure and consultation, the President of Parliament calls on the Commission to forward the confidential information in question. Before the expiry of that deadline, the Commission informs Parliament in writing of its final position.[103] The reference to the EP should not be misleading to represent that every Member of the EP would be able to give such opinions regarding the classification level. With

[100] Council Decision 2009/968/JHA of 30 November 2009 adopting the rules on the confidentiality of Europol information [2009] OJ L332/17, art 11(3). However, in practice, this happens rarely, Respondent No 1.

[101] Framework Agreement on relations between the European Parliament and the European Commission [2010] OJ L304/47, Annex II paras 2(3) and 2(4).

[102] ibid Annex II para 2(3).

[103] ibid Annex II, para 2(4).

respect to the Council, the EP has no opportunity to show its disagreement over what it would consider an unnecessary classification decision, as the Inter-institutional Agreement in 2014 foresees no such review mechanism. This agreement does not lay down a detailed procedure to be followed in cases of doubt regarding the confidential nature of information or its appropriate level of classification.[104]

This lack of procedures for review is not accidental, but rather the Council took a clear position during the negotiations of the agreement that it did not want its decision to classify a document to be assessed by the EP. This position of the Council is identified from both the interviews conducted with Council officials as well as documents pertaining to the negotiations.[105] The Inter-institutional Agreement regarding the exchange of classified information in the CFSP of 2002 does not stipulate a possibility for the EP to express its view on the classification decisions. The EP is not satisfied with this outcome and expressly stated it regrets that 'unlike the Framework Agreement between the Commission and Parliament, the agreement does not lay down a detailed procedure to be followed in cases of doubt regarding the confidential nature of an item of information or its appropriate level of classification'.[106] Besides the Council, the EP does not have review or consultation prerogatives towards EU agencies or bodies dealing with classified information. The only option for the EP to raise attention if it considers that an executive claim to secrecy is unwarranted is vis-à-vis the Commission, although it should be emphasized that it is not an obligation for the Commission to follow the EP's opinion on the classification marking.

The lack of powers of the EP in a more strict sense, referring specifically to the decisions within the EUCI system, does not imply that it lacks other oversight mechanisms and prerogatives through which it could check executive action and seek disclosure of secrecy. Particularly noteworthy are examples where individual MEPs summon executive institutions to the Court or where the EP does this at an institutional level. For instance, under the public access to documents regime as provided in Regulation

[104] European Parliament decision of 13 September 2012 on the conclusion of an inter-institutional agreement between the European Parliament and the Council concerning the forwarding to and handling by the European Parliament of classified information held by the Council on matters other than those in the area of the common foreign and security policy (2012/2069(ACI)), point 5.

[105] ibid; Respondents Nos 6, 13, 16.

[106] European Parliament decision of 13 September 2012 (n 104) point 5.

1049/01, Sophie In 't Veld, a Dutch ALDE MEP has sought to disclose executive secrecy pertaining to international relations both from the Commission on the negotiations around the Anti-Counterfeiting Trade Agreement (ACTA)[107] and from the Council regarding the TFTP.[108] In addition to judicial avenues as a means to disclose executive secrecy, the EP uses its veto powers acquired in the post-Lisbon context, by refusing or delaying consent to international agreements in its political efforts to disclose executive secrecy. For example, the EP refused consent to the EU–US SWIFT Agreement and delayed consent to USA and Australia Passenger Name Records (PNR) Agreements. Regarding the SWIFT Agreement, the EP gave its consent at a later stage but scholars note there were 'no remarkable differences between the first and second SWIFT agreements'.[109] Rather, the difference was that during the second round, the EP was fully informed at all stages of the negotiations, hence it succeeded in disclosing executive secrecy for oversight purposes.[110]

EU secrecy under administrative review

Investigating maladministration is the key function of the EO, which is precisely what is needed in cases involving secrecy considering that the latter may shield embarrassing or incriminating information. The EO has dealt with two types of cases regarding classified information: first, cases on the refusal of EU institutions to grant public access to documents, and second, inquiries of maladministration. The role of the EO with regard to cases on the refusal of public access is to determine whether the institution's claim to secrecy is justified. The EO has the power to request the documents and determine if public access should be granted or whether disclosure would undermine the interests that the institutions claim to protect. This review mechanism is not strictly addressed at classified information but rather involves any document the disclosure of which has been refused by the institution. Looking at the practice of the EO, it seems that

[107] Whereas the litigant in that case was unsuccessful, the ACTA was subsequently abandoned after protracted major public pressure opposing the agreement.

[108] Case T-301/10 *In 't Veld* v *Commission* EU:T:2013:135.

[109] See Juan Santos Vara, 'The Role of the European Parliament in the Conclusion of the Transatlantic Agreements on the Transfer of Personal Data after Lisbon' (2013) CLEER Working Papers 2013/2, <http://www.asser.nl/upload/documents/20130226T013310-cleer_13-2_web.pdf> accessed 25 July 2018, on how the EP vetoed PNR and other agreements.

[110] ibid 20.

it has never asked an institution to declassify a document and when review of denied access requests pertain to Article 4(1) of Regulation 1049/01, similarly to the Court, the EO conducts a narrow procedural review. The EO has pointed out that the standard of review it carries out is compatible with that of EU courts.[111] The review of refusal of public access to documents on the grounds of the protection of public interest regarding international relations is limited to the verification of compliance with procedural requirements and duty to state reasons as well as the assessment of the accuracy of factual statements and lack of errors or misuse of powers.[112]

The EO does not review whether a classification label is justified and necessary. In cases dealing with the refusal of public access requests based on protection of international relations,[113] the EO refers to documents whose disclosure was refused in a brief manner, merely stating that disclosure of such documents should be reconsidered. An institution that refuses access to sensitive information must give reasons for its refusal. The role of the EO is limited to verifying whether the institution has complied with this duty. Hence, the review of the EO is not based on whether a document should be classified or declassified; rather it is focused on whether the reasons provided as to why the document should be undisclosed to the public are satisfactory. Regarding the scope of the duty to state reasons, the decisions of the EO point out that it follows the reasoning of the Court. While in its earlier cases, the EO considered that a brief statement of reasons could suffice in cases where more elaborate statements could undermine the very interest the institution seeks to protect,[114] over the years the EO has expanded the duty to state reasons into an obligation to show how disclosure would specifically and actually undermine the protected interest,[115] and

[111] Draft recommendations of the European Ombudsman in the inquiry into complaint 1398/2013/ANA against the European Commission, made in accordance with Article 3(6) of the Statute of the European Ombudsman, point 66.

[112] ibid; Decision of the European Ombudsman closing her inquiry into complaint 1633/2008/DK against the European Commission, point 17; Decision of the European Ombudsman closing her inquiry into complaint 488/2007/PB against the European Commission, point 50.

[113] See, eg, Inquiry into complaint 1398/2013/ANA.

[114] Decision of the European Ombudsman closing his inquiry into complaint 523/2009/TS against the Council of the European Union, points 20 and 22; Decision of the European Ombudsman closing his inquiry into complaint 944/2008/OV against the Council of the European Union, point 30.

[115] Decision of the European Ombudsman closing his inquiry into complaint 1051/2010/BEH against the European External Action Service (EEAS), point 42.

that such a risk is foreseeable and not merely hypothetical.[116] The EO is entitled to inspect the document and it can verify whether public access was justifiably denied regardless of whether EU institutions provide a brief or a detailed statement of reasons.[117] If the EO finds that partial or complete public access to the disputed document could be granted, it will make recommendations to that end and give the institution in question a deadline within which it has to implement the recommendations.[118] The EO may review executive claims to secrecy through conducting inquiries for maladministration. However, the EO's practice thus far does not include cases relating exclusively to classified information in the sense of the misuse of classification authority or revelations of embarrassing information for the EU institutions.

The EO has a stronger position than the EP with regard to assessing secrecy claims, and shares more similarities with the Court regarding the evaluations in cases of public access requests. In terms of implications for the institutions, however, the EO's review is more limited than the Court's considering that the latter delivers legally binding judgments as opposed to recommendations. The EU executive institutions do not have the sole prerogative to determine the level of secrecy in the EU when it comes to classified information. Each oversight institution has some powers to limit the claims to secrecy. The EP has the most direct mechanism for giving an opinion regarding the classification decision on whether it should be classified or the level of classification, but this is strictly limited to the Commission. The Council was specifically opposed to the EP having such

[116] Decision of the European Ombudsman closing the inquiry into complaint 2275/2013/ANA against the European Commission, point 27; Decision of the European Ombudsman closing the inquiry into complaint 2266/2013/JN against the European Commission, points 40 and 41; Draft recommendations 1398/2013/ANA (n 111) point 64; Decision of the European Ombudsman closing her inquiry into complaint 1454/2012/ANA against the European Commission, point 51; Decision of the European Ombudsman in her inquiry into complaint 2393/2011/RA against the European Parliament, point 53.

[117] Cases where the European Ombudsman inspected the file and found denial of disclosure justified: Decision 2275/2013/ANA (n 116), points 28–30; Draft recommendations 1398/2013/ANA (n 111), point 68; Decision 1454/2012/ANA (n 116) point 52; Decision of the European Ombudsman closing her inquiry into complaint 339/2011/AN against the European Commission, points 38–40; Decision 1051/2010/BEH (n 115) points 43–50; Decision 523/2009/TS (n 114) points 20–22; Decision of the European Ombudsman closing her inquiry into complaint 90/2009/(JD)OV against the Council of the European Union, points 27–36; Decision 944/2008/OV (n 114) points 28–30.

[118] See, eg, Draft recommendations 1398/2013/ANA (n 111) points 70–72, art V.

powers with regard to classified documents, regardless of the policy area.[119] The Court and the EO have review mechanisms that are focused on the failure of the executive institutions and bodies to disclose information and address the implications arising from non-disclosure. These arrangements for review of secrecy in the EU provide a mixed picture: whilst some limitations exist and all EU branches of oversight have some powers for review, it is worthwhile to look more closely at whether the extent of executive discretion in secrecy is within the remits of the EU's constitutional obligations to principles of democracy and openness.

An 'Executive Privilege' for Official Secrets in the EU?

Is an 'executive privilege' de facto being established in the EU? Looking comparatively in the US context, 'executive privilege' gives the President and high-level executive branch officials the power to withhold information from Congress, the courts and the public.[120] Established in the case of *US v Nixon*,[121] this privilege is not mentioned in the US Constitution, yet this is not the only aspect that makes its applicability highly disputed.[122] Rather, it is questionable whether it grants a power to the executive branch that is disproportionate to that foreseen by the US Constitution and leads to an unacceptable practice from a democratic accountability perspective.[123] In the EU context, whilst the current legal framework establishes privileged access to classified documents for EU oversight institutions, it

[119] As we saw, this applies to both the 2014 and the 2002 agreements: Inter-institutional Agreement of 12 March 2014 between the European Parliament and the Council concerning the forwarding to and handling by the European Parliament of classified information held by the Council on matters other than those in the area of the common foreign and security policy [2014] OJ C95/1; Inter-institutional Agreement of 20 November 2002 between the European Parliament and the Council concerning access by the European Parliament to sensitive information of the Council in the field of security and defence policy [2002] OJ C298/1.

[120] Mark J Rozell, *Executive Privilege: Presidential Power, Secrecy, and Accountability* (3rd edn, University Press of Kansas 2010).

[121] *United States v Nixon* 418 US 683 (1974).

[122] Heidi Kitrosser, 'Secrecy and Separated Powers: Executive Privilege Revisited' (2007) 92 Iowa Law Review 489, 514–15, 542–43.

[123] Heidi Kitrosser, *Reclaiming Accountability: Transparency, Executive Power, and the U.S. Constitution* (University of Chicago Press 2015).

also maintains a rigid application of the originator control, which ultimately provides discretion to executive institutions on whether information would be shared. In practice, the originator discretion has been applied to deny access to classified documents to all three oversight institutions analysed here. The application of the originator rule is also wide—it encompasses EU institutions, MS, and third countries and organizations. In fact, as the cases such as *OMPI* and *Fulman* illustrate, EU executive institutions are prevented from sharing classified documents with EU oversight institutions due to the compound administrative procedures as the documents originate from national authorities that in turn deny granting access to EU oversight institutions. Hence, the current law and practice of the originator principle blocks privileged access for EU oversight institutions not only as a matter of choice of EU executive institutions, but also due to national and third country policy choices. Such choices are defended by executive institutions on basis of protection of national security interests and claimed to be within their powers to withhold information fully. More importantly, the executive institutions become the final arbiter on whether the information should be disclosed to the oversight institution when the originator rule is invoked. In the EU context, it is noteworthy that this level of final control emerges not from constitutional norms but it has been developed by the executive institutions themselves, under external pressure from military actors such as NATO,[124] and in turn it has been used as a condition to establish security agreements for the exchange of classified information with EU oversight actors. In a slow and shadowy manner, the executive institutions, particularly the Council, introduced a practice of secrecy that leads to stronger powers for them and their position of control over the accessibility of classified information, as was elaborated in detail in Chapter 2.

Inaccessibility to classified information leads the oversight actors to become incapable of exercising their oversight responsibilities. The discretion of executive actors regarding limits of access should not expand to the extent of obstructing oversight processes. Although in the case of *Sison II*, discussed above, it was noted that a wide margin of executive discretion regarding non-disclosure is permitted and possibly the requesting party could even face deep secrecy, such limitations cannot be applicable for oversight institutions considering the constitutional stipulations of

[124] See Chapter 2.

oversight, institutional balance, and sincere cooperation. If the Court were to interpret the originator rule in the context of privileged rather than public access, as was the case in *Sison II*, such a level of secrecy would not be acceptable since the Court faces a different set of questions when it comes to institutional balance and the constitutional architecture of peer-to-peer accountability. For example, the Court does clearly provide its own final authority to decide on the fundamental rights implication in cases of secrecy consideration in security cases, such as a fair trial and the right to defence. It could be imaginable that the Court would aim towards protecting the constitutional rights of the EO and the EP for access in order to conduct oversight. It is noteworthy that the Court interprets the principle of sincere cooperation and information-sharing obligations between the institutions rather broadly in this regard. This becomes most clear in the *Mauritious* case concerning obligations of the Council to share information even for matters strictly pertaining to the CFSP, which is exactly the type of sensitive area of EU law with limited EU level oversight. The Court most clearly stated the obligation for MS to share information, regardless of the area, due to the principle of sincere cooperation.[125]

Privileged access to EUCI would lose meaning and purpose for oversight institutions if limitations were invoked precisely for the key information that oversight institutions utilize. Drawing an analogy with the Court's interpretation regarding public access in cases such as *Sweden v Commission* and *Council v Hautala*, the Court would not allow a limitation of public access right that leads it to be 'frustrated without an objective reason and that the effectiveness of the right would be substantially reduced'.[126] The Court finds unacceptable that 'documents of the same kind and of the same importance for shedding light on the [European Union] decision-making process could be granted or refused depending solely on the origin of the document'.[127] An additional argument in favour of narrowing the applicability of the originator rule is that national law cannot impose limitations on the realization of EU law and prerogatives. The problem of course is that the originator rule does not merely derive from

[125] Case C-658/11 *European Parliament v Council of the European Union* EU:C:2014:2025, para 85.

[126] Case C-64/05 P *Sweden v Commission* EU:C:2007:802, para 64; *Hautala v Council* (n 65) para 26.

[127] *Sweden v Commission* (n 126) para 72.

the national level but it has been incorporated at the EU level and internalized by the oversight institutions. However, MS or third parties do not have a 'general and unconditional right of veto, so that it could in a discretionary manner oppose the disclosure of documents originating from it and held by an institution'.[128] Similarly, national security cannot be broadly invoked as a limitation to comply with sharing information. Although Article 346(1a) TFEU provides that 'no Member States shall be obliged to supply information the disclosure of which it considers contrary to the essential interest of its security', the Court has already given a narrow interpretation to such exceptions. In *Commission v Finland*, the Court has held that derogations provided for in Article 346(1a) must be interpreted strictly and that the provision cannot be understood in such a way as to confer on MS a power to depart from the application of EU law.[129] Crucially, the Court stated that national security justification as such does not provide a basis for the MS not to provide information. The MS invoking Article 346(1a) must actually prove that its application is necessary in order to protect its essential security interests and in principle make information available.[130] Lastly, the originator control leads to consequences of classification and block information that is disproportionate because it does not only affect the original document but also the deriving documents. This effectively leads to the EU documents de facto never breaking away from the national and foreign classification decision. Instead, the originators ensure a permanent link and discretion, which could possibly result not only in blocking privileged access but also in creating over-classification. This further illustrates that the establishment and practice of the originator control reflects the rigid security-driven logic and the technicalities of the classification without a consideration of consequences beyond the executive's needs. It reflects the one-sidedness of the EUCI regime that caters to executives and their control, but blocks constitutional EU oversight prerogatives. Such practice cannot be deemed in line with the EU's principles and legal commitments to democratic principles and openness.[131]

[128] ibid para 75. [129] Case C-284/05 *Commission v Finland* EU:C:2009:778, para 47.

[130] ibid para 53. See Panos Koutrakos, *The EU Common Security and Defence Policy* (OUP 2013).

[131] Art 1 TEU, art 10 TEU, art 11 TEU, art 15 TFEU, and art 41 of the Charter of Fundamental Rights of the European Union [2012] OJ C326/391.

Conclusions

Official secrets challenge the flow of information to oversight institutions and they also pose limits to the exercise of EU fundamental rights. The analysis demonstrated that legally EU oversight institutions enjoy a privileged access to classified information, which derives specifically from their constitutionally stipulated role in oversight. However, this privileged access is not absolute but rather limited by the rule of originator control, which extends to the point of fully blocking access to classified information for oversight actors. The EU oversight actors are reliant on executive actors for access to official secrets and face a clear limitation that can be invoked for their privileged right to access. This limitation is stipulated internally within the rules of oversight actors, hence they are based on EU law, as well as included in all arrangements and agreements regarding classified information that the EU has with third parties as well as with the MS. This level of wide discretion on the side of executive institutions to decide on access to official secrets is not in line with the democratic constraints on secrecy. The single most important aspect regarding oversight institutions is that they do not fully depend on the discretion of executive actors regarding access to information. In an institutional setting the empowerment of the secret-keeper over the disclosure of secrecy should be matched with prerogatives of the outsiders to avoid or prevent a misbalance of powers. In the EU context, the complexity of access to classified information is also exacerbated by compound administrative procedures. This leads to information often deriving from national authorities that retain the discretion to decide whether such information is to be shared, with whom and when. Whilst the chapter also showed that the case law of the Court supports a narrow discretion on the part of the MS for refraining to disclose information and rather cooperate with EU institutions in light of the principle of sincere cooperation, in practice official secrets, especially those pertaining to national security, are often not shared with EU oversight institutions. In fact, in the case of the Court, this issue has even motivated the revision of the Rules of Procedure in order to allow the Court to access to official secrets in a manner that the Court is deemed trustworthy by the MS in light of the new security procedures in place. Yet, the procedure of judicial review introduced a new level of secrecy in EU Courts that is against the prior case law of the Court on minimum requirements of disclosure to the applicant and it is also not compatible with the case law of the ECtHR on access to justice.

This chapter also showed that review of official secrets by EU oversight institutions is varied. Each oversight institution has some powers to limit the claims to secrecy. The purpose of these external checks on executive discretion to secrecy is to ensure that secrecy is applied only when necessary and that affected rights, such as the right of public access to documents and the right of access to justice, are only limited to the extent that is necessary, while additional safeguards are provided. The EP has the most direct mechanism for giving an opinion regarding the classification decision on whether it should be classified or the level of classification, but this is strictly limited to the Commission. The Council was specifically opposed to the EP having such powers with regard to classified documents, regardless of the policy area. The Court and the EO have review mechanisms that are focused on the failure of the executive institutions and bodies to disclose information and address the implications arising from non-disclosure. Examined separately or taken together overall, these review processes still leave the question open on whether the extent of executive discretion in secrecy is within the remits of the EU's constitutional obligations to principles of democracy and openness as well as fundamental rights. Hence, the chapter examined whether executive discretion in secrecy is sufficiently bound in the EU or rather can we observe a slow emergence of a de facto 'executive privilege'. This chapter partly answers this question by pointing to the significant limitations in the processes of access to and review of official secrets. In the following chapter, the discussion focuses on whether the ramifications of official secrets for oversight and fundamental rights would also justify such concerns.

5

Closed Parliamentary Oversight and Secret Evidence in EU Courts

Abstracts
This chapter examines parliamentary and judicial oversight practices resulting from rules on official secrets. It shows how these practices fundamentally affect public deliberation and access to justice in the EU. Closed parliamentary oversight does not sufficiently take into account the necessities of public deliberation and focuses predominantly on peer accountability. Secret evidence in EU courts fails to meet the standards of access to justice as set in previous case law of the CJEU as well as the European Court of Human Rights. The latter has an established case law under which circumstances and conditions the use of secret evidence may be considered lawful. By looking at closed oversight and secret evidence, this chapter shows that EU oversight institutions have taken the necessary steps to address the problems of access to classified documents, but have done so without sufficient regard to the arising consequences for key EU principles and fundamental rights.

Introduction

> What I have learned in my long experience, what I can say for democracy is that there is no final or ultimate solution.
>
> It is a process . . . constant checks and balances.
>
> We have to make sure to create a margin or borders of checks but we must understand that there will be cases that outline these borders.[1]

Democratic constraints on official secrets establish 'borders of checks'. These borders are meant to ensure the lawfulness of the use of official

[1] Respondent No 25.

secrets. Such constraints are difficult to be maintained in the context of the EU, where there is a growing tension between networked executives and intelligence cooperation, on the one hand, and compartmentalized oversight structures, on the other hand. Official secrets increase the existing information asymmetries and enable the creation of new ones spread throughout the multi-layered structures of the EU. To address what became an acute problem for oversight—that is access to classified documents due to limitations imposed by official secrets, which was only increasing information asymmetries—EU oversight institutions revised their rules of procedure to accommodate security for classified documents and hence ensure access.

This chapter focuses on the practice of parliamentary and judicial oversight in the EU as a result of the revised procedural rules on official secrets. Both the European Parliament (EP) and the Court of Justice of the European Union (CJEU) have made significant changes to their oversight arrangements through their rules of procedure leading to closed parliamentary oversight and the use of secret evidence in court. Unlike these institutions, the European Ombudsman (EO) does not have a separate set of rules for classified information or special arrangements for classified information.[2] As the Statute addresses classified information as a category that requires special handling by the EO when such information is requested from the EU administration in line with its prerogatives to initiate an inquiry or address a complaint received by individuals. The EO reviews the requested document in a confidential setting. However such closed oversight does not directly result from the new rules of official secrets in the EU, hence in the current discussion the focus is specifically on the changes that the EP and the Court have made due to the EU's regulation of secrecy.

The chapter shows that the revised procedures for oversight fundamentally affect public deliberation and access to justice in the EU. Closed parliamentary oversight does not sufficiently take into account the necessities of public deliberation and focuses predominantly on peer accountability.

[2] Note, however, that the Statute of the European Ombudsman mentions the following in the preamble: 'the Ombudsman should have agreed in advance with the institution or body concerned regarding the conditions for treatment of classified information or documents and other information covered by the obligation of professional secrecy'. See Decision of the European Parliament of 9 March 1994 on the regulations and general conditions governing the performance of the Ombudsman's duties [1994] OJ L113/15, as amended by decision of 14 March 2002, OJ L92/13 and decision of 18 June 2008, OJ L189/25 (the Statute of the European Ombudsman).

Secret evidence in EU Courts fails to meet the standards of access to justice as set in previous case law of the CJEU as well as the European Court of Human Rights (ECtHR). The latter has an established case law and clear requirements under which circumstances and conditions the use of secret evidence may be considered lawful. The chapter identifies the aspects of the EU secret evidence procedure that do not align with those standards. By looking at closed oversight and secret evidence, this chapter shows that EU oversight institutions have taken the necessary steps to address the problems of access to classified documents, but have done so without sufficient regard to the arising consequences for key EU principles and fundamental rights.

Parliamentary Oversight behind Closed Doors

Parliaments accommodate the necessities of secrecy and maintain high security protections of official secrets when conducting oversight. Often such arrangements result in closed parliamentary oversight. Closed oversight means that both the manner in which the oversight is conducted and the results of the oversight process are unavailable to the public. From an accountability perspective, closed oversight is not necessarily problematic as it ensures the purpose of scrutinizing executive power. However, seen from the perspective of public deliberation as the final constraint of secrecy, openness should have a higher level of applicability. This in turn implies that the general public should know whether a secret is being kept and what the results of oversight processes are through reports or deliberation. As it has been noted elsewhere, in a representative democracy 'worthy of its name one of the truly distinctive qualities of parliaments is their publicness, the fact that they constitute a public forum as opposed to an accountability relationship among peers'.[3]

The necessity of openness for deliberation creates a higher threshold on the question of to what extent secrecy should be limited because it always requires that some information is directly available to the citizens. The purpose of mechanisms that support deliberation as a democratic process is to provide citizens with an active and participatory role

[3] Deirdre Curtin, 'Challenging Executive Dominance in European Democracy' (2013) Amsterdam Centre for European Law and Governance Working Paper Series 2013—09, 32.

in decision-making. It hence requires an institutional setting under which citizens are informed about processes of oversight and the exercise of secrecy. From this perspective, core choices about secrecy should be made in an open manner and through public debate. As argued by Thompson in 'Democratic Secrecy', more clarity should be established between what is considered secret and what is open and available for citizens to discuss in what he calls first and second order of publicity.[4] Namely, while first order publicity implies the secrets themselves can remain hidden due to the harm of legitimate interests if disclosed, second order publicity refers to the *processes* under which decisions are made as to what is legitimate to constitute a secret in the first place and how should those secrets be kept. This second order publicity, as this chapter shows, is lacking in the EU. For example, the EP would know that Europol is conducting an investigation about cybercrime in the EU, but they do not need to know which individuals are being investigated or more specific information about their location, which could possibly jeopardize the outcome of the investigation. Hence, this means the EP or citizens do not have access to first order secrets. Yet a public debate can be held on how Europol exercises its powers without full access to all protected documents regarding the specificities of the case. In the context of the EU often access to classified documents is very limited and parliamentarians would only receive access to such documents behind closed doors without enabling this second part of open review and deliberation. Hence, the following subsection examines how the EP exercises its powers of oversight when confronted with the legal requirements of safeguarding official secrets. It aims to identify and discuss to what extent the EP safeguards official secrets at the detriment of democratic processes of public deliberation.

Parliamentary oversight and arrangements for official secrets

> Keeping oversight means two main things, first having the powers and second mobilising the public. I think that the European Parliament has focused and still does the first thing; it is always trying to secure its powers—it is used to do that—it knows how to do that. Debate is completely underdeveloped.[5]

[4] Dennis Thompson, 'Democratic Secrecy' (1999) 114 Political Science Quarterly 181.
[5] Respondent No 26.

Drawing a balance between the needs for effective parliamentary oversight and safeguarding official secrets is a challenging task for parliaments. For the EP this challenge is multiplied considering that its powers of oversight have been lacking behind the increased executive prerogatives, both in law and in practice. As frankly expressed by a former Member of the EP, in trying to ensure the exercise (and increase) of its powers, the EP has not always managed to equally incite or develop a public debate and engage EU citizens. There are two aspects of parliamentary oversight to examine in more detail when official secrets are involved: First, whether and to what extent oversight is conducted behind closed doors when parliamentary bodies are given access to official secrets. Second, whether and to what extent the results of parliamentary review are accessible and public. From a public deliberation perspective, even if there is a level of closed oversight, the outcomes of the oversight process should be public. Such outcomes may be a public statement, a report, or a (recorded) debate. Any of the latter options provides citizens with access to materials and information that enables them to establish their own opinion and understanding on the issue of oversight.

In terms of access to official secrets, the EP asserts its powers of oversight. Yet the MEPs that are granted access to official secrets undergo a strict security procedure in order to review the documents. For example, in accordance with Article 6(5) of the Inter-institutional Agreement between the Council and the EP meetings that involve a discussion including official secrets take place behind closed doors.[6] Documents are distributed at the beginning of the meeting and collected again at the end, documents may not be copied by any means, such as photocopying or photographing, no notes may be taken, and the minutes of the meeting cannot make any mention of the discussion of the item containing classified information.[7] These are the strict requirements under which any access and review of classified documents must take place. For documents classified at a higher level than the level of '*Confidential*', the Council makes arrangements on an ad hoc basis regarding their access and review. The experience of the MEPs under this Agreement shows that those documents may only be

[6] See Inter-institutional Agreement of 12 March 2014 between the European Parliament and the Council concerning the forwarding to and handling by the European Parliament of classified information held by the Council on matters other than those in the area of the common foreign and security policy [2014] OJ C95/1.

[7] ibid arts 5–6.

accessed at the Council's premises and under strict security, where all the above-mentioned conditions apply. Institutional instruments which would allow the EP to be able to make public a clear demarcation of what remains closed are not foreseen in the current framework on classified documents, including the EP's own procedural rules on classified information. Instead, the EP has internalized equally strong principles of the classification system, such as the originator control giving full authority of disclosure to the originating source of classified information and potentially blocking access for MEPs.

Parliamentary questions are the only form of public oversight.[8] They are also published on the EP's website as well as in the EU's official journal. The caveat here is that the content of classified information will not be discussed. Hence, when oversight processes are open, crucial questions regarding classified information may be left unanswered by invoking executive confidentiality. This in turn has an implication that both processes of review, that is behind closed doors oversight and when questions are publicly posed, do not lead to any public information that can be useful and relied upon by citizens or civil organizations for any external scrutiny or debate. Such scrutiny would in turn be valuable not merely towards the actions of the executive institutions but also towards the EP and would provide a necessary external check as to whether the EP conducts its oversight role with sufficient rigour. Yet, this aspect in EU parliamentary oversight is lacking.

The second aspect of evaluation of closed oversight is whether the outcomes of such oversight are public. In the EU context, due to closed oversight and the obligations of the EP not to disclose classified documents in any manner, the specific outcomes of the oversight process are not made public. Classified information and its access by MEPs are not allowed to be included even in the meeting minutes.[9] The consequences of closed oversight when considered with the fact that the EP has no institutional measures to alert the public (besides individual MEPs alerting the press for example) raise concerns because research has shown that in such instances 'democratic controversy, transparency and critical debate' are mostly avoided.[10] In the case of the EP, it is argued that parliamentary oversight

[8] Rule 130 EP Rules of Procedure, July 2014.

[9] Art 6 (5) 2014 Council Agreement; Art. 6(6) Council 2014 Agreement (n 6).

[10] Sergio Carrera, Nicholas Hernanz, and Joanna Parkin, 'The "Lisbonisation" of the European Parliament: Assessing Progress, Shortcomings and Challenges for Democratic

committees have changed their working methods and have adapted to executive working methods.[11] Whilst this change of working methods for the EP might be positive from a perspective of gaining access to official secrets, when seen from the core functions of the EP, it seems secrecy and the protection of official secrets might have been given priority over public deliberation.

Lack of publicness and public deliberation

On the basis of EP's resolutions and statements regarding official secrets and the EP's efforts to gain access, it is noticeable that the institutional focus and efforts were centred on gaining access to official secrets. The EP's main concern has been not to be an outsider to the information circle about important EU developments in the area of security and foreign relations. Less attention was paid to the implications of access to official secrets for the EP's other functions, such as public deliberation. Research shows that holding actors to account is to a large extent about 'managing and cultivating one's reputation vis-à-vis different audiences. It is about being seen as a reputable actor in the eyes of one's audience(s), conveying the impression of performing competently one's (accountability) roles, thereby generating reputational benefits.'[12] In such reputational terms, the EP maintains a level of oversight that conveys 'the impression of performing competently one's (accountability) roles' but it leaves open doubts as to what extent such oversight truly checks executive discretion on secrecy and to what extent the borders of checks are maintained in a firm manner to ensure the lawfulness of official secrets. From a procedural perspective, the issue is that these changes to oversight arrangements have been made mostly behind closed doors or through internal rules that do give an opportunity for a public debate on where the lines between safeguarding official secrets and effective oversight be drawn. This in turn implies that in the EU context there is also a lack of publicity not only as to what can become a secret, but also on how oversight of secrets works. The EP might aim to assert its

Accountability in the Area of Freedom, Security and Justice' (2013) CEPS Paper in Liberty and Security in Europe No 58, 4.

[11] ibid.

[12] Madalina Busuioc and Martin Lodge, 'The Reputational Basis of Public Accountability' (2015) LSE Discussion Paper No 78 <http://www.lse.ac.uk/accounting/CARR/pdf/DPs/CARR-DP78-BusuiocLodge.pdf> accessed 25 July 2018; Erving Goffman, *Presentation of Self in Everyday Life* (Penguin 1959) 243.

role in oversight, yet oversight behind closed doors does not enable citizens to gain a better understanding of or clarity about the allocation of responsibilities on what the EU does and whether these decisions are made at the national or European level. Furthermore, it results in parliamentary oversight arrangements that disproportionally favour peer-to-peer accountability, without sufficient—or any—involvement of citizens and civil society as external scrutiny and relevant stakeholders for debate on the margins of EU secrecy. This form of oversight weakens the core constitutional function of public deliberation for the EP. Whether and to what extent official secrets also negatively impact judicial review and the core protections of fundamental rights is the focus of the next section.

Judicial Review and Official Secrets in the EU

The Court allows different levels of secrecy limitations to the right of access to justice and the right of public access to documents. Such differences are based on the necessities and rationales of these different rights. Public access to information norms aim to support the realization of democratic principles, such as accountability and participation, whereas the right of the individual to her file is crucial for a meaningful exercise of essential procedural rights and access to justice specifically. In the context of security measures, judicial review may be the ultimate safeguard. As Advocate General Sharpston emphasized in the *OMPI* case, in the context of security measures against terrorism, judicial review 'is all the more essential because it constitutes the *only safeguard* ensuring that a fair balance is struck between the need to combat international terrorism and the protection of fundamental rights'.[13] Another important aspect is the difference in transparency cultures of the Member States (MS) regarding public access to information.[14] Whereas some MS might not ensure the right to public access to documents at all or leave a very broad scope to administrative discretion, others have a strong (constitutional) tradition to maintain the openness

[13] Case C-27/09 P *French Republic v People's Mojahedin Organization of Iran*, Opinion of AG Sharpston EU:C:2011:482 (Sharpston Opinion), para 75, author's emphasis.

[14] Paul Craig, *EU Administrative Law* (OUP 2012) see especially 356–66. See also Deirdre Curtin, 'Digital Government in the European Union: Freedom of Information Trumped by "Internal Security"' in Alasdair Roberts (ed), *National Security and Open Government: Striking the Right Balance* (The Maxwell School of Syracuse University 2003).

and availability of public information.[15] This is in contrast with procedural rights of a fair trial and right to defence, which are common in all legal orders of MS and furthermore are stipulated in the European Convention of Human Rights (ECHR).[16]

In both types of cases, the Court ensures a limitation to the institutions' discretion and aims to ensure that the relevant right is upheld through the requirement of a statement of reasons. However, this statement of reasons is rather 'thin' and hence it is questionable to what extent it could be seen as sufficient scrutiny of the institution and a safeguard of the right. The Court has stated that the degree of precision of the statement of reasons 'must be weighed against practical realities and the time and technical facilities available for making the decision'.[17] For international relations, under the exception of Article 4(1)(a) Regulation 1049/01, the Court leaves a margin for institutional discretion by only requiring a short statement of reasons from the party. The Court justifies such brevity 'by the need not to undermine the sensitive interests protected by the exceptions … through disclosure of the very information which those exceptions are designed to protect'.[18] Similarly, in cases of the sanctions regime, the Court accepts a short statement of reasons. For example, in the case of *Council v Fulmen*,[19] the Court held that the statement of reasons may be brief and it is considered as a satisfactory level of information *if* the individual is able to first, understand what the person is accused of and second, on basis of such information the individual is able to dispute either the accuracy or the relevance of the information. The evidence does not need to be detailed, as the Court held in *Al-Aqsa v Council*.[20] Scholars have pointed out that in cases of sanctions, the Court has adopted a structurally lower standard of review in order to avoid repeated annulments.[21] Yet, more worrisome than the lack of an elaborate statement of reasons is the General Court's (GC) new

[15] See also Ulf Oberg, 'EU Citizen's Right to Know: The Improbable Adoption of a European Freedom of Information Act' (1999) 2 Cambridge Yearbook of European Legal Studies 303.

[16] See art 6 ECHR.

[17] Case T-228/02 *OMPI* EU:T:2006:384, para 141; Case C-350/88 *Delacre and Others v Commission* EU:C:1990:71, para 16.

[18] See Case C-266/05 P *Sison v Council* (known as *Sison II*) EU:C:2007:75, para 82; Case T-110/03 *Sison v Council* EU:T:2005:143, paras 62 and 63.

[19] Case C-280/12 P *Council v Fulmen and Mahmoudian* EU:C:2013:775, paras 61, 62, 68.

[20] Joined Cases C-539/10 P and C-550/10 P *Al-Aqsa v Council* and *The Netherlands v Al-Aqsa* EU:C:2012:711.

[21] See also Christina Eckes, *EU Counter-Terrorist Policies and Fundamental Rights: The Case of Individual Sanctions* (OUP 2009).

procedural rules that allow for secret evidence during judicial review when classified documents are involved. In the next subsection, I examine the scope of this procedure and its implications for access to justice after elaborating how review of classified information took place prior to the changes of the Procedural Rules.

EU judicial review prior to the official secrets revisions

A variety of security policies in the Area of Freedom, Security and Justice and Common Foreign and Security Policies gave rise to tensions between closed evidence and access to justice, particularly cases relating to anti-terrorism measures such as individual sanctions[22] or expulsion measures under grounds of public security.[23] The EU Courts were repeatedly confronted with the claims of the Council and/or MS that some information was of confidential nature and too security sensitive to be disclosed to the defendant. In some of these cases, secrecy claims extended not only to the defendant, but to the Court as well, that is denying even the EU Court access to closed material.

This is relevant in order to understand how the EU Courts approached claims to closed evidence prior to Article 105. Firstly, illustrated by the *Kadi* case, the Court made its own assessment whether the material was security sensitive, as claimed by the Council, and hence had to be kept secret from the defendant.[24] If the Court found that the reasons provided by the Council do not preclude partial disclosure, the Court asked the institution to disclose the information.[25] In cases where the institution refused to disclose the information, the Court only based its assessment on the material that had been disclosed. However, if the Court found that the claim to closed evidence was well founded, that is the security sensitivity of the information justified keeping the material undisclosed to the defendant, the Court affirmed its authority to conduct the *final* assessment as to whether

[22] Council Common Position 2001/931/CFSP of 27 December 2001 on the application of specific measures to combat terrorism [2001] OJ L344/93; Council Regulation (EC) No 2580/2001 of 27 December 2001 on specific restrictive measures directed against certain persons and entities with a view to combating terrorism [2001] OJ L344/70.

[23] Derogation from free movement of person on the basis of art 45(3) TFEU and art 52 TFEU. MS may derogate from EU law on the basis of security and also in the areas of the free movement of goods (art 36 TFEU) and capital (art 65 TFEU).

[24] Joined Cases C-584, C-593, and 595/10 P *European Commission and Others v Yassin Abdullah Kadi* EU:C:2013:518 (*Kadi II*).

[25] ibid.

and to what extent the failure to disclose the classified information to the individual affected her ability to defend her rights and the Court took this into consideration in its final judgment.[26] Yet, an important caveat to cases prior to Article 105 is the Court's ability to access closed material. In a number of cases MS refused to grant access to closed material to the Court by invoking the Court's lack of security rules as an obstacle to sharing information.

Secondly, the Court strongly maintained a minimum threshold of disclosure to the defendant. This requirement of the Court was core in safeguarding the right of access to justice prior to the revised rules of procedure. In cases concerning counter-terrorist measures or expulsion on the basis of public security, the Court had consistently held that some information must be available to the individual even if such disclosure was minimal.[27] In the case of *OMPI*, the first decision of the Court in which it annulled an autonomous EU list of terrorist suspects,[28] the Court clearly held that without the relevant information the person adversely affected by the measure would not be in the position to submit her observations to correct an error or produce information in favour of her position and crucially, that the Court itself must be able to take a fully informed decision.[29]

Lastly, the Court maintained a procedural safeguard to ensure fair trial by requiring a statement of reasons by the institution invoking closed evidence. For example, the *ZZ* case shows that for the expulsion of an EU citizen on the basis of national security concerns, the individual must be given a precise and comprehensive statement of the grounds of the decision.[30] If providing a comprehensive statement would imply the disclosure of national security sensitive information, the authorities nevertheless

[26] ibid para 129; Case C-300/11 *ZZ v Secretary of State for the Home Department* EU:C:2013:363, para 67.

[27] See Case T-284/08 *People's Mojahedin Organization of Iran v Council* (OMPI/PMOI III) EU:T:2008:550, paras 71–73; Case C-27/09 P *France v People's Mojahedin Organization of Iran* EU:C:2011:853. See also Christina Eckes, 'Decision-making in the Dark? Autonomous EU Sanctions and National Classification' Amsterdam Centre for European Law and Governance Working Paper Series 2012-02, 12–13.

[28] See Eckes, *EU Counter-Terrorist Policies and Fundamental Rights: The Case of Individual Sanctions* (n 21) 306.

[29] As Eckes (n 21) 307 points out, the 'Court could hardly have expressed criticism more clearly' towards the executive institution regarding the secret nature of the procedure that led to the listing of OMPI and resulted in the Court not being in a position to take an informed decision.

[30] *ZZ v Secretary of State for the Home Department* (n 26).

remain obliged to provide a *summary of reasons*. The Court stressed that the individual must have 'full knowledge of relevant facts'.[31] In the case of *Council v Fulmen*,[32] the Court held that the statement of reasons could be brief *if* the individual was able to first, understand what the person is accused of and second, on the basis of such information, to dispute either the accuracy or the relevance of the information. The Court confirmed in *Al-Aqsa v Council*[33] that the statement of reasons does not need to be detailed.

These three aspects taken together ensured to a sufficient extent that the Court was able to safeguard access to justice rights for the individual whilst maintaining a level of official secrets that ensured the security interests of the executive authorities. Yet, these arrangements were not deemed satisfactory by national authorities to trust the Court with the sharing of their national classified documents. Rather, more emphasis on the security and secrecy of information was required from the Court, leading the Court to review its Rules of Procedure. Under the consultation of the Council's Security Committee, new changes were introduced. The following subsection focuses on the new procedure of review of classified documents.

Secret evidence and access to justice

As discussed above, in a large number of cases pertaining to the individual sanctions regime, national authorities consistently refused to share classified documents with the EU Courts. In such instances, it was a practice that the Court did not take into account the arguments raised by the executive institutions on the basis of undisclosed material. The Court repeatedly annulled the Council's decisions precisely on the basis of secrecy and lack

[31] *Kadi II* (n 24) para 100.

[32] *Council v Fulmen and Mahmoudian* (n 19) paras 61, 62, 68.

[33] *Al-Aqsa v Council* and *The Netherlands v Al-Aqsa* (n 20). A relevant distinction is whether the individual is listed for the first time or whether it is a recurring measure. When the individual is initially listed, the statement of reasons does not need to be issued before the measure is applied so as to preserve the element of 'surprise' that secrecy offers. In the application of security measures, secrecy may be used to create a situation where the intended target is left unprepared to take counteraction. In sanctions cases, in order for the measure to be successful, the individual should not be aware that her assets will be frozen. In specific circumstances it is also possible that 'restrictions on access may concern the specific content of or particular reasoning of [the restrictive] decision, or even the identity of the authority that took it'. See *OMPI* (n 17) para 148. Regarding the subsequent listing, considering that the element of surprise is no longer necessary, the institution must provide the 'actual and specific reasons' for the justification of the continuation of the measure *OMPI*, para 143.

of access to the classified information. This persistent issue of lack of access to classified documents for the Court led to revisions of the Court's rules of procedure that introduced secret evidence. [34]

In April 2015, the GC adopted its new Rules of Procedure, which were fully negotiated and established behind closed doors. Article 105 of the proposed Rules of Procedure, explicitly stipulated the treatment of confidential information and material for the first time in the Court's history. This provision, 'intended to fill a legislative gap',[35] stipulates what is called secret evidence as a possible basis for the Court's decisions.[36]

According to Article 105 of the Rules of Procedure of the GC, if the material is confidential and shared with the GC it will not be submitted to the other party. Consequences of different natures regarding disclosure to the other party could follow, depending on the GC's evaluation whether the material should indeed be undisclosed on the basis of security concerns for the EU or its MS. On the one hand, the GC could ask the submitting party to disclose the information to the other main party if the GC finds that it would not damage the interests protected. If the submitting party refuses or is unresponsive to the GC's request, the latter will not take the confidential material into consideration in its overall review of the case. In fact, this procedure has already been applicable in previous cases at the Court such as *ZZ* or *OMPI* before any revisions to the procedural arrangements. On the other hand, if the GC finds that the disclosure of the confidential material vis-à-vis the other main party could be harmful, the GC 'shall not communicate that information or material to that main party'.[37] In line with Article 105(6), the party may only receive 'a non-confidential version or a non-confidential summary of the information or material, containing the essential content thereof and enabling the other main party, to the greatest extent possible, to make its views known'. This second new option for the GC raises questions of the compatibility of the provision of non-disclosure with the right to a fair trial.

Yet, the clearest limitation of access to justice is the stipulation under Article 105(8) of the Rules of Procedure. Under this provision, the Court

[34] Vigjilenca Abazi and Christina Eckes, 'Closed Evidence in EU Courts: Security, Secrets and Access to Justice' (2018) 55 Common Market Law Review 753.

[35] Council of the European Union, Draft Rules of Procedure of the General Court, 17 March 2014, Council Doc 7795/14, 102.

[36] Rules of Procedure of the General Court [2015] OJ L105/1, art 105(6).

[37] ibid art 105(5).

may base its judgment on secret evidence without disclosing even a non-confidential summary to the applicant. This level of secrecy in judicial review marks a clear departure from the Court's approach in its case law prior to the introduction of Article 105, according to which a minimum of information must be disclosed to the applicant. The provision seems to fully relinquish the possibility of the 'gist' of information, an issue that Advocate General Sharpston has also argued in favour of in order for the provision to actually be in accordance with Article 6 of the ECHR. [38] The 'gist' of disclosure implies that the party would be:

> provided with sufficient information about the allegations against him to enable him to give effective instructions to the special advocate and that any difficulties caused to the defendant by a limitation on his rights [be] sufficiently counterbalanced by the procedures followed by the judicial authorities.[39]

Although limitations to the adversarial principle are possible, under which all information and material must be fully communicated between the parties,[40] it is questionable whether this new arrangement of the GC accommodates secrecy claims more favourably and to the detriment of essential procedural safeguards. Serious doubts have been expressed regarding the compatibility of this new provision in the GC's Rules of Procedure with Article 6 of the ECHR.[41] The following subsection identifies the specific aspects of the secret evidence procedure that are problematic, and even incompatible, with the established standards on access to justice and the lawful use of secret evidence.

Lawfulness of secret evidence: The 'gist' of disclosure

Access to justice is a fundamental right in the EU. The GC interprets EU fundamental rights in accordance with the approach taken by the ECtHR. The latter is a direct result of the fact that Article 53 of the Charter of

[38] Cian C Murphy, 'Secret Evidence in EU Security Law: Special Advocates before the Court of Justice?' (2012) Centre for European Law, Working Papers in European Law, Working Paper 02/2012 <https://www.kcl.ac.uk/law/research/centres/european/research/CELWPEL022012FINAL.pdf> accessed 25 July 2018.

[39] Opinion of AG Sharpston in *France v People's Mojahedin Organization of Iran* (n 13) para 244.

[40] See Rules of Procedure of the General Court, art 64.

[41] Maya Lester, 'Organisations Call on European Court to Consult on Classified Evidence Rule Change' (*European Sanctions*, 27 July 2013) <http://europeansanctions.com/2013/07/27/organisations-call-on-european-court-to-consult-on-classified-evidence-rule-change/> accessed 25 July 2018. See Abazi and Eckes (n 34).

Fundamental Rights requires that a Charter right corresponding to a right under the Convention should be interpreted in the same way as the Convention right and that protection under the Charter must at all times respect the minimum standard of the Convention.[42] Primary EU law also requires that the EU's general principles are inter alia based on the ECHR.[43] The case law of ECtHR establishes a number of specific requirements under which the use of secrecy would be considered lawful, also examined elsewhere.[44] Such requirements pertain both to the procedure in which secret evidence is introduced in the EU as well as the substantive aspects of the margin of review for the courts. First and foremost, the use of secret evidence must be seen as an exception, which in turn is narrowly interpreted and its use must be necessary in the specific case. Related to this, the authority for the decision on the discretion of classified information must be set for an independent court that has in turn full access to information. Furthermore, if information is withheld additional safeguards must be introduced to ensure the impartiality of the court.

The core and minimum requirement of the adversarial principle is that at all times the gist of information is disclosed to the applicant. This key requirement sets the core and basic criterion for the lawful use of secret evidence. To what extent the applicant receives any information on the evidence that constitutes a basis for the judgment by the Court is a determinant on whether there is any safeguard for access to justice and the defence of the applicant. The case law of the ECtHR as well as the CJEU prior to the revised rules has been clear and consistent that a minimum level of information should always be disclosed to the applicant. Such minimum level of disclosure is particularly urgent in cases where the measures have a severe effect on the applicant, such as is the case with sanctions.

[42] While the Charter only refers to the Convention itself and not to the case law of the ECtHR (except in its Preamble), the ECJ has ruled in *J.McB. v L.E.* that where rights in the Charter correspond to rights in the ECHR, it will follow the case law of the ECtHR; Case C-400/10, *J.McB v L.E.* EU:C:2010:582.

[43] Art 6(3) TEU.

[44] See Abazi, Eckes (n 34). See cases that pertain to closed evidence at the ECtHR: *Rowe v UK* Appl No 28901/95, judgment of 16 February 2000, paras 60–63; *Atlan v UK* Appl No 36533/97, judgment of 19 June 2001; *Dowsett v UK* Appl No 39482/98, judgment of 14 May 20021; *Fitt v UK*, Appl. No. 29777/96, judgment of 16 February 2000; *Jasper v UK* Appl No 27052/95, judgment of 16 February 2000; *Edwards v UK* Series A No 247-B, judgment of 25 November 1992; *Botmeh and Alami v UK* Appl No 15187/03, judgment of 7 June 2007.

The lack of disclosing even the gist of information to the applicant under Article 105(8) of the Rules of Procedure of the Court fails to meet the standards of disclosure as set by the ECtHR as well as the case law established by the CJEU prior to the revised rules. It is unclear why the Rules of Procedure of the GC do not follow the case law and the requirements on the gist of disclosure to the extent that it goes against the right of access to justice. The Court has taken into account the security concerns of national authorities regarding sharing of classified documents, however this level of secrecy as part of judicial review is not in line with prior case law or the standards of review as set by the ECtHR. In this regard, and similarly as the EP explained above, the Court seems to have disproportionally focused on ensuring arrangements that work in favour of receiving access to classified documents, but without taking sufficiently into account to what extent such implications harm fundamental EU rights, such as access to justice.

Conclusions

This chapter showed how the practice of oversight has been fundamentally affected by the rules on classified information since both the EP and the CJEU have made changes to their oversight arrangements leading to closed oversight and secret evidence in the EU. With the aim of ensuring access to classified information, these EU oversight institutions have made changes that significantly alter public debate and right of access to justice in the EU. What is remarkable about these changes to the procedural rules is that they have been developed and adopted by the EP and the CJEU mostly behind closed doors whilst they negatively impact core constitutional prerogatives and obligations.

These changes to the oversight arrangements are not proportionate to the EP's obligations for public deliberation or with the Court's standard of review in safeguarding the fundamental right of access to justice. In this respect, the revised procedures for oversight of classified documents are problematic both from a procedural standpoint, as these processes of oversight were revised behind closed doors, as well as from a substantive perspective, taking into account that they fundamentally alter and negatively affect constitutional principles and rights. Although these revisions have followed legally set paths for the Rules of Procedure, that is both the Court and the EP have certain discretions in terms of changing their

Rules of Procedures, it is questionable whether changes that have such a profound impact on principles and rights in the EU should be fully under the discretion of internal procedural rules and without any public debate on the matter.

These changes to procedural rules have not tackled the main problem that they were initially set out to address, which is the accessibility to classified information for oversight institutions. The latter still depends on executive discretion through the originator rule. Rather than revising the originator rule such as through adopting more constraints in its application, the oversight institutions have internalized this rule and it is now ingrained in the overall system of official secrets in the EU. This in turn has led to a negative implication for the role of oversight institutions in the arrangements of official secrets in the EU. Namely, instead of contributing towards making the EU classification regime more prone to the presumption in favour of openness, the oversight institutions have actually adopted the logic of secrecy and security as put forward by executive institutions. This logic in turn directly clashes with the key constitutional principles and rights, which oversight institutions are meant to safeguard in the EU legal order.

Conclusion

Abstracts
This concluding chapter brings to the fore the main findings of this book. It also offers observations for the implications of official secrets and what they tell us about oversight in the EU. The chapter summarizes that the establishment and the practice of official secrets ignore democratic constraints, they provide for an almost absolute discretion to executive actors and inaccessibility of official secrets is a recurrent problem for oversight institutions. Official secrets and oversight in the EU have been pragmatically settled behind closed doors. Yet, as a legal order committed to constitutional values of democracy, the book concludes that the EU should publically debate a law that affirms openness as a guiding principle in how secrets are kept.

This book is situated within and drew from two distinct academic debates: on the one hand, the book explored official secrets on the basis of the vast literature on secrecy drawing from political science and democratic theory. On the other hand, the book examined the intricacies of EU law, specifically its constitutional underpinnings and administrative practice. The effort of this book was to synergize the knowledge from these rich discussions in order to provide the first comprehensive and systematic analysis of official secrets and oversight in the EU.

The book sought to assess how the rules and practices of EU official secrets, and the legal and institutional responses to it, have affected institutional relations, particularly in oversight, as well as fundamental rights, especially access to justice and access to information. The book was centred on four main themes. Firstly, the book examined the *governance of official secrets* understood as the decision-making structures, regulatory frameworks, and rules that regulate the flow of information with a specific focus on its emergence and expansion in the EU. Secondly, the book delved into administrative practices of official secrets and through original interviews drawn from forty interviews with relevant stakeholders, in order to detail how *executive discretion* works in practice. The book also examined executive discretion in the design of the regulatory framework. Thirdly, the book showed the dynamics of *oversight* relations and the reoccurring challenges for access to classified documents for the European Parliament (EP), the Court of Justice of the European Union (CJEU), and the European Ombudsman (EO). Whilst initially contesting the regime of official secrets the book shows how oversight institutions co-opt into the rationales of official secrets, especially with the increased security role of the EU. Lastly, the book focused on the implications of official secrets for *fundamental rights* in the EU, particularly access to justice and access to information. Drawing from relevant case law on access to justice by the CJEU as well as the European Court of Human Rights (ECtHR), the book argued that current rules allowing for secret evidence fail to meet the standards of protection of access to justice.

From a democratic perspective, the book argued that current governance of official secrets is problematic and pointed to the structural and substantial changes in the exercise of oversight and fundamental rights in the EU. It would be normatively desirable for oversight institutions to assume responsibility and pave the way forward to establish a law of official secrets that would be publicly debated and guided by EU constitutional principles.

Findings

A guiding principle in the design of the regulatory framework of official secrets, which would adhere to constitutional principles of democracy and openness, is to establish institutional arrangements that safeguard necessary secrets without impeding democratic processes that rely on openness. This book proposed democratic constraints for EU governance of official secrets ensuring this principle. The findings regarding the EU's institutional arrangements follow the established three main democratic constraints to official secrets. To recall, firstly, openness is essential for both the processes of accountability and deliberation. Hence, the book argued that limits to openness must be legitimate and necessary. Secondly, accessibility to the relevant information is the first and key step for the initiation of oversight, which therefore poses the additional constraint that openness cannot be limited to the extent that oversight ceases. Thirdly, with respect to public deliberation, openness cannot be limited to the extent that the public does not know whether a secret is being kept or does not know the outcome of oversight.

Limited review in ensuring a legitimate governance of official secrets

The basic and most difficult issue to ascertain is whether a claim to classify a document as an official secret is necessary and legitimate save for cases where the abuse of power or negligence is obvious. This constraint is not only directed at a singular case of invoking the authority to classify documents, but it also relates to how the system of official secrets is established. This constraint was assessed in different chapters of the book relating to the regulation of official secrets, the practice of establishing individual decisions of classification, as well as whether and how the CJEU, the EP, and the EO assess executive claims to official secrets and safeguard openness to the extent that is necessary for effectuating individual rights and public deliberation.

Chapter 2 demonstrates that the executive institutions, particularly the Council, have led to the establishment of the regulation of official secrets in the EU. Executive actors have been solely and completely in charge of the design of the architecture of official secrets in the EU. The Council, and the Commission to some extent, established the rules of official secrets in a piecemeal approach, with separate internal rules for each institution, agency, or body. This patchwork regulation of official secrets is established in a shadowy manner and defended by EU officials as the only possible manner to establish rules due to the lack of explicit legal bases in the Treaties. This lack of a legal act unifying the governance of official secrets led to a concerted push by the Council, in particular its Security Committee, for a horizontal 'harmonization' of rules through peer pressure and common standards encompassing not only the executive actors but also oversight institutions. Remarkably, the oversight actors did not establish their rules in a more open manner or openly debate the consequences of such rules for openness. These efforts towards introducing similarities in the rules are not steered towards openness. Limitations of public access to documents and openness in the EU more generally are not considered as a matter for concern or a constraint on the regulation of official secrets in the EU, which in turn implies that the logic of necessary and legitimate secrets is lacking from an openness perspective in the EU regulation of classified information.

Chapter 3 addresses who has the power to make the assessment of whether a claim to classify documents is necessary and legitimate. This is particularly relevant to the individual decisions of classifications made in EU practice as well as to the oversight actors' *ex post* evaluation. Every EU official can potentially classify documents. The initial decision to classify a document is not supported or guided in any manner, which would make the official with classifying authority more aware and prudent of the consequences of her decision from an openness perspective. The determination of what is necessary and hence legitimate to be classified in the EU is strictly limited to security concerns. The decision to classify raises further concerns when we turn to the legal terminology applicable for the four different labels of classification: '*Restricted*', '*Confidential*', '*Secret*', '*Top Secret*'. The interests that are supposed to be protected are stated in a broad manner and in practice they can encompass anything from negotiation mandates, to background facts or simply the interests of the official with classifying authority. As some candid statements from EU officials illustrated, it is also the case that some officials use the security label as a signal of importance for their work in what was noted as 'stamps-of-importance'.

Some level of discretion is always involved when making decisions whether to classify a particular document. This is a crucial aspect of the system of classifying information and one that EU officials are aware of as something that is inevitable in the system. This therefore makes the sanctioning of the decision to classify or instilling other internal mechanisms of review very important in order to keep administrative discretion in check. Nevertheless in the EU the predominant manner of classifying documents is through derivative classification, which implies that EU officials reproduce, extract, or summarize classified information and apply classification markings derived from the original source material. In most cases, the latter is information deriving from the Member States (MS). The derivative classification operates strictly from a security perspective and enforces a more rigid secrecy culture as it makes the highest classification label applicable to the entire document when, for example, a variety of documents with different security labels are used. Furthermore, it creates an element of non-responsibility for the EU officials, as the official merely needs to reproduce the classification stamp without challenging it. In fact, from a security perspective, maintaining the originator's security label is seen as a positive aspect of the rules because it provides the necessary assurances of a rigid security culture. Through derivative classification the national culture of secrecy pierces through at the EU level. Although derivative classification reduces the EU level discretion on classifying, it certainly does not imply that over-classification is avoided since, as EU officials' statements reveal, some national capitals have a tendency to over-classify.

Against this background, Chapter 4 raised the pertinent question of the external review of the assessment of necessary and legitimate secrecy. EU executive institutions do not have the sole prerogative to determine the level of secrecy in the EU when it comes to classified information. Each oversight institution has some powers to limit the claims to official secrets.

The EP has the most direct mechanism for giving an opinion regarding the classification decision of whether a document should be classified or the level of classification, but this is strictly limited with regard to documents of the Commission. The Council was specifically opposed to the EP having such powers with regard to classified documents, regardless of the policy area. The Court and the EO have review mechanisms that are focused on the failure of the executive institutions and bodies to disclose information and address the implications arising from non-disclosure.

The Court exercises a 'marginal' review in cases pertaining to the right of public access to information and allows a higher margin of executive discretion for non-disclosure. The Court assesses whether the procedural rules and duty to state reasons have been complied with, whether the facts have been accurately stated, and whether there has been a manifest error of assessment of the facts or misuse of power. Yet the Court seems to gradually establish a differentiation on the applicability of the exceptions under Article 4(1)(a) of Regulation 1049/01. In this vein, if the undisclosed document concerns public interests and relates to possible future legislative changes and in particular fundamental rights, the Court seems to favour disclosure even in connection with security and international relations exceptions and hence limits the extent of executive secrecy in these fields. In cases when access to justice is at stake, the Court explicitly affirms its authority to conduct the final assessment as to whether and to what extent the failure to disclose classified information to the individual concerned affects her ability to defend her rights and takes this into consideration in the final judgment. Yet, in line with the revised Rules of Procedure of the General Court, a severe option is included of not providing the individual or her lawyer with any access to official secrets whilst taking into account such documents in the final judgment. Hence, whilst the powers of the Court for access to and review of official secrets has increased, this has had a directly negative effect on the access to those documents by the individual and her lawyer.

The EO has the power to request the documents and determine if public access should be granted or whether disclosure would undermine the interests that the institution claims to protect. In line with the cases examined, practice shows that the EO has never asked an institution to declassify a document. It is not within the scope of the EO's review to examine whether a classification marking is justified and necessary. In cases dealing with the refusal of access based on the protection of international relations, the EO refers to documents whose disclosure was refused in a brief manner, merely stating that disclosure of certain documents should be reconsidered. The institution that refuses access to sensitive information must give its reasons for refusal. The role of the EO is limited to verifying whether the institution has complied with this duty.

Closed oversight and continuous challenges of access to official secrets

An additional constraint in line with the theoretical framework established in this book is that openness cannot be limited to the extent to which the realization of oversight is obstructed. Oversight institutions must have the means to know or to access official secrets independently from the discretion of the secret-keeper. The external oversight institutions should not fully rely on the willingness of executive institutions to disclose official secrets. However, this normative perspective is not upheld in the case of the EU. The current oversight structure in the EU faces typical challenges of oversight in security policies due to the struggle regarding access to classified information as a result of predominant executive discretion.

Chapter 4 shows that by law the institutions enjoy 'privileged' access to classified information, which derives specifically from their constitutionally stipulated role in oversight. This implies that access is strictly related to the institution's prerogatives and that the information is not made publicly accessible. However, limitations to access are very significant and they concern the rule of originator control that extends to the point of fully blocking access to classified information for oversight actors. EU oversight actors are reliant on executive actors for access to official secrets and face a clear limitation that can be invoked against their privileged right to access. This limitation is stipulated both internally within the rules of oversight actors, hence it is based on EU law, as well as being included in all external arrangements and agreements that the EU has with third parties and with MS.

Many of the problematic aspects regarding access to classified information have their origin in the executive engineering of the regulatory regime. This is the case because, as Chapter 2 argues, the system of official secrets in the EU is established and functions to foster a rigid security culture and openness considerations are lacking. The establishment of the EU regulation of secrecy was predominately driven by administrative pragmatism, is influenced by NATO military secrecy, and is strictly security-oriented.

Chapter 2 further reveals that the executive actors have discretion to decide on whether information should be disclosed to the oversight institution when the originator rule is invoked. This level of final control does not emerge from constitutional norms but has been developed in the EU by the executive institutions themselves. The originator control leads to consequences of classification and blocking information that is disproportionate because it not only affects the original document but also the deriving documents. This effectively leads to the EU documents de facto never breaking away from national and foreign classification decisions. Instead, the originators ensure a permanent link and discretion, which could possibly result not only in blocking privileged access but also in creating over-classification.

Paradoxically, in the period when the oversight institutions had not yet established internal rules on official secrets and hence their oversight practices did not incorporate secrecy, the oversight of executive action was more rigid and the institutional battles to gain access to classified information were more pronounced. This arose because there was stronger opposition to and rejection of the rules of official secrets, and particularly the EP made efforts to point out the secretive way in which the executives established the system. In fact, the EP was for a long period fully opposed to the establishment of the regulation of official secrets in the EU. The CJEU too was firm and categorically did not accept secret evidence, that is material that is undisclosed to the party. The internalization of rules on official secrets by EU oversight institutions is a turning point for secrecy and its practice and oversight in the EU. Partly, EU oversight institutions incorporated the originator control because they had no option to do otherwise at the time the legal arrangements for access to EU executive classified information were made. To some extent, however, the oversight institutions have accepted the originator rule without fully realizing its limitations. The current oversight structures in the EU no longer challenge the manner in which official secrets operate and have become part of the sharing ring of classified information.

Hindering public deliberation

For the realization of deliberation, openness cannot be limited to the extent that the public would not know at all whether something is being kept secret or know the outcomes of oversight. The book shows that in the EU deep secrecy is possible in cases concerning the right of public access to documents. Deep secrecy refers to information or documents whose very existence is unknown as opposed to shallow secrets, where the content of the document is protected (undisclosed) but its existence is public or could be disclosed. The Court affirmed that the originator of sensitive information, which could be an EU institution or agency, MS, or a third party, is justified in refusing not only to disclose the document's content but also its *very existence* on basis of Article 9(3) of Regulation 1049/01 and that the identity of the originator could also remain undisclosed.

Chapter 5 elaborates on the relevance of openness in oversight for facilitating public deliberation. However, EU oversight actors did not fully debate or realize what the effects of the rules of official secrets would be for their core functions of oversight, deliberation, and protecting EU fundamental rights. Firm conclusions on this matter cannot be drawn since both the EP and the General Court (GC) made the changes to their rules in a secret manner, without any involvement by outside concerned parties and in fact instead, in the case of the GC, explicitly rejected public legal opinion submitted to it by advocates of access to justice. It remains speculative whether oversight institutions could have established different legal arrangements about rules of official secrets with more public pressure, but we clearly see that closed-door meetings of oversight actors have led to institutional arrangements that are unsatisfactory from a democratic perspective. Closed oversight creates the effect that oversight actors become part of the system that legitimizes the governance of official secrets, but creates a further separation and distance between oversight institutions and the citizens whose rights and interests they are meant to protect.

From a perspective of deliberation and public knowledge, the role of MEPs is not merely to ensure that executive actors are not breaching their powers, but it is fundamental that they provide the link between what takes place at the executive decision-making level and the citizens. It is necessary from this perspective that the MEPs discuss and communicate how the interests and rights of citizens are affected. However, due to closed oversight and the obligations of the EP not to disclose official secrets, the specific outcomes of oversight processes are not made public. Access to classified information and the issues contained therein are not allowed to be included in the meeting minutes. The EP has no other institutional measures through which it could alert the public and raise concerns regarding issues covered by official secrets, which could possibly lead to the avoidance of policy controversy, transparency, and critical debate. Individual MEPs could, for example, alert the press on some issues they consider relevant for further discussion. However, this manner of bringing attention to policy questions could also be driven by political interests that are not only concerned with public debate and transparency. Parliamentary questions are the only institutional form of public oversight. They are also published on EP's website as well as in the EU's official journal. The caveat here is that the content of classified information is not discussed. Hence, oversight processes that are open may leave crucial questions regarding classified information unanswered by invoking executive confidentiality.

The EU oversight institutions aim to assert their role in oversight, yet oversight behind closed doors does not enable citizens to gain a better understanding of or clarity about the allocation of responsibilities on what the EU does and whether these decisions are made at the national or European level.

Constitutional Implications

Peer-to-peer accountability

The governance of official secrets in the EU creates a structural imbalance of power. The EU oversight institutions are reliant on the discretion of secret-keepers to actually conduct their constitutional prerogatives and core functions in the EU. The main implication for the oversight institutions that have internalized and incorporated the rules of official secrets is that establishing oversight arrangements disproportionally favours peer-to-peer accountability while leading to closed oversight and secret evidence. These new oversight arrangements create further distance from the potential for public deliberation in the EU and give rise to serious concerns about the impact on fundamental rights, particularly on effective judicial protection. Rules of official secrets have re-structured oversight in the EU because the EU oversight institutions have changed their review procedures to safeguard official secrets. In their efforts to conduct oversight in the face of new security policies in the EU that require the use of secrecy, EU oversight institutions have adjusted to secrecy and security rationales. This, however, has come at the cost of negative implications for public deliberation and fundamental rights. Official secrets rules are essential for exchanging classified information and, in turn, indispensable for the functioning of security policies. However, the extent to which this system goes unchallenged and the extent to which access to classified information is the main focus of the oversight institutions is unsatisfactory from the perspectives of openness and fundamental rights.

Closed oversight and secret evidence is not unique to the EU. Indeed comparative examples from MS show that they too, despite long traditions of civil liberties, have adapted to and adopted oversight processes that seriously challenge public deliberation and fundamental rights in the face of security and the necessary secrecy rules in this regard. Moreover, the oversight of intelligence agencies has traditionally been more secluded from public view. What is different in the EU, however, is that oversight processes were negotiated by the executive and oversight institutions themselves instead of by publicly debated and constitutionally set arrangements. Rather, these changes have been established in inter-institutional agreements and internal rules of procedure fully negotiated behind closed doors and most of the documents remain undisclosed or are severely redacted even a decade after these arrangements were made.

Security and autonomy: Relations with Member States

Rules of official secrets have been a factor that enabled the EU to make itself independent from the MS, both in information input and the rules for arranging classified information. Furthermore, official secrets regulation has enabled the EU to build relations with important third parties that would not have been possible otherwise and hence increase its own sources of security information. This has put the EU on the map with respect to the exchange of sensitive information with important actors. Gaining more autonomy through secrecy was an opportunity recognized by EU security actors, specifically Secretary General Solana during his time in office, for the establishment of the classification system and developing an independent EU network for the exchange of official secrets.

The system of classified information has positive implications for the security of the EU and the ability of EU security agencies to receive and exchange classified information. The EU's security policies extend inter alia to military and non-military operations in third countries, sanction regimes as a means of counter-terrorism measures, as well as intelligence reporting and analysis. All these issues rely on the exchange of sensitive information and in turn require that the EU is an informed security actor.

The governance of official secrets has direct implications on the relationship with the MS. In the first instance, it reveals the MS' centrism in EU security policies. A significant aspect in this regard is the EU's dependency on the MS for the exchange of classified documents. In general, MS have retained a dominant position in this sphere and their relation to the system of classified information has taken place in accordance with their national rules. Consequently, their classification culture became indirectly 'binding' on the EU. Historically, MS have different approaches to classification and some do over-classify. Yet, it also shows that the EU has also used the rules of official secrets as a matrix for separation from the MS. The EU has provided itself with the means to create some independence from the MS regarding security due to its direct external cooperation with relevant third parties. Moreover, the EU has direct influence on how the MS share official secrets. In this respect, the Decision of the Secretary General on measures for the protection of classified information adopted in July 2000 also committed the MS to *the extent required* for the proper functioning of the Council. This was a first attempt to encourage the MS to apply EU rules on classification as opposed to national ones more actively.

Towards Official Secrets and Oversight Aligned with EU Constitutional Principles

The basic dilemma of official secrets and oversight is, as noted at the outset of this book, how to delineate necessary official secrets and to ensure the processes of oversight while safeguarding them. The practice in official secrets is characterized by the particularities of the structure and institutional workings of the EU. This adds a layer of complexity with regard to secrecy and oversight as compared to the common national setting. EU practice reveals that the EU is not a producer of original secrets but to a large extent derives its official secrets from the MS and third parties. This means that rigid rules on the exchange of classified information in the EU are more applicable and significant. It also implies that in most situations, EU oversight institutions will request privileged access to derivative official secrets, leading de facto to an external authority, whether the originator body at the national level or of a third state, to decide on the disclosure of the official secrets for the EP, the Court, and the EO.

The EU is characterized by the plurality of executive institutions. In this respect, the exchange of classified information and possible information asymmetries that arise can be seen not only from the angle of the executive towards oversight actors, but also from the angle of the relations between executive actors. Research indicates that MS' executive bodies are reluctant to share classified information with EU-level security and intelligence agencies, but further empirical research could map this underexplored aspect more broadly in the EU, including at a horizontal level.

EU oversight differs from national oversight. First, EU oversight differs in the respect that the EP and the Council consist of different political majorities. The EP is directly elected at EU level whereas the Council has a direct link to the national electorate. Hence, disagreements in policy making are likely, making the availability of the same classified information to the EP relevant for an informed debate and policy choices. Yet, simultaneously within the EU institutional structure, the Council acts as an executive actor and hence has an information advantage as it actually receives official secrets directly from other executive actors. Second, in the procedure of preliminary reference, which is specific to the EU judicial system, the Court does not have a fact-finding function, but merely guides itself through the information submitted to it by the national court. In this respect, the accessibility of classified information at the national level is important for the Court to be able to reach an informed judgment at the EU level, yet EU rules cannot establish procedures of what information national executive agencies give to national courts. Lastly, with regard to the EO, its authority does not extend to national administration and the latter is only obliged to submit classified information to the extent that it concerns the application of EU law. Yet, in practice issues are more intermingled, making the availability of information more limited for the EO.

This book argues that the presumption in favour of openness could be spelled out at the broad policy level of regulating secrecy and with regard to the specific decision to classify documents. At a policy level, applying the presumption in favour of openness means having an EU public debate on official secrets, especially about where and how to draw the difficult lines among oversight, secrecy, and security. Rules of official secrets in the EU have a tremendous impact on oversight and fundamental rights and hence should not be at the full discretion of internal regulation and closed-door debates between EU institutions. The biggest issue with EU administrative practice is that once a classified document is created, it keeps expanding into a number of other classified documents. This does not mean that EU officials prefer secrecy or intentionally over-classify. Yet, due to the structure and rules of classified information, even if one document is classified it amplifies into many more. In current EU practice, there is no internal incentive or pressure to reconsider classification decisions from a perspective of openness and the consequences of over-classification. An EU official has much to lose if she does not classify a document she should have, whereas there are no internal checks or incentives that provide for mechanisms to prevent over-classification. Instead of this, considerations in favour of openness should guide the decision of the official and, specifically, this would mean that the briefing process that every EU official receives at the start of her employment contract could be focused on directly linking classifying information with its openness implications. Moreover, a written justification for the decision to classify a specific document could accompany the document and make it clear what specific reasons make secrecy legitimate and necessary. The registration of classified documents and public records are other specific means of applying the aspect of openness within the classification procedure. Keeping track of classified information is relevant for the usability of the information but even more so for possible declassification purposes. Lastly, more openness and accessibility to documents could be ensured if EU practice favoured and made it a principle that only specific sensitive parts of a document are classified and not necessarily the entire document.

Ultimately, EU constitutional values of democracy and openness should guide and constraint the governance of official secrets, leading to a foundation that acknowledges the functional necessity of official secrets without undermining oversight and fundamental rights.

Annex: List of Respondents

Europol Official, The Hague, 2012 #1
Europol Official, The Hague, 2013 #2
Europol Official, The Hague, 2013 #3
Former Europol Official, The Hague, 2012 #4
Council Official, Brussels, 2013 #5
Council Official, Brussels, 2013 #6
Council Official, Brussels, 2013 #7
Council Official, Brussels, 2013 #8
Council Official, Brussels, 2013 #9
Council Official, Brussels, 2013 # 10
Council Official, Brussels, 2013 # 11
Former Council Official, Brussels, 2013 # 12
Council Official, Brussels, 2013 # 13
Council Official, Brussels, 2013 # 14
Commission Official, Brussels, 2013 #15
Commission Official, Brussels, 2013 # 16
EEAS Official, Brussels, 2013 #17
EEAS Official, Brussels, 2013 #18
EEAS Official, Brussels, 2013 #19
EEAS Official, Brussels, 2015 #20
EEAS Official, Brussels, 2015 #21
EEAS Official, Brussels, 2015 #22
EULEX Official, Pristina, 2013 #23
EULEX Official, Pristina, 2013 #24
European Parliament Respondent, Amsterdam, 2013 #25
European Parliament Respondent, Amsterdam, 2014 #26
European Parliament Respondent, Brussels, 2014 #27
Expert Respondent, Amsterdam, 2014 #28
Expert Respondent, Washington DC, 2014 # 29
Expert Respondent, Washington DC, 2014 #30

Expert Respondent, Washington DC, 2014 #31
Expert Respondent, Maryland, 2014 # 32
Expert Respondent, Cambridge, 2014 # 33
Expert Respondent, New York City, 2014 #34
Expert Respondent, New York City, 2014 # 35
Expert Respondent, New York City, 2014 # 36
Expert Respondent, New York City, 2014 #37
Expert Respondent, Chicago, 2014 # 38
Expert Respondent, The Hague, 2014 #39
Expert Respondent, Amsterdam, 2015 #40

BIBLIOGRAPHY

Abazi V, 'The Future of Europol's Parliamentary Oversight: A Great Leap Forward?' (2014) 15(6) German Law Journal 1121.

Abazi V, 'European Parliamentary Oversight Behind Closed Doors' (2016) 5 Cambridge International Law Journal 31.

Abazi V, 'Transparency in the Institutionalisation of Transatlantic Relations: Dynamics of Official Secrets and Access to Information in Security and Trade' in E Fahey (ed), *Institutionalisation Beyond the State: Transatlantic Relations in Data, Privacy and Trade Law* (Springer 2018).

Abazi V and Adriaensen J, 'Allies in Transparency? Parliamentary, Judicial and Administrative Interplays in the EU's International Negotiations' (2017) 5(3) Politics & Governance 75.

Abazi V and Eckes C, 'Closed Evidence in EU Courts: Security, Secrets and Access to Justice' (2018) 55(3) Common Market Law Review 753.

Abazi V and Hillebrandt M, 'The Legal Limits to Confidential Negotiations: Recent Case Law Developments in Council Transparency: *Access Info Europe* and *in 't Veld*' (2015) 52(3) Common Market Law Review 825.

Abazi V and Tauschinsky E, 'Reasons of Control and Trust: Grounding the Public Need for Transparency in the European Union' (2015) 11(2) Utrecht Law Review 78.

Adamski D, 'How Wide is "The Widest Possible?" Judicial Interpretation of the Exceptions to the Right of Access to Official Documents Revisited' (2009) 46(2) Common Market Law Review 521.

Adamski D, 'Approximating a Workable Compromise on Access to Official Documents: The 2011 Developments in the European Courts' (2012) 49 Common Market Law Review 521.

Adrian V, *Mechanisms of Democracy: Institutional Design Writ Small* (OUP 2007).

Aftergood S, 'If in Doubt, Classify' (2008) 37 Index on Censorship 101.

Aftergood S, 'Reducing Government Secrecy: Finding What Works' (2009) 27 Yale Law & Policy Review 399.

Aftergood S, 'An Inquiry into the Dynamics of Government Secrecy' (2013) 48 Harvard Civil Rights—Civil Liberties Law Review 511.

Alemano A, 'Unpacking the Principle of Openness in EU Law: Transparency, Participation and Democracy' (2014) 39 European Law Review 72.

Alemanno A and Stefan O, 'Openness at the Court of Justice of the European Union: Toppling a Taboo' (2014) 51 Common Market Law Review 97.

Alexy R, *A Theory of Constitutional Rights*, J Rivers tr (OUP 2002).

Arnull A, *The European Union and its Court of Justice* (OUP 1999).

Arnull A and Wincott D, *Accountability and Legitimacy in the European Union* (OUP 2002).
Ashton C, 'Quiet Diplomacy Will Get Our Voice Heard' *The Times*, 17 December 2009.
Austin-Smith D and Riker WH, 'Asymmetric Information and the Coherence of Legislation' (1987) 81 American Political Science Review 897.
Bales R, *Personality and Interpersonal Behaviour* (Holt, Rinehart, and Winston 1970).
Balzacq T and Puybareau B, 'The Economy of Secrecy: Security, Information Control, and EU–US relations' (2018) 41(4) West European Politics 890.
Barber B, *Strong Democracy: Participatory Politics for a New Age* (University of California Press 1984).
Beidelman TO, 'Secrecy and Society: The Paradox of Knowing and the Knowing of Paradox' Program of African Studies, Northwestern University, No 5 (1993).
Bensman J and Lilienfeld R, *Between Public and Private: Lost Boundaries of the Self* (Free Press 1979).
Bentham J, 'Of Publicity' in J Bowring (ed), *Essays on Political Tactics in the Works of Jeremy Bentham* (William Tate 1839).
Berkowitz BD and Goodman AE, *Best Truth: Intelligence in the Information Age* (Yale University Press 2002).
Bieber R, Jacque JP, and Weiler JHH (eds), *An Ever Closer Union?* (The European Perspectives Series 1985).
Birchall C, 'Introduction to "Secrecy and Transparency": The Politics of Opacity and Openness' (2011) 28 Theory, Culture and Society 7.
Birkinshaw P, *Freedom of Information: The Law, the Practice and the Ideal* (4th edn, CUP 2010).
Birkinshaw P and Varney M, *European Union Legal Order after Lisbon* (Kluwer Law International 2010).
Bitter S, 'Loyalty in the European Union—A Review' (2002) 3 German Law Journal.
Blank L, 'Introduction' in S Maret and J Goldman (eds), *Government Secrecy: Classic and Contemporary Readings* (Libraries Unlimited 2009).
Blockmans S, 'Between Dream and Reality: Challenges to the Legal Rapprochement of the Western Balkans' in P Van Elsuwege and R Petrov (eds), *Legal Approximation and Application of EU Law in the Eastern Neighbourhood of the European Union: Towards a Common Regulatory Space?* (Routledge 2014).
Blockmans S, Hillion C, Cremona M, Curtin D, De Baere G, Duke S, Eckes C, Van Vooren B, Wessel R, and Wouters J, *EEAS 2.0: A Legal Commentary on Council Decision 2010/427/EU Establishing the Organisation and Functioning of the European External Action Service* (extern rapport) (Centre for European Policy Studies 2013).
Bobbio N, *The Future of Democracy*, R Dellamy ed, R Griffin tr (Polity 1991).

Bodei R, 'From Secrecy to Transparency: Reason of State and Democracy' (2011) 37 Philosophy and Social Criticism 889.

Boer de N, 'Secret Evidence and Due Process Rights under EU Law: *ZZ*' (2014) 51 Common Market Law Review 1235.

Boer de M, Hillebrand C, and Nolkehillebrand, A 'Legitimacy Under Pressure: The European Web of Counter-Terrorism Networks' (2008) 46 Journal of Common Market Studies 101.

Bogdandy van A and Sonnevend P (eds), *Constitutional Crisis in the European Constitutional Area: Theory, Law and Politics in Hungary and Romania* (Hart Publishing 2015).

Bok S, *Secrets: On the Ethics of Concealment and Revelation* (Pantheon Books 1982).

Bok S, 'The Limits of Confidentiality' (1983) 13 The Hasting Center Report 24.

Bovens M, 'Analysing and Assessing Accountability: A Conceptual Framework' (2007) 13 European Law Journal 447.

Brandsma G, 'Accountability Deficits in European "Comitology" Decision-Making' (2007) 11 European Integration Online Papers http://eiop.or.at/eiop/pdf/2007-004.pdf.

Brunkhorst H, Eigmüller M, and Fossum JE, 'European Transformations: Are the Crises Really Over or Is it Just the End of their Beginning?' (2017) 23 European Law Journal 310.

Bugaric B, 'Openness and Transparency in Public Administration: Challenges for Public Law' (2004) 22 Wisconsin International Law Journal 483.

Bunyan T, *Secrecy and Openness in the EU* (Kogan Page Limited 1999).

Burca de G and Witte de B, 'The Delimitation of Powers between the EU and its Member States' in A Arnull and D Wincott (eds), *Accountability and Legitimacy in the European Union* (OUP 2002).

Busuioc M, *European Agencies: Law and Practices of Accountability* (OUP 2013).

Carrera S, Hernanz N, and Parkin, J, 'The "Lisbonisation" of the European Parliament: Assessing Progress, Shortcomings and Challenges for Democratic Accountability in the Area of Freedom, Security and Justice' CEPS Working Paper No 58 (2013).

Chafetz J, 'Whose Secrets?' (2013) 127 Harvard Law Review Forum 86.

Chalmers D, Davies G, and Monti G, *European Union Law* (2nd edn, CUP 2010).

Chambers S, 'Behind Closed Doors: Publicity, Secrecy, and the Quality of Deliberation' (2004) 12 Journal of Political Philosophy 389.

Chaturvedi T, *Secrecy in Government* (Indian Institute of Public Administration 1980).

Chinen MA, 'Secrecy and Democratic Decisions' (2008) 127 Quinnipiac Law Review 101.

Christiansen Th and Piattoni S, *Informal Governance in the European Union* (Edward Elgar Publishing Inc 2003).

Chrysschoou D, *Theorizing European Integration* (Sage Publications 2001).

Colby WE, 'Intelligence Secrecy and Security in a Free Society' (1976) 1 International Security 3.
Conway G, 'Recovering a Separation of Powers in the European Union' (2011) 17(3) European Law Journal 304.
Corbett R, 'Governance and Institutional Developments' (1994) 23 Journal of Common Market Studies 2.
Corbett R, *The European Parliament's Role in Closer EU Integration* (Palgrave Macmillan 1998).
Costa O and Brack N, *How the EU Really Works* (Ashgate 2014).
Costas J and Grey C, *Secrecy at Work: The Hidden Architectures of Organisational Life* (Stanford University Press 2016).
Costello C, 'Administrative Governance and the Europeanization of Asylum and Immigration Policy' in H Hofmann and A Türk (eds), *EU Administrative Governance* (Edward Elgar 2006).
Cox AT, *The Myths of National Security: The Peril of Secret Government* (Beacon Press 1975).
Craig P, *EU Administrative Law* (OUP 2012).
Craig P, 'Brexit, A Drama: The Interregnum' (2017) 36 Yearbook of European Law 3.
Craig P and Burca de G, *EU Law: Text, Cases and Materials* (5th edn, OUP 2011).
Cremona M, 'The Union as a Global Actor: Roles, Models and Identity' (2004) 41 Common Market Law Review 553.
Cremona M, 'Justice and Home Affairs in a Globalised World: Ambitions and Reality in the tale of the EU-US SWIFT Agreement' Institute for European Integration Research Working Paper 4/2011 (2011).
Cronin T, *Direct Democracy: The Politics of Initiative, Referendum, and Recall* (Harvard University Press 1989).
Cross MKD, *Security Integration in Europe: How Knowledge-based Networks Are Transforming the European Union* (University of Michigan Press 2011).
Cross MKD, 'Secrecy and the Making of CFSP' (2018) 41(4) West European Politics 914.
Cryer R (ed), *Research Methodologies in EU and International Law* (Hart Publishing 2011).
Curtin DM, 'Digital Government in the European Union: Freedom of Information Trumped by "Internal Security"' in A Roberts (ed), *National Security and Open Government: Striking the Right Balance* (The Maxwell School of Syracuse University 2003).
Curtin D, *Executive Power of the European Union: Law, Practices, and Living Constitutions* (OUP 2009).
Curtin DM, 'Top Secret Europe' Inaugural lecture delivered at the University of Amsterdam, 20 October 2011.
Curtin DM, 'Judging EU Secrecy' (2012) Cahiers de Droit Européen 457.
Curtin DM 'Official Secrets and the Negotiation of International Agreements. Is the EU Executive Unbound?' (2013) 50 Common Market Law Review 423.

Curtin DM, 'Challenging Executive Dominance in European Democracy' (Amsterdam Centre for European Law and Governance Working Paper Series 2013–09).

Curtin DM, 'Overseeing Secrets in the EU: A Democratic Perspective' (2014) 52 Journal of Common Market Studies 684.

Curtin DM, Hofmann H, and Mendes J, 'Constitutionalising EU Executive Rule-Making Procedures: A Research Agenda' (2013) 19 European Law Journal 1.

Curtin DM, Klip A, Mccahery J, and Mmits J, *European Integration and Law* (Intersentia 2006).

Curtin D and Leino P, 'Openness, Transparency and the Right of Access to Documents in the EU' Robert Schuman Centre for Advanced Studies Research Paper No RSCAS 2016/63.

Curtin DM and Meijer AJ 'Does Transparency Strengthen Legitimacy?—A Critical Analysis of European Union Policy Documents' (2006) 11 Information Polity 109.

Curtin DM and Nollkaemper A, 'Conceptualizing Accountability in International and European Law' (2005) 36 Netherlands Yearbook of International Law 3.

Curtin DM and Wessel RA (ed), *Good Governance and the European Union. Reflections on Concepts, Institutions and Substance* (Intersentia 2005).

Dahl RA, 'The Concept of Power' (1957) 2 Behavioral Science 201.

Dahl RA, 'Procedural Democracy' in RE Goodin and P Pettit (eds), *Contemporary Political Philosophy: An Anthology* (Blackwell 1997).

Dalgaard-Nielsen A, 'Homeland Security: American and European Responses to September 11th' in J Pilegaard (ed), *The Politics of European Security* (Danish Institute for International Studies 2004).

Dawson D, 'How Does the European Court of Justice Reason? A Review Essay on the Legal Reasoning of the European Court of Justice' (2014) 20(3) European Law Journal 423.

Dawson M and De Witte F, 'Constitutional Balance in the EU after the Euro-Crisis' (2013) 76(5) The Modern Law Review 817.

Deckmyn V, *Increasing transparency in the EU?* (European Institute of Public Administration 2002).

De Baere G, *Constitutional Principles of EU External Relations* (OUP 2008).

DeSanti VM, 'A Policy Framework on the Dissemination of Government Electronic Information: Some Remarks' (1993) 10 Government Information Quarterly 256.

Dicey AV, *The Law of the Constitution*, JWF Allison (ed) (OUP 2013).

Dinan D (ed), *Origins and Evolution of the European Union* (2nd edn, OUP 2014).

Doninck van V, 'Report on Corruption Claims within EU Mission in Kosovo' (2015) *EUReporter*.

Driessen B, 'The Council of the European Union and Access to Documents' (2005) 30 European Law Review 675.

Driessen B, *Transparency in EU Institutional Law* (2nd edn, Kluwer Law International 2012).

Dworkin RM, 'The Model of Rules' Faculty Scholarship Series, Paper 3609 (1967).

Eckes C, *EU Counter-Terrorist Policies and Fundamental Rights: The Case of Individual Sanctions* (OUP 2009).

Eckes C, 'Decision-making in the Dark? Autonomous EU Sanctions and National Classification' in I Cameron (ed), *EU Sanctions: Law and Policy Issues Concerning Restrictive Measures* (Supranational Criminal Law Series, Book 15, Intersentia 2013).

Eckes C and Konstadinides T (eds), *Crime within the Area of Freedom, Security and Justice: A European Public Order* (CUP 2011).

Editorial, 'Between the Constitutional Document and the Constitutional Settlement' (2014) 10 European Constitutional Law Review 375.

Eeckhout P, 'The EU's Common Foreign and Security Policy after Lisbon: From Pillar Talk to Constitutionalism' in A Biondi, P Eeckhout, and S Ripley (eds), *EU Law after Lisbon* (OUP 2012).

Ellington T, 'Closed Mouths and Closed Doors: Why Democratic Theory Must Address Official Secrecy' Paper presented at the annual meeting of the The Midwest Political Science Association, Palmer House Hilton, Chicago, Illinois (2004).

Elworthy S, 'Balancing the Need for Secrecy with the Need for Accountability' (1998) 143 The RUSI Journal 5.

Emiliou N, 'Opening Pandora's Box: The Legal Basis of Community Measures before the Court of Justice' (1994) 19 European Law Review 488.

Epstein D and O'Halloran S, *Delegating Powers* (Columbia University Press 1999).

Fasone C, 'European Economic Governance and Parliamentary Representation: What Place for the European Parliament?' (2014) 20 European Law Journal 164.

Fasone C, 'Powers of Parliaments in Euro-crisis Budgetary Reforms' Paper presented at 'Constitutional Change Through Euro-Crisis Law' Workshop, EUI (2014).

Feldman D, 'The Nature of Legal Scholarships'(1989) 25 Modern Law Review 498.

Fenster M, 'The Opacity of Transparency' (2006) 91 Iowa Law Review 885.

Fenster M, 'The Implausibility of Secrecy' (2012) 65(2) Hastings Law Review 309.

Fenster M, *The Transparency Fix: Secrets, Leaks and Uncontrollable Government Information* (Stanford University Press 2017).

Fine GA and Holyfield L, 'Secrecy, Trust, and Dangerous Leisure: Generating Group Cohesion in Voluntary Organizations' (1996) 59 Social Psychology Quarterly 22.

Fisher E, 'The European Union in the Age of Accountability' (2004) 24 Oxford Journal of Legal Studies 495.

Fossum JE and Schlesinger P, *The European Union and the Public Sphere* (Routledge 2007).

Fox J, *Government Transparency and Policymaking* (Yale University Press 2005).

Franck TM and Weisband E (eds), *Secrecy and Foreign Policy* (OUP 1974).

Franck TM and Weisband E 'Secrecy in the Foreign Relations of Three Democracies: A Comparative Analysis' (1973) 50 Chicago-Kent Law Review 1.

Frankel M, 'Freedom of Information: Some International Characteristics' (Working Paper: the Campaign for Freedom of Information 2001).

Fried C, 'Privacy' (1966) 77 Yale Law Journal 475.

Friedrich CJ, *The Pathology of Politics: Violence, Betrayal, Corruption, Secrecy and Propaganda* (Harper and Row Publishers 1972).

Froomkin D, 'The Inverse of Oversight: CIA Spies on Congress' (2014) *The Intercept*.

Frost A, 'Restoring Faith in Government: Transparency Reform in the United States and the European Union' (2003) 9(1) European Public Law 87.

Fuchs M, 'Judging Secrets: The Role Courts Should Play in Preventing Unnecessary Secrecy' (2006) 58 Administrative Law Review 131.

Galloway D, 'Classifying Secrets in the EU' (Working Paper presented at Transparency and Access to the Records and Archives of the EU Institutions Seminar, the European University Institute 2013).

Galloway D, 'Classifying Secrets in the EU' (2014) 52 Journal of Common Market Studies 668.

Galnoor I, 'Government Secrecy: Exchanges, Intermediaries, and Middlemen' (1975) 35 Public Administration Review 32.

Galnoor I, *Government Secrecy in Democracies* (New York University Press 1977).

Gibbs D, 'Secrecy and International Relations' (1995) 32 Journal of Peace Research 213.

Goede de M, 'The SWIFT Affair and the Global Politics of European Security' (2012) 50 Journal of Common Market Studies 214.

Goede de M and Wesseling M, 'Clashing Cultures of Secrecy: Tracking Terrorism Financing and the Paradox of Publicity' Paper presented to the Annual Meeting of the Council of European Studies, University of Amsterdam (2013).

Goitein L (2011) *Reducing Over-classification Through Accountability* (New York University School of Law 2011).

Grant RW and Keohane RO, 'Accountability and Abuses of Power in World Politics' (2005) 99 American Political Science Review 29.

Green HP, 'Born Classified in the AEC—A Legal Perspective' (1981) 37 Bulletin of the Atomic Scientists 28.

Grønbech-Jensen C, 'The Scandinavian Tradition of Open Government and the European Union: Problems of Compatibility? (1998) 5(1) Journal of European Public Policy 185.

Guterson H, *Nuclear Rites A Weapons Laboratory at the End of the Cold War* (University of California Press 1998).

Gutmann A and Thompson, D, *Democracy and Disagreement* (Harvard University Press 1998).

Habermas J, *Between Facts and Norms: Contributions to a Discourse Theory of Law and Democracy*, W Rehg tr (MIT Press 1996).
Harlow C, 'European Governance and Accountability' in N Bamforth and P Leyland (eds), *Public Law in a Multi-Layered Constitution* (Hart Publishing 2003).
Hayden MV, 'Balancing Security and Liberty: The Challenge of Sharing Foreign Signals Intelligence' (2005) 19 Notre Dame Journal of Law, Ethics & Public Policy 247.
Hayes-Renshaw F and Wallace H, *The Council of Ministers* (MacMillan Press 1997).
Heald D, 'Varieties of Transparency' in C Hood and D Heald (eds), *Transparency: The Key to Better Governance?* (OUP 2006).
Held D, *Models of Democracy* (Stanford University Press 2006).
Henkin L, 'The Right to Know and the Duty to Withhold: The Case of the Pentagon Papers' (1971) 120(2) University of Pennsylvania Law Review 271.
Heritier A, *Explaining Institutional Change in Europe* (OUP 2007).
Hernon P, 'Information Life Cycle: Its Place in the Management of U.S. Government Information Resources' (1994) 11 Government Information Quarterly 147.
Hewlett RG, 'Born Classified in the AEC—A Historian's View' (1981) 37 Bulletin of the Atomic Scientists 20.
Heywood A, *Political Theory: An Introduction* (Palgrave Macmillan 2004).
Hilbert RA, *The Classical Roots of Ethnomethodology* (University of North Carolina Press 1992).
Hillebrandt M, Curtin D, and Meijer A, 'Transparency in the EU Council of Ministers: An Institutional Analysis' (2014) 20(1) European Law Journal 1.
Hislop D, *Knowledge Management in Organizations: A Critical Introduction* (OUP 2005).
Höing O and Wessels W, 'The European Commission's Position in the Post-Lisbon Institutional Balance: Secretariat or Partner to the European Council?' in M Chang and J Monar (eds), *The European Commission in the Post-Lisbon Era of Crises: Between Politial Leadership and Policy Management* (Peter Lang 2013).
Holt PM, *Secret Intelligence and Public Policy: A Dilemma of Democracy* (Holt Books 1995).
Horn E, 'The Logics of Political Secrecy' (2011) 28 Theory, Culture and Society 103.
Ilchman WF and Uphoff NT, () *The Political Economy of Change* (University of California Press 1971).
Jacqué J, *Review of the EULEX Kosovo Mission's Implementation of the Mandate with a Particular Focus on the Handling of the Recent Allegations* (2015) http://eeas.europa.eu/statements-eeas/docs/150331_jacque-report_en.pdf; http://eeas.europa.eu/statements-eeas/docs/150331_jacque-report-annexes_en.pdf.
Jorgensen KE, *The European Union and International Organizations* (Routledge 2009).

Juncker J, 'A New Start for Europe: My Agenda for Jobs, Growth, Fairness and Democratic Change' Speech given to the European Parliament on 15 July 2014.

Kaiser FM, 'The Amount of Classified Information: Causes, Consequences, and Correctives of a Growing Concern' (1989) 6 Government Information Quarterly 247.

Kant I, *To Perpetual Peace: A Philosophical Sketch*, Hackett Publishing, 2003.

Katyal KM, 'Internal Separation of Powers: Checking Today's Most Dangerous Branch from Within' (2006) 115 Yale Law Journal 2314.

Katz ST, *Government Secrecy: Decisions Without Democracy* (People for the American Way 1987).

Kelly A, *The Psychology of Secrets* (Springer 2002).

Kelly C, 'Managing the Relationship Between Knowledge and Power in Organisations' (2007) 59 New Information Perspectives 125.

Kelsen H, *The Essence and Value of Democracy*, N Urbinati and C Invernizzi Accetti eds, B Graf tr (Rowman & Littlefield 2013).

Kirchner EJ and Sperling J, *EU Security Governance* (Manchester University Press 2007).

Kitrosser H, 'Secrecy and Separated Powers: Executive Privilege Revisited' (2007) 92 Iowa Law Review 491.

Kitrosser H, 'Congressional Oversight of National Security Activities: Improving Information Funnels' (2008) 29 Cardozo Law Review 1049.

Kitrosser H, 'What If Daniel Ellsberg Hadn't Bothered?' (2011) 45 Indiana Law Review 89.

Kitrosser H, *Reclaiming Accountability: Transparency, Executive Power, and the U.S. Constitution* (University of Chicago Press 2015).

Kluth M and Pilegaard J, 'The Making of the EU's External Action Service: A Neorealist Interpretation' (2012) 17(2) European Foreign Affairs Review 303.

Koutrakos P, *The EU Common Security and Defence Policy* (OUP 2013).

Kochenov D and Bard P, 'Rule of Law Crisis in the New Member States of the EU: The Pitfalls of Overemphasising Enforcement' (27 July 2018) Reconnect Working Papers (Leuven) No 1.

Krauss S, 'The European Parliament in EU External Relations: The Customs Union with Turkey' (2000) 5 European Foreign Affairs Review 215.

Konstadinides T, 'Drawing the Line Between Circumvention and Gap Filling: An Exploration of the Conceptual Limits of the Treaty's Flexibility Clause' (2012) 31 Yearbook of European Law 227.

Kozak DC and Keagle JM, *Bureaucratic Politics and National Security: Theory and Practice* (Lynne Rienner Publishers 1988).

Kramer RM, *Organizational Trust* (OUP 2006).

Krishna V and Morgan J, 'Asymmetric Information and Legislative Rules: Some Amendments' (2001) 95 American Political Science Review 435.

Kronman AT, 'Mistake, Disclosure, Information, and the Law of Contracts' (1978) 7 The Journal of Legal Studies 1.
Kuner C, 'PRISM and Privacy: Will this Change Everything?' (2013) 3 International Data Privacy Law 217.
Labayle H, 'Principles and Procedures for Dealing with the European Union Classified Information in Light of the Lisbon Treaty' Study for the European Parliament, Brussels (2010).
Labayle M, The New Commission's Role in Freedom, Security and Justice in the Post-Lisbon Context: New Era or Missed Opportunity?' in M Chang and J Monar (eds), *The European Commission in the Post-Lisbon Era of Crises: Between Politial Leadership and Policy Management* (Peter Lang 2013).
Leino P 'Case C-353/99 P, *Council* v. *Heidi Hautala*, judgment of the Full Court of 6 December 2001, nyr, appeal against the judgment of the Court of First Instance of 19 July 1999 in Case T-14/98, *Hautala* v. *Council*, [1999] II-2489' (2002) 39 Common Market Law Review 621.
Leino P, 'Case C-64/05 P, *Kingdom of Sweden* v. *Commission of the European Communities and Others*, Judgment of the European Court of Justice (Grand Chamber) of 18 December 2007, nyr' (2008) 45 Common Market Law Review 1469.
Leino P, 'Just a Little Sunshine in the Rain: The 2010 Case Law of the European Court of Justice on Access to Documents' (2011) 48 Common Market Law Review 1215.
Leino P, 'Transparency, Participation and EU Institutional Practice: An Inquiry into the Limits of the "Widest Possible"' EUI Working Papers LAW 2014/3.
Lester M, 'Organisations Call on European Court to Consult on Classified Evidence Rule Change' (2013) *European Sanctions Blog*.
Lester M, 'Draft European Court Rules Propose Secret Hearings' (2014) *European Sanctions Blog*.
Lodge J, 'Transparency and Democratic Legitimacy' (1994) 32(3) Journal of Common Market Studies 343.
Lodge J, 'EU Homeland Security: Citizens or Suspects?' (2004) 26(3) Journal of European Integration 253.
Lodge J, 'Communicating (in)Security: A Failure of Public Diplomacy?' Research Paper No 3, The Challenging Landscape of European Liberty and Security (2006).
Lowry RP, 'Toward a Sociology of Secrecy and Security Systems' in SK Tefft (ed), *Secrecy: A Cross-Cultural Perspective* (Human Sciences Press 1980).
Magnette P, 'Between Parliamentary Control and the Rule of Law: The Political Role of the Ombudsman in the European Union' (2003) 10 Journal of European Public Policy 677.
Mokrosinska D, 'The People's Right to Know and State Secrecy' (2018) 1 Canadian Journal of Law & Jurisprudence 87.

Mair P, *Ruling the Void: The Hallowing of Western Democracy* (Verso 2013).
Majone G, 'Europe's "Democratic Deficit": The Question of Standards' (1998) 4(1) European Law Journal 5.
Majone G, *Dilemmas of European Integration: The Ambiguities and Pitfalls of Integration by Stealth* (OUP 2005).
March JG and Olsen JP, *Democratic Governance* (Free Press 1995).
Maret S and Goldman J, *Government Secrecy: Classic and Contemporary Readings* (Emerald 2011).
Martenczuk B and Thiel van, S, *Justice, Liberty, Security: New Challenges for EU External Relations* (Brussels University Press 2008).
Marx GT, 'The Law's Secrets' (1990) 88(6) Michigan Law Review 2276.
Maskin E and Tirole J, 'The Politician and the Judge: Accountability in Government' (2004) 94(4) American Economic Review 429.
Meijer A, 'Understanding the Complex Dynamics of Transparency' (2013) 73 Public Administration Review 429.
Mendes J, *Participation in EU Rule-making: A Rights-based Approach by Joana Mendes* (OUP 2011).
Menéndez AJ, 'The Refugee Crisis: Between Human Tragedy and Symptom of the Structural Crisis of European Integration' (2016) 22 European Law Journal 388.
Merlingen M and Ostrauskaite R, *European Security and Defense Policy: An Implementation Perspective* (Routledge 2008).
Metzger GE, 'The Interdependent Relationship Between Internal and External Separation of Powers' Columbia Public Law Research Paper No 09–213 (2009).
Meyer-Resende M, 'Democracy Reporting International, Discussing International Standards for Democratic Governance: A Preliminary Research Report' Discussion Paper No 2 (2007).
Meyer-Resende M, *Democracy Revisited: Which Notion of Democracy for the EU's External Relations?* (Office for Promotion of Parliamentary Democracy (OPPD) 2009).
Mill JS, *Considerations on Representative Government* (Parker Son and Bourn 1861).
Monar J, 'The EU's Growing External Role in the AFSJ Domain: Factors, Framework and Forms of Action' (2014) 27 Cambridge Review of International Affairs 147.
Monar J, Rees W, and Mitsilegas V, *The European Union and Internal Security: Guardian of the People?* (Palgrave Macmillan 2003).
Moncrieffe JM, 'Accountability: Ideals, Ideas, Constraints' (2001) 8 Democratization 26.
Moravcsik A, 'In Defense of the "Democratic Deficit': Reassessing Legitimacy in the European Union' (2002) 40(4) Journal of Common Market Studies 603.
Moynihan D, *Secrecy: The American Experience* (Yale University Press 1999).
Mulgan R, '"Accountability": An Ever-Expanding Concept?' (2000) 78 Public Administration 555.

Murphy CC, 'Secret Evidence in EU Security Law: Special Advocates before the Court of Justice?' Centre for European Law, Working Papers in European Law, Working Paper 02/2012.

Müller-Wille B, 'Intelligence and Democratic Accountability: A Blessing, not a Curse' (2006) 15 European Security 491.

Mutz D, *Hearing the Other Side: Deliberative versus Participatory Democracy* (CUP 2006).

Naurin D, *Dressed for Politics: Why Increasing Transparency in the European Union Will Not Make Lobbyists Behave any Better Than They Already Do* (Göteborg 2004).

Naurin D, 'Taking Transparency Seriously' Sussex European Institute Working Paper No 59 (2002).

Naurin D, *Deliberation Behind Closed Doors. Transparency and Lobbying In The European Union* (ECPR Press 2007).

Naurin D, 'Transparency, Publicity, Accountability—The Missing Links' (2006) 12 Swiss Political Science Review 90.

Nielsen N, 'US Gag Order on EU Police Agency Stirs Controversy' (2015) *EUobserver.*

Norman L, 'EU Governments Approve Secret Evidence in Sanctions Cases' *The Wall Street Journal,* 10 February 2015.

Nuttall S, *European Political Cooperation* (OUP 1992).

Oberg U, 'EU Citizen's Right to Know: The Improbable Adoption of a European Freedom of Information Act' (1999) 2 Cambridge Yearbook of European Legal Studies 303.

Olsen JP, 'The Institutional Basis of Democratic Accountability' (2013) 36 *West European Politics* 447.

Parry C, 'Legislatures and Secrecy' (1954) 67 Harvard Law Review 737.

Pasquier M and Villeneuve J, 'Organizational Barriers to Transparency: A Typology and Analysis of Organizational Behaviour Tending to Prevent or Restrict Access to Information' (2007) 73 International Review of Administrative Sciences 147.

Pech L, '"A Union Founded on the Rule of Law": Meaning and Reality of the Rule of Law as a Constitutional Principle of EU Law' (2010) 6 European Constitutional Law Review 359.

Pech L and Scheppele KL, 'Illiberalism Within: Rule of Law Backsliding in the EU' in *Cambridge Yearbook of European Legal Studies* (CUP 2017).

Peers S, 'The New Regulation on Access to Documents: A Critical Analysis, University of Essex' Queen's Papers on Europeanization, No 6/2002.

Peers S and Costa M, 'The Accountability of Delegated and Implementing Acts after the Treaty of Lisbon' (2012) 18 European Law Journal 427.

Peters A, () 'Transparency, Secrecy, and Security' in J Iliopoulos-Strangas, O Diggelmann, and H Bauer (eds), *Rule of Law, Freedom and Security in Europe* (Nomos 2010).

Pettit P, *On the People's Terms: A Republican Theory and Model of Democracy* (CUP 2012).
Phillips WG, 'Secret Government: The Classification System' in N Dorsen et al (eds), *None of Your Business* (Viking Press 1974).
Pierson P, 'The Path to European Integration: A Historical Institutionalist Analysis' (1996) 29(2) Comparative Political Studies 123.
Pollock M, *Engines of European Integration: Delegation, Agency, and Agenda Setting in the EU* (OUP 2003).
Pop V, 'Eurogroup Chief: "I'm for Secret, Dark Debates"' (2011) *EUobserver*.
Posner EA, 'Before You Reboot NSA, Think About This: The Paradox of Reforming the Secrecy-Industrial Complex' (2013) *The New Republic*.
Posner EA and Vermeule A, 'The Credible Executive' University of Chicago Law and Economics, Olin Working Paper No 309 (2006).
Posner RA, 'The Right to Privacy' Sibley Lectures, Paper 22 (1978).
Pozen DE, 'The Mosaic Theory, National Security and the Freedom of Information Act' (2005) 115 Yale Law Journal 628.
Pozen DE, 'Deep Secrecy' (2010) 62(2) Stanford Law Review 257.
Pozen DE, 'The Leaky Leviathan: Why the Government Condemns and Condones Unlawful Disclosures of Information' (2013) 127 Harvard Law Review 512.
Puetter U, *The European Council and the Council: New Intergovernmentalism and Institutional Change* (OUP 2014).
Rawls J, *A Theory of Justice. Revised Edition* (OUP 1999).
Rayner L, 'The EU Foreign Ministry and Union Embassies' The Foreign Policy Centre (2005).
Reichard M, *The EU-NATO Relationship: A Legal and Political Perspective* (Ashgate Publishing 2006).
Relyea HC, 'Opening Government to Public Scrutiny: A Decade of Federal Efforts' (1975) 35 Public Administration Review 3.
Rettman A, 'Ashton Names EU Foreign Service Priorities at Low-key Launch Event' (2012) *EUObserver*.
Rettman A, 'MEPs Ask Tough Questions on EU mission in Kosovo' (2014) *EUObserver*.
Rittberger B and Goetz KH, 'Secrecy in Europe' (2018) 41(4) West European Politics 825.
Roberts AS, 'Entangling Alliances: NATO's Security Policy and the Entrenchment of State Secrecy' (2003) 26 Cornell International Law Journal 329.
Roberts AS, *Blacked Out: Government Secrecy in the Information Age* (CUP 2006).
Roberston KG, *Public Secrets: A Study in the Development of Government Secrecy* (St. Martin's Press 1982).
Robertson KG, *Secrecy and Open Government: Why Governments Want You to Know* (MacMillan Press 2003).

Rosanvallon P, *Counter-Democracy: Politics in an Age of Distrust*, A Goldhammer tr (CUP 2008).
Rosén G, 'Can You Keep a Secret? How the European Parliament got Access to Sensitive Documents in the Area of Security and Defence' RECON Working Paper 22 (2011).
Rosén G, 'EU Confidential: The European Parliament's Involvement in EU Security and Defence Policy' (2015) 53 Journal of Common Market Studies 383.
Rossi LS, 'Does the Lisbon Treaty Provide a Clearer Separation of Competences between EU and Member States?' in A Biondi, P Eeckhout, and S Ripley (eds), *EU Law after Lisbon* (OUP 2012).
Rossi L and Vinagre e Silva, P, *Public Access to Documents in the EU* (Hart Publishing 2017).
Rourke F, *Secrecy and Publicity: Dilemmas of Democracy* (John Hopkins Press 1961).
Rozell MJ, *Executive Privilege: Presidential Power, Secrecy, and Accountability* (3rd edn, University Press of Kansas 2010).
Rozell MJ, *Executive Privilege: The Dilemma of Secrecy and Democratic Accountability* (John Hopkins University Press 1994).
Rubin AJ, 'Lawmakers in France Move to Vastly Expand Surveillance' *The New York Times*, 5 May 2015.
Ruffert M, 'European Debt Crisis and European Union Law' (2011) 48(6) Common Market Law Review 1777.
Saffon M and Urbinati N, 'Procedural Democracy, the Bulwark of Equal Liberty' (2013) 41 Political Theory 441.
Sagar R, 'On Combating the Abuse of State Secrecy' (2007) 15 Journal of Political Philosophy 404.
Sagar R, 'Who Holds the Balance?: A Missing Detail in the Debate over Balancing Security and Liberty' (2009) 41 Polity 166.
Sagar R, *Secrecy and Leaks: The Dilemma of State Secrecy* (Princeton University Press 2013).
Samaha A, 'Government Secrets, Constitutional Law, and Platforms for Judicial Intervention' (2005) 53 UCLA Law Review 909.
Sandholtz W and Stone Sweet A, *European Integration and Supranational Governance* (OUP 1998).
Sauter W, 'Proportionality in EU law: A Balancing Act?' TILEC Discussion Paper, DP 2013–003 (2013).
Scharpf F, *Governing Europe: Effective and Democratic?* (OUP 1999).
Schechner S and Dalton M, 'French Constitutional Court Approves New Powers for Intelligence Services' *Wall Street Journal*, 24 July 2015.
Scheppele KL, *Legal Secrets: Equality and Efficiency in the Common Law* (University of Chicago Press 1988).
Schilde KE, 'Cosmic Top Secret Europe? The Legacy of NATO and Cold War US Policy on European Union Information Policy' (2015) 24 European Security 167.

Schmitter PC, 'Political Accountability in "Real-Existing" Democracies: Meaning and Mechanisms' European University Institute (2007).

Schulhofer SJ, 'Secrecy and Democracy: Who Controls Information in the National Security State?' Public Law and Legal Theory Research Paper Series, Working Paper No 10-53, 15 (2010).

Schulhofer SJ, 'Oversight of National Security Secrecy in the United States' in D Cole, F Fabbrini, and A Vedaschi (eds), *Secrecy, National Security and the Vindication of Constitutional Law* (Edward Elgar 2013).

Schütze R, *European Constitutional Law* (CUP 2012).

Shamir A, 'How to Share a Secret' (1979) 22 Communications of the Association for Computing Machinery 612.

Shane PM, 'Negotiating for Knowledge: Administrative Responses to Congressional Demands for Information' (1992) 44 Administrative Law Review 197.

Simmel G, 'The Sociology of Secrecy and of Secret Societies' (1906) 11 American Journal of Sociology 441.

Stasavage D, 'Open or Closed Door? Transparency in Domestic and International Bargaining' (2004) 58(4) International Organization 667.

Stärkle G, 'La Protection et le Traitement des Informations Classifiées dans le Cadre de la Politique de Sécurité et de Défense Commune (PSDC) au sein des Institutions et Agences de l'Union Européenne' (2011) 47 Cahiers de Droit Européen 155.

Steinhauer J and Weisman J, 'U.S. Surveillance in Place Since 9/11 Is Sharply Limited' *The New York Times*, 2 June 2015.

Steunenberg B, () *European Parliament: Moving toward Democracy in the EU* (Rowan &Littlefield Publishers Inc 2002).

Stigler G, 'The Economics of Information' (1963) 69 Journal of Political Economy 213.

Stiglitz J, 'The Private Uses of Public Interests: Incentives and Institutions' (1998) 12 Journal of Economic Perspectives 7.

Stiglitz JE, 'On Liberty, the Right to Know, and Public Discourse: The Role of Transparency in Public Life, in Globalizing Rights' the Oxford Amnesty Lectures (1999).

Stuntz WJ, 'Secret Service: Against Privacy and Transparency' (2006) *New Republic*.

Sunstein CR, 'Government Control of Information' (1986) 74 California Law Review 889.

Tefft SK (ed), *Secrecy: A Cross-Cultural Perspective* (Human Sciences Press 1980).

Thompson DF, 'Democratic Secrecy' (1999) 114(2) Political Science Quarterly 181.

Thompson ED and Kaarst-Brown ML, 'Sensitive Information: A Review and Research Agenda' (2005) 56 Journal American Society for Information Science and Technology 245.

Trybus M and White N (eds), *European Security Law* (OUP 2007).

Tsadiras A, 'Unravelling Ariadne's Thread: The European Ombudsman's Investigative Powers' (2008) 45 Common Market Law Review 757.
Tsebelis G and Garrett G, 'The Institutional Foundations of Intergovernmentalism and Supranationalism in the European Union' (2001) 55 International Organization 357.
Thym D, 'The "Refugee Crisis" as a Challenge of Legal Design and Institutional Legitimacy' (2016) 53 Common Market Law Review 1545.
Turner M and Pratkanis A, 'Twenty-five Years of Groupthink Theory and Research: Lessons from Evolution of a Theory' (1998) 73 Organisational Behavior and Human Decision Process 105.
Urbinati N, *Democracy Disfigured: Opinion, Truth and the People* (Harvard University Press 2014).
Vara JS, 'The Role of the European Parliament in the Conclusion of the Transatlantic Agreements on the Transfer of Personal Data after Lisbon' CLEER Working Papers 2013/2 (2013).
Walker N (ed), *Europe's Area of Freedom, Security and Justice* (OUP 2004).
Wallace H, The Council: An Institutional Chameleon? (2002) 15(3) Governance 325.
Walsh JI, 'Intelligence-Sharing in the European Union: Institutions Are Not Enough' (2006) 44 Journal of Common Market Studies 625.
Warren C and Laslett B, 'Privacy and Secrecy: A Conceptual Comparison' in K Tefft (ed), *Secrecy: A Cross-Cultural Perspective* (Human Sciences Press 1980).
Weber M, *Economy and Society*, G Roth and C Wittich (eds) (Bedminster Press 1968).
Weiler J, 'eEuropean Democracy and its Critique' (1995) 18(3) West European Politics 4.
Weisband F, *Secrecy and Foreign Policy* (OUP 1974).
Weiss RS, *Learning from Strangers. The Art and Method of Qualitative Interview Studies* (Free Press 1994).
Wessel RA and Hertog den L, 'EU Foreign, Security and Defence Policy: A Competence-Responsibility Gap?' in MD Evans and P Koutrakos (eds), *International Responsibility: EU and International Perspectives* (Hart Publishing 2012).
Wessels W, 'Democratic Control in the Member States of the European Council and the Euro zone Summits' Study requested by the European Parliament's Committee on Constitutional Affairs (2013).
Westin A, *Privacy and Freedom* (Atheneum 1967).
Whitman RG, 'NATO, the EU and ESDP: An Emerging Division of Labour?' (2004) 25 Contemporary Security Policy 430.
Wilde de M, 'Locke and the State of Exception: Towards a Modern Understanding of Emergency Government' (2010) 6 European Constitutional Law Review 249.
Wilson W, 'The Study of Administration' (1887) 2 Political Science Quarterly 197.
Wilson W, *The New Freedom: A Call for the Emancipation of the Generous Energies of a People* (The Country Life Press 1916).

Wisniewski E, 'The Influence of the European Parliament on the European External Action Service' (2013) 18 European Foreign Affairs Review 81.
Witte de B, 'An Undivided Union? Differentiated Integration in Post-Brexit Times' (2018) 55(2/3) Common Market Law Review 227.
Woodward R, 'Establishing Europol' (1994) 1 European Journal on Criminal Policy and Research 7.
Zimmer Ch, Schneider G, and Dobbins M, 'The Contested Council: Conflict Dimensions of an Intergovernmental EU Institution' (2005) 53 Political Studies 403.
Zwaan de J Jans J, and Nelissen F, *The European Union: An Ongoing Process of European Integration* (T.M.C Asser Press 2004).

INDEX